The Moral Work of Anthropology

Anthropology at Work

Series Editors:
Jakob Krause-Jensen, Aarhus University
Emil André Røyrvik, Norwegian University of Science and
Technology (NTNU)

Editorial Committee:
Ann Jordan, University of North Texas
Michael Blim, City University of New York, Graduate Center
James Carrier, University of Indiana
Brian Moeran, University of Hong Kong
Halvard Vike, University of South-Eastern Norway
Marina Welker, Cornell University

We dedicate much of our lives to work, and work defines both people and their relationships to a great extent. The social and cultural processes of work require investigation, not least in our time of globalization and crises in capitalism. The series offers ethnography-based, anthropological analyses of work in its diverse contexts and manifestations.

The Moral Work of Anthropology

Ethnographic Studies of Anthropologists at Work

Edited by
HANNE OVERGAARD MOGENSEN
and
BIRGITTE GORM HANSEN

berghahn
NEW YORK · OXFORD
www.berghahnbooks.com

First published in 2021 by
Berghahn Books
www.berghahnbooks.com

Library of Congress Cataloging-in-Publication Data

Names: Mogensen, Hanne Overgaard, editor. | Hansen, Birgitte
Gorm, editor.
Title: The moral work of anthropology : ethnographic studies of
anthropologists at work / edited by Hanne Overgaard Mogensen
and Birgitte Gorm Hansen.
Description: New York, N.Y. : Berghahn Books, 2021. | Series:
Anthropology at work ; volume 2 | Includes bibliographical
references and index.
Identifiers: LCCN 2020051899 (print) | LCCN 2020051900 (ebook) |
ISBN 9781800731127 (hardback) | ISBN 9781800731134 (ebook)
Subjects: LCSH: Anthropological ethics.
Classification: LCC GN33.6 .M674 2021 (print) | LCC GN33.6 (ebook) |
DDC 174/.9301--dc23
LC record available at https://lccn.loc.gov/2020051899
LC ebook record available at https://lccn.loc.gov/2020051900

British Library Cataloguing in Publication Data

A catalogue record for this book is available from the British Library

ISBN 978-1-80073-112-7 hardback
ISBN 978-1-80073-113-4 ebook

Contents

🙌 🙌 🙌

Introduction
An Ethnography and Anthropology of Anthropologists

Hanne Overgaard Mogensen, Birgitte Gorm Hansen
and Morten Axel Pedersen

– Why do so many anthropologists say that they are not real/true
  anthropologists?
– Why are anthropologists so preoccupied with their moral
  commitments?
– Why do so many anthropologists want to save the world?
– Why do so many anthropologists emphasize complexity?
– Why do so many anthropologists hesitate to explicate anthropological
  practice?
– Why do so many anthropologists disown power?

The above questions arose as a result of the initial analysis of material from research carried out in Denmark from 2015 to 2019 on the practice of anthropology. This book is an attempt to answer these questions.

The humanities are presently being pushed to justify their relevance and existence. Yet there is at the same time an increasing demand for the humanities to respond to an ever-widening range of scientific questions and societal problems. In recent years there has also been an increasing demand for anthropologists and anthropological knowledge both inside and outside of academia. It was against this background that the research project originally set out to ethnographically explore what anthropologists actually do when at work in these professional arenas and communities.

The ethnographic fieldwork on which the book is based has primarily been carried out among anthropologists and their collaborators in Denmark. There are, however, some exceptions to this: one study was conducted in a consultancy firm abroad, some anthropologists were trained abroad but working in Denmark, and the researchers' participation in various networks and international conferences on anthropology and its application are also drawn upon as ethnography. Nonetheless, the bulk of our ethnographic material on how anthropology is practised originates from a Danish context.

As our research progressed, one specific issue emerged that seemed to matter a great deal within each of the communities of anthropological practice under investigation, namely that of 'morality'. Accordingly, the contributions to this collection address the ways in which anthropologists at work seek to do what they consider right or good. In other words, what is the kind of morality that is performed by anthropologists at work and what are the effects of this morality both on the anthropologists themselves and the people with whom they work and collaborate? The book addresses these questions through ethnographic studies of anthropologists at work in four professional arenas: healthcare, business, management and interdisciplinary research. More specifically, it demonstrates the ways in which anthropologists, whether doing research, selling insights, managing newspapers or caring for patients, perform particular moral values, striving to become certain kinds of virtuous subjects. We study anthropology as a social practice inside and outside academia, which in both sites may involve research as well as non-research tasks, but all of which, it is argued, are undergirded by a particular kind of morality.

The book is situated at the intersection of two prominent anthropological subfields, namely 'applied or public anthropology' and 'the anthropology of ethics and morality'. Below we will discuss these in turn. But first a bit more about the study.

The Study

Our four arenas of research can all be seen as good examples of some of those interdisciplinary and non-academic engagements and collaborations from which it has been argued that anthropology has drawn its vitality since the crisis of representation in the 1980s (Marcus 2008: 1,3) as will also be discussed below. But the choice of arenas was also shaped by the experience of the researchers involved and activities taking place at the Department of Anthropology in Copenhagen where the research project was based.

Medical anthropology and business and organizational anthropology have for a long period been prominent fields of research and teaching at the department in Copenhagen (as also testified by the fact that master's programmes in 'business and organizational anthropology' and 'the anthropology of health' have been offered there for the past fifteen years). Adding to this, Danish anthropologists have become increasingly involved in interdisciplinary projects, and the Danish departments of anthropology have played an active role in several interdisciplinary degrees and research centres. Another factor that informed our delimitation and design of the project was our realization that an increasing number of anthropology graduates were being employed in managerial and leadership positions outside of academia. While this development could no doubt partly be explained simply by the general academic qualifications obtained by these graduates, several people with whom we discussed this also suggested that anthropological skills set these anthropologically trained managers apart from other managers, and so we decided to include management as our fourth arena of research. Other arenas could have been included. Many graduates end up in public administration, which could also have been a field of study in itself. It is to some extent included in the study on medical anthropologists, since some of these end up in the administration of the health and welfare system. Global development is another important field at the department in Copenhagen, both in terms of teaching, research and employment of graduates, and probably the first field which saw anthropologists and anthropological concepts move in and out of academia. However, it no longer makes up as large a proportion of the national anthropological labour market as it did earlier.[1]

The sub-projects differed in terms of length and set-up and in terms of the background of the researcher. Two (and at the time of the research, three) of the authors are tenured staff at the Copenhagen department. Accordingly, they had less time for doing fieldwork than did the postdoc and PhD student involved in the project; however, they all have extensive working experience with the field they write about. Mogensen has carried out research in medical anthropology (primarily in Africa) throughout her academic career, and did consultancy work in relation to international health for different development organizations before embarking upon her academic career. M.A. Pedersen has originally carried out long-term fieldwork in Mongolia, but has since 2014 been involved in the development of an interdisciplinary research, education and outreach centre known as the Copenhagen Centre of Social Data Science (SODAS) at the Faculty of Social Sciences in Copenhagen. Jöhncke was the head of the so-called Anthropological Analysis Unit at the department for ten years, and was in this capacity responsible for collaborative research and teaching projects with private corporations, public institutions and civil society organizations. Chapters by these authors are largely based on short bursts of fieldworks spread out over the course of two to three years, as well as on their previous long-term experience with the fields they write about. The postdoc and the PhD student did longer periods of fieldwork. Cullen worked in different organizations and as a consultant in private companies before returning to academia to do a PhD on business anthropology, and Gorm Hansen came from a background in psychology and science and technology studies, and did her PhD on research managers before embarking upon a postdoc on anthropologists-cum-managers. L.R. Pedersen has done fieldwork on anthropologists as consultants and has co-written a chapter with Gorm Hansen on the process of studying anthropologists ethnographically and the moral concerns it involves for the researcher.

All researchers carried out biographical interviews within their field with particular attention being paid to cases of collaboration and key competences of their anthropological interlocutors, but some researchers (Cullen and Gorm Hansen) were also present for longer periods in the work settings they studied. They have, however, both chosen a writing style where they focus on one or a few interlocutors. M.A Pedersen's chapter relies heavily on auto-ethnographic data and insights from his work at SODAS. In sum, the studies were different in length and shape, but all of the researchers had previous experience with the fields they studied.

The researchers have all worked at the department of Anthropology at Copenhagen University for longer or shorter periods in their career. With one exception (Gorm Hansen who is trained as a social psychologist), they all received some (or all) of their education at one of the two university departments of anthropology in Denmark. However, the joint discussions of material across different sub-projects benefited from a diversity in prior fieldwork, and theoretical interests of the researchers, some of which included the phenomenological tradition, science and technology studies, economic anthropology and the ontological turn in anthropology. The moral project of anthropologists stood out as a cross-cutting issue of significance, which we therefore decided to devote attention to.

More information about the individual studies is found in the chapters. We will now turn to the two subfields of anthropology: 'applied' or 'public' anthropology and 'the anthropology of ethics and morality', at the intersection of which the book is situated.

'Academic' versus 'Applied' Anthropology, and Beyond

The theme of the 116th Annual Meeting of the American Anthropological Association (AAA) in 2017 was 'Anthropology Matters'! As was stated in the call for papers: 'The Anthropocene, packed with meaning and crisis, needs anthropologists with critical skills in empowering subaltern voices and practices'. The conference itself opened with words of concern about worldwide threats to fundamental principles of fairness, equity, open mindedness, respect, compassion, caring and love, but also with the reassurance that anthropologists are taking action and are working towards what is right, and what is just. The opening ceremony continued with a keynote by Paul Farmer, the co-founder and chief strategist of 'Partners in Health', an NGO providing community-based care to impoverished communities around the world, and Jim Yong Kim, the President of the World Bank (2012–2019). The President of the American Anthropological Association, Alisse Waterston, introduced them with the words: 'I cannot think of a better way to get our week going than have Jim and Paul reflect with us about their work, the role of engaged and applied anthropology, and what they think it will take to make a more just and sustainable world'.

The message that was delivered at this opening ceremony – the biggest annual event for anthropologists, not only from the US, but from all over the word – was unequivocal: the justification for anthropology is its ability to make the world a better place, and it is the responsibility of anthropologists to do so through applied and engaged work. Decades of debates over the relation between academic and applied anthropology were not brought up. Questions about what was meant by 'a more just world' were not raised. These are however exactly the questions we intend to look at in this book. We will do so by first turning to the history of the relation between academic and applied anthropology, and what David Mills refers to as the history of a discipline denying its own utility while also being dependent on it (2006: 56). Afterwards we will move on to the question of what anthropologists mean by 'a more just world'.

For Radcliffe-Brown, one of the founding fathers of the discipline, there was no opposition between research and its application. On the contrary. His ambition was to develop a natural science of society (Radcliffe-Brown and Eggan 1957) which, just like (other) natural sciences, could be used to manipulate natural (social) phenomena (Campbell 2014). Malinowski also advocated for the role of anthropologists as policy advisers to African colonial administrators, and Radcliffe-Brown and Malinowski were both involved in the debate over segregation policies in South Africa in the 1920s and 1930s. Malinowski argued for the need to segregate black and white populations in order to protect indigenous cultures, whereas Radcliffe-Brown argued for the impossibility of doing so, considering that the different groups were already deeply integrated and mutually dependent on each other, and that they were each contributing to the functioning of the overall social structure of the South African society (Niehaus 2018). Ethical and political questions deriving from theoretical positions and societal engagement were thus inherent to the discipline from the very beginning.

The first part of the twentieth century saw repeated attempts by anthropologists at the Royal Anthropological Institute in the UK to convince the Imperial government that anthropology served a useful purpose and deserved funding (Wright 2006: 56). However, after the Second World War, attempts were made to distance anthropology from the 'tainted' work of policy and applied involvement. During a debate in the Association of Social Anthropologists (ASA) in the UK in 1946 on whether members should address issues of applied anthropology and provide scope for discussing colonial problems, Max Gluckman, among others, strongly argued against that kind of involvement, fearing that the demands of colonial governments would lead to the defilement of basic research (Mills 2003). Anthropology's association with colonial administration had brought an unease to the discipline, which became one of the major contributing factors behind the efforts to clearly separate 'pure' and 'impure', or academic and applied anthropology. Anthropology's attitude towards its application can be characterized as one of serial ambivalence according to Wright (2006: 56), and as Shore and Wright note, the usefulness of anthropological knowledge has been held hostage by the culture of the discipline itself and a preoccupation with the purity of academic boundaries, applied work being seen not only as 'un-theoretical', but also impure and polluting (1997: 142).

In spite of this ambivalence and unease, anthropology has been applied outside of academia all along. After the Second World War, the concept of development became one of the dominant ideas of the twentieth century, embodying a set of aspirations and techniques aimed at bringing about 'positive changes' or 'progress' in former colonies now referred to as the less-developed South or Third World. Relations between anthropologists and the world of development ideas and practices date from the early days of the 'development industry' (the 1950s) and have continued, in various forms, up to today. The relation between the two parallels the one between academic and applied anthropology more generally speaking; that is, it encompasses positions from sympathetic involvement to stances of disengaged critique or even outright hostility and arguments that the idea of development is in direct opposition to the cultural relativist project of anthropology (Lewis 2012: 469–70).

Anthropologists studying businesses and working for private enterprises are not a new phenomenon either, as shown by a number of scholars (Baba 2006, 2014; Mills 2006; Cefkin 2009; Jordan 2003). An insightful overview of intersections between anthropology and business over time is given by L.R. Pedersen (2018: 47–76). Here it suffices to say that there were examples of early collaborations between anthropology and the corporate world (e.g. the Hawthorn studies in the 1920s and 1930s; see also Schwartzman 1993: 6), but also that after the Second World War (in the 1950s) there was a period in which resistance towards anthropology's involvement with business grew in the established anthropological community. This resistance was linked to the general unease with 'impure' applied anthropology, the insistence upon anthropology as a theoretical and inherently critical project, and the resistance to studying 'modern' societies, to 'studying up', and to working for the capitalist system (L.R. Pedersen 2018: 53). It was therefore not until the 1990s that business anthropology became established as a sub-discipline within anthropology.

With postmodernism, the crisis of representation and the reflexive turn of the 1980s (Clifford and Marcus 1986; Marcus and Fischer 1986), there was, on the one hand, a return to concerns with power and discourse and a heightened critique from within the discipline of its own relation with power and hence application of knowledge outside of academia. On the other hand, the reflexive turn in anthropology in the 1980s pushed anthropologists to identify their subject beyond the study of the 'primitive' and 'exotic'. Anthropology's area of enquiry is now often found in modern institutions and amongst national and transnational agents of governance and finance (Matsutake Worlds Research Group 2009: 398; Marcus 2005, 2008). It is exactly from these diverse interdisciplinary and non-academic engagements and collaborations that the discipline draws its present vitality (Marcus 2008: 1, 3). Anthropological knowledge is more than ever contingent on the production of other forms of knowledge, outside of academic institutions, and anthropologists at work are no longer simply 'apprentices' of a new 'exotic' culture. They are, rather, 'collaborators' of their subjects with whom they share interests, concerns, ideas and projects. Reflecting these developments, influential voices talk about a 'collaborative turn' within anthropology, to capture the fact that anthropologists are now beginning to systematically study and theorize the wide range of collaborations that they and their colleagues are part of (Lassiter 2005).

It was also in the 1980s that ethnography – primarily perceived as a method – became widely used beyond academic anthropology, for example as a tool for innovation, product development and corporate growth (L.R. Pedersen 2018: 54), and in the development world, where decentralization, participation and bottom-up approaches became key concepts, and ethnographic methods – in ways that have often been referred to as 'quick and dirty' – moved beyond academia and into the development industry (Lewis 2012; Mosse 2013). In the 1980s and 1990s, a renewed interest arose in the application of anthropology outside of academia, and there have been attempts since then to steer away from the academic-applied dichotomy and talk instead about 'practice' (Wright 2006). Still, a distinction is often made between 'applied anthropology', understood as research on topics deemed to be of practical relevance, and 'practicing anthropologists' working outside of academia and carrying out non-research tasks, that is, operating in contexts where they may not even work as anthropologists but still apply anthropological approaches (Nolan 2003). Academia has been reluctant to accept that knowledge generated from work in policy and practice could constitute a legitimate basis for constructing theory (Shore and Wright 1997: 143) and that conceptualizing is also a kind of practice (Holbraad and Pedersen 2017); even when it is argued that basic research and so-called applied anthropology are not mutually exclusive endeavours as applied work always draws on theories and methods from academia (Pink 2006: 8), they are still referred to as two separate domains. An implicit distinction thus continues to be made between 'academic theory and knowledge' on the one hand, and its 'application in practice' on the other.

Numerous publications deal with the 'application' or 'practice' of anthropology (e.g. Jordan 1994, 2003; Hill and Baba 1997; Nolan 2003, 2013, 2017; Pink 2006; Strang 2009) as do several journals based in both the US and the UK: *Anthropology in Action*; *Journal for Applied Anthropology in Policy and Action*, a journal of the ASA network of Applied Anthropologists; *Human Organization and Practicing Anthropology*, a journal of the Society for Applied Anthropology; and *Annals of Anthro-*

pological Practice (known as the *NAPA Bulletin* until 2011), published by NAPA (National Association for the Practice of Anthropology), the section of the American Anthropological Association (AAA) that represents practicing anthropologists. Other scholars discuss 'engaged anthropology', that is, an anthropology speaking about crucial issues in contemporary society or becoming engaged as activists on behalf of the people they study (e.g. Low and Merry 2010; Benson 2014; Beck and Maida 2015).

A series of books deals with anthropologists working outside of academia, such as *Theoretical Scholarship and Applied Practice* by Pink, Fors and O'Dell (2017), discussing ways in which theoretical research has been incorporated into the practices of anthropologists outside of academia. Pink (2006) focuses on anthropologists employed as consultants or in salaried posts to actually provide anthropological research, insights or expertise to companies or organizations. Mosse (2011) discusses anthropologists working in international development and, more specifically, knowledge practices in the realm of international development, the object of this review article thus being international development rather than anthropology as such. Cefkin (2009) focuses on research by anthropologists on and in the corporate world, and again the object is the corporate world rather than anthropology as such. MacClancy (2017) discusses the experience of anthropologists working in government. In his book, *Anthropology and Public Service*, he outlines examples of the multiple trails that anthropological careers may move along, but discusses to a much smaller extent what it is that characterizes the practices of the anthropologists in question. In this book we intend to direct our gaze to anthropology and anthropologists themselves.

The self-reflective turn of the 1980s and the renewed interest in the practice of anthropology has spurred a debate on when and with what credentials one might call oneself an anthropologist. Is it defined by academic qualifications or by a particular anthropological way of thinking? It is clear by now that anthropologists do not wish to be defined simply by their methods. Anthropology, Pink states, is also a particular type of approach, a set of ideas that informs anthropologists' understanding of the world, a particular way of constructing and analysing problems (2006: 10). But Pink does not specify what these are and instead she notes that there are many different ways in which one can be an anthropologist and that there is no reason to try to essentialize anthropology as a discipline. As we will return to in later chapters, this reluctance to explicate, this fear of essentializing anthropological competences, is paradoxically one of the notable characteristics of anthropology.

In our project we asked not how to define anthropology, but what characterizes the practices of those who were trained as anthropologists, whether they work inside or outside of academia, carrying out anthropological research for a company or an organization or doing other tasks with an anthropological approach. Whether we are dealing with anthropologists' participation in the provision of healthcare or interdisciplinary research on science and technology, business or management, we stipulated that we were dealing with social practices of collaboration and that through ethnographic immersion into these collaborations we could move beyond the distinction between the abstract knowledge of basic research and its application and make explicit hitherto tacit dimensions of anthropological knowledge and competences. It became clear, as we started analysing our material from the four sub-studies, that what characterized the social practices of anthropologists across the different fields was not so much a particular set of competences, but rather a particular preoccupation with moral questions. We did not at the outset of the project have a specific interest in questions of ethics and morality, but ongoing comparisons of material from the different professional arenas that we studied have made it clear to us that there is a noteworthy consistency in the way in which anthropologists pose moral questions in relation to themselves and their work.

Questions of ethics and responsibility have, as noted above, been inherent to anthropologists' work since the time of Radcliffe-Brown and Malinowski, but as Pink reminds us, new working contexts, methodologies and research sponsors that anthropologists face today have new kinds of implications for ethics in anthropological research and representation (2006). When one does applied work one is confronted with a series of ethical choices, she further says, but some types of applied work are perhaps more universally morally justified; for example, acting as an expert in the asylum courts is easy to justify morally (Good in Pink 2006: 11), whereas some anthropologists would feel uncomfortable working for the Ministry of Defence, for multinational companies that are integral to global capitalism or for organizations involved with fox hunting (Pink 2006: 12). Ethical questions apply not only to the choice of whom to work with or for. During their work, anthropologists become tied up in complex series of loyalties and moral responsibilities and should ask themselves to whom and under what circumstances anthropologists are responsible: to their interlocutors, to the consumers, the institutions, the production company, the university, the client paying for results (ibid.)? Pink ends this discussion of ethics in the introduction to *Applications of Anthropology: Professional*

Anthropology in the Twenty-first Century by stating that what NAPA and SFAA (Society for Applied Anthropology) ethical guidelines do is to construct applied anthropology as an ethical project with a mission: it should contribute anthropological insights to society and might serve as a *moral corrective* (Pink 2006: 13, our italics).

What is clear from this is that Pink – like the organizers of the annual conference of the American Anthropological Association in 2017 and the interlocutors in our study – takes it for granted that anthropology has a 'mission' and should serve as a 'moral corrective' in society. What we intend to do in this book is to try to unpack this 'mission' or ambition to serve as a 'moral corrective'. We will argue that what seems to define anthropologists, not just the so-called applied or practicing anthropologist, but anthropologists both within and outside of academia, in Denmark (where most of our interlocutors' work) or elsewhere, is exactly this idea of a particular 'mission' and the ability of anthropologists to serve as a 'moral corrective' in society. Anthropology is not the only discipline or profession with a mission, but anthropologists are remarkably unreflective about their own moral project, especially considering the discipline's preoccupation in recent years with the moral projects of others. Therefore we ask: what is the kind of world that a training in anthropology makes us feel morally obliged to work towards?

In order to address this question, let us first look at the ways in which anthropologists have studied the moral worlds of people other than themselves.

The Anthropology of Anthropological Ethics

Over the last decade or so, the 'anthropology of ethics' (Faubion 2011) or 'moral anthropology' (Kapferer and Gold 2018) has emerged as an important and fast-growing subfield within anthropology. Following Mattingly and Throop (2018: 267), we use the two terms 'ethics' and 'morality' interchangeably. While the point here is not to make a comprehensive review of this literature, a quick gloss over some its most influential scholars and 'schools' will serve as a useful point of departure for an explication of our own specific concerns. Broadly speaking, we can distinguish between three approaches to the study of ethics and morality in anthropology, namely, what might for present purposes be called 'virtue ethics', 'ordinary ethics' and 'experience ethics'. In a recent review article Mattingly and Throop distinguish between 'three philosophical frameworks [that] have been most influential thus far in the ethical turn: (a) ordinary language philosophy and a focus on ordinary ethics, (b) phenomenology and an emphasis on moral experience, (c) Foucauldian and neo-Aristotelian traditions of virtue ethics' (2018: 475).

Inspired by ordinary language philosophers like Wittgenstein and Cavell, prominent everyday ethics anthropologists such as Veena Das (2012) and Michael Lambek (2010) maintain that the locus of moral agency is to be found in the human subject's everyday relations and/or acts of care and responsibility for others. Largely unarticulated, these ordinary ethics can only be unearthed via long-term fieldwork with its unique possibilities (and obligations) for participation and involvement in the suffering and hardships of key interlocutors. This focus on the ordinary and the everyday to some extent overlaps with that of experience ethical scholars like Jarrett Zigon (2007) and Jason Throop (2014) for whom the moral dimension of human existence is part of a broader backdrop of embodied experiences and tacit knowledge, which forms the everyday practical doxa against which reflexive thinking and normative moral rules are the exceptions. But what distinguishes at least some of these phenomenological scholars from the ordinary language ones is the emphasis they place on situations of crisis. Indeed, for Jarrett Zigon, it is only during moments of 'moral breakdown' that otherwise tacit ethical questions and behaviours are made explicit as the extraordinary situation forces people to make difficult moral choices and propels them to potentially reorient their moral compasses. Finally, the virtue ethical approach places emphasis on the conscious and reflective dimension of moral life. Drawing on Foucault's later work and other philosophical work on virtue ethics (e.g. Macintyre 1981), anthropologists like James Laidlaw (2014) and Joel Robbins (2004) have published influential analyses of the moral work that people do on themselves in order to become specific kinds of virtuous subjects.

Due to the increasing popularity and influence of these approaches and various combinations between them, the discipline of anthropology has seen 'an astonishing efflorescence of theoretical and ethnographic efforts to describe, recognize, locate, and analytically delimit moral dimensions of human existence' (Mattingly and Throop 2018: 476). Nonetheless, as Mattingly and Throop then go on to say, 'there is something still nascent and unfinished about the whole enterprise. Certainly, no clear consensus has coalesced about what its most important questions are, what is most crucial to foreground, why it needs its own "turn", or what terminology one should use when speaking of or analysing ethical life' (2018: 476). We entirely concur with this observation, but would here also like to qualify or add to it. For it seems to us that one of the key issues that have not hitherto been foregrounded enough is the ethical values and moral worlds of the anthropologists themselves. It is true that there is an extensive literature on ethnographic research ethics including, most recently, Josephides and Grønseth (2017; see also American Anthropological Association 2012; Iphofen 2013). Little or none of this work, however, has been based on systematic empirical research of the ethical ideas and practices of different anthropological individuals and communities, with a view to comparing, conceptualizing and theorizing them. In other words, whereas there has been both a great deal of work within the anthropology of ethics and also many books written that are concerned with how to practice anthropology ethically, very little attention has been given to an important yet overlooked field of inquiry that can be said to crisscross and potentially transcend these two literatures – namely, what might be called the 'anthropology of anthropological ethics'.

So how does one go about opening up this largely unexplored field of enquiry? How, to paraphrase Mattingly and Throop (2018: 476), are we to identity the right terminology one should use when speaking of or analysing [this distinct] ethical life? In the section that follows below, we shall suggest that a possible answer to this question can be found in the literature about and concept of 'moral economies'. But before doing so, let us reflect a little more on the interesting question as to why it might be that so few anthropologists have shown any ethnographic interest in anthropology's own ethical values.

In the introduction to the edited volume *Moral Anthropology: A Critique*, Kapferer and Gold criticize the anthropology of ethics and morality for 'reducing the radical critical potential of anthropology' (2018: 3) and for 'manifest[ing] a moralism underneath, a repressed or suppressed moralism despite declarations against it, that extends from the Western imperialism of the past' (2018: 11). While we do not necessarily agree with this rather harsh verdict, it seems to us that its two editors are getting at something important in suggesting that this anthropological subfield 'does not sufficiently acknowledge the extent to which it is a product of its own situation' (2018: 18). More precisely, Kapferer and Gold argue, anthropologists are insufficiently aware of their own positioning within a broader intellectual economy and disciplinary politics, which to an increasing degree has pushed anthropology towards occupying a marginal and labile identity position. In that sense, as they put it, the anthropology of ethics and morality is a reaction (perhaps unconscious) to structural changes in the discipline that have dissipated or fractured a sense of a coherent and relatively distinct project. This is an effect both of the great expansion in the number of practicing anthropologists combined with the growth of sub disciplinary areas within anthropology. As a result . . . anthropology has been emptied of much of its erstwhile distinction, becoming more a subbranch of other disciplines in the sense of being defined by their perspectives and paradigms . . . Being an anthropologist has value as a statement of identity, but it has lost much of the methodological and theoretical worth it had begun to achieve in the course of establishing itself as an academic discipline . . . The moral turn in anthropology can be seen as a return to the concerns and methodological issues that gave anthropology a relatively distinct coherence. (2018: 10–11)

What Kapferer and Gold are suggesting, then, is that the expansion of anthropology since its establishment has brought about a shift in anthropological identity. Having originally found its professional pride and purpose in the (purportedly) unique questions, methods and concepts associated with the discipline's modernist heyday, anthropology's 'value as a statement of identity' has over recent decades become tied, to an increasing degree, to questions of ethics and morality. We entirely agree with this, which is also in tune with discussions (and critics) of the more general turn away from the 'grand narratives' of mid-twentieth-century social science and humanities to the more particularistic, individualistic and 'critical' (including self-critical) approaches that took off from the 1980s and onwards (Marcus and Fisher 1986; Friedman 1994). Certainly, Kapferer and Gold make a strong case for the view that the rise of moral anthropology represents a (subconscious) return to the 'coherence' and 'distinction' of the past, but with the key difference that the 'grand narratives' of then have now been exchanged for the 'moral narratives' of today.

The Case of Denmark

Before specifying the conceptual framework through which we shall analyse the ethical idea(l)s of anthropology, let us now return to the question of when and why anthropology began branching out from academia, focusing on Denmark as the critical case of some international trends that changed anthropology from an academic discipline, critical about its own application, to a professional practice being carried out in many arenas of society.

In Denmark, anthropology has remained a highly competitive option for choice of university education for more than four decades and has attracted some of the brightest students. After graduating anthropologists are employed in a broad range of positions in the public as well as the private sector (Capacent 2009; Hansen and Jöhncke 2013). Anthropologists graduating from one of the two major universities in Denmark (Copenhagen and Aarhus) complete a five-year specialized degree in anthropology and emerge with a very strong identity as anthropologists. Their 'anthropological identity' does weaken over time as they gain different kinds of work experience and obtain other kinds of professional identity alongside their anthropological identity, but what our study has shown is that the same moral questions continue to guide many of them in their working life in a remarkably persistent way.

Anthropology has become a relatively large discipline in Danish universities compared to many other countries. The two large and original departments in Copenhagen and Aarhus have in the last two decades been supplemented by studies in other universities within subfields such as the anthropology of education, of technology and of marketing and management. Outside of academia, anthropologists have long been part of various kinds of professional collaborations and these have in many ways contributed to shaping the discipline and the way in which anthropology is currently being taught in universities in Denmark. Different kinds of initiatives have been taken by the major university departments in an attempt to build bridges between academia and the labour market. The students are taught compulsory courses in applied anthropology and anthropology as a profession and are encouraged to carry out fieldwork in collaboration with external partners.

At the heart of the research vision of the Department Anthropology at the University in Copenhagen, where the authors of this book were affiliated while carrying out their research, lies a commitment to *engaged* anthropology, which seeks to combine, in different and often *experimental* ways, a critical attention to pressing social problems and their potential solutions with a strong desire to formulate cutting-edge anthropological theories based on solid bodies of *ethnography*, also referred to by the department as 'The Triple E'. A unit has been established within the Department at the University of Copenhagen for the development and conduct of collaborative research and teaching projects with private corporations and public institutions as well as civil society organizations. The general purpose of this unit, referred to as

'AnthroAnalysis, Center for Applied Anthropology', is to contribute to the development and use of anthropological perspectives in practice, and to help inspire anthropologists and collaborative partners alike to take the use of the discipline still further into new areas and forms of application. As is stated on the homepage of this unit: 'It is part of an ongoing effort to build stronger links between university research and knowledge needs in different sectors of society – challenging and transforming both sides in the process'.

Researchers at the university departments also still carry out long ethnographic fieldwork in far-away places, and the academic community of anthropologists in Denmark has a high level of internationalization, including many international scholars, and most anthropological publications are in English. But anthropology in Denmark is at the same time a discipline that has put great effort into adapting to political and economic reforms in Denmark and new working conditions, both inside and outside of academia.

The humanities and the social sciences are presently being pushed to justify their relevance and existence in Denmark, as is also the case in many other countries, but there has also been a noteworthy increase in the demand for anthropologists on the Danish labour market. This paradox, as well as the attempts made by the Department of Anthropology in Copenhagen to bridge the divide between basic and applied research, need to be understood in the context of the growth of the Danish welfare state in the second half of the twentieth century and neo-liberal reforms in Denmark since the 1980s.

In Denmark, where all universities are state universities, there is a direct link between national research and education policy and changes in research and teaching at universities. Universities in Denmark have always educated people for a labour market, defined by the political project of the state, as discussed by O.K. Pedersen (2011) in his book *Konkurrencestaten* (The Competition State) which has had a considerable influence on the debate in Denmark since its publication. He refers to three different phases in the history of political culture in Denmark, from 1850 to 2010: 1) the formation of the nation state (1850–1950); 2) the development of the welfare state (1950–1990); and 3) the development of what he refers to as the 'competition state'.

The development of the nation state depended on tools such as a national language, a shared understanding of the culture and history of the nation, and the shaping of the individual through educational institutions. Therefore, during the nineteenth and the first half of the twentieth century, the humanities, especially those contributing to this nationalist project, became solidified in Danish universities (ibid.

169–77). During the next phase (1950–1990), democracy and participation in the welfare state took centre stage, through the promotion of values like community, equality and equal opportunity, and through the building of public institutions that could counter social inequalities. The social sciences (economy, political science, sociology) grew vastly at the university during this period, educational institutions now being expected to educate professionals for the fast-growing state bureaucracy and the increasing number of welfare institutions (ibid. 177–86). During this period, anthropology in Copenhagen was moved from the humanities, from being based at the National Museum of Denmark, to the faculty of social sciences.[2] The third phase, the 'competition phase', O.K. Pedersen argues, started around the 1990s. In the 1970s and 1980s a critique of the growing welfare state developed, and a transition to a new ideology was heralded at the time of financial crisis in the 1970s (ibid.: 187; O.K. Pedersen 2013). The result was a wave of neoliberal reforms and financial cuts, and the introduction of new public management tools in the public sector in the 1980s and 1990s (Kaspersen and Nørgaard 2015: 74–86), and the expectation that universities now educate people not only for the public but also the private sector.

While public employees' time and resources for each child, pupil, client, citizen, patient or student decreased in the 1980s and 1990s, anthropology as a discipline focusing on culture, and on the people's/patients'/users' perspective and experience, grew. In the 1980s the anthropology of development and medical anthropology became established subfields at the university departments in both Copenhagen and Aarhus, accompanied by a renewed interest in the application of anthropology. The Danish Development Agency (within the Danish Ministry of Foreign Affairs) has been a generous sponsor of anthropological research since the 1980s and 1990s and has therefore played a significant role in shaping – and making possible – research in those parts of the world where the development agency worked, in particular with regard to themes of particular interest to the agency (e.g. health in Africa and Asia). Alongside anthropologists' increasing involvement in development, requests were made from the Danish healthcare system and patient organizations in Denmark that anthropologists contribute to studying patients' experience of sickness and treatment, and medical anthropology became a significant subfield in the 1980s in Denmark, as it also did internationally.

The 1990s involved continued organizational rationalizations and an entry of market principles into the public sector, but during this decade a new market also opened for anthropologists in terms of collaboration with a whole range of professionals: corporate consultants, designers, IT specialists and others. Medical anthropology continued to grow, design anthropology and business and organizational anthropology became established as subfields, and the political demand for interdisciplinary research pushed anthropologists into a large range of collaborative projects, where they were often expected to explain culture and uncover the needs and perspectives of people. Ethnography was seen as a promising new means for mapping human behaviour (L.R. Pedersen 2018: 56).

After the turn of the century, the government launched a mission for Denmark to become a leading 'knowledge economy', as a way to counter the threat of globalization. In a strategy document issued by the Danish Government in 2006 the agenda is clear: 'We need to ensure that Denmark has the power to compete so we will remain among the richest countries in the world . . . The knowledge, ideas and work of people are the key to using the possibilities given to us by globalization. Therefore, Denmark needs to have a world-class educational system. We need to be a leading knowledge-society with research on the highest international level' (Government of Denmark 2006: 4–5). The concepts of a knowledge society or knowledge-based economy have been used interchangeably in a European context and date back to the mid-1990s. The specific concepts relating to a knowledge-based economy coalesced into a general policy, in no small part due to the OECD, which systematically developed indicators to measure the success rate of economies in terms of how knowledge was produced, disseminated and integrated in national economies (Godin 2006; Wright and Ørberg 2011). Like many other European countries, Denmark has taken up the OECD focus on knowledge production as a path to growth and value creation as a way to strengthen a traditional industrial production system. At a time when Denmark was actually doing rather well, not just financially but also in terms of international assessments of the quality of research and higher education, there was nevertheless a growing concern that an increasingly globalized market would become a threat to the nation (Gorm Hansen 2011: 29).

In a report published by the Danish Government in 2003, 'New Paths between Research and Industry from Insights to Invoice', the Danish Government stated: 'It is the goal of the government that Denmark be able to measure itself against the best in the world when it comes to interaction between industry and knowledge institutions . . . We are not good enough [yet] at ensuring that industry, knowledge and perspectives are mirrored in research and education' (Government of Denmark 2003: 5). Even though Denmark did well in terms of knowledge production, the new indicators developed by the OECD brought issues of knowledge dissemination to the forefront (Gorm Hansen 2011: 31).

This agenda echoed international trends where OECD countries in particular leaned heavily on the idea that knowledge production was going through necessary historical shift: the so-called leap from 'mode 1' to 'mode 2' knowledge production. This idea was first suggested by the now highly impactful book: *The New Production of Knowledge: The Dynamics of Science and Research in Contemporary Societies* (Gibbons et al. 1994),[3] which was later followed up in the writings of one of the authors, Helga Nowotny (Nowotny et al. 2001, Nowotny 2003). The 1994 book describes knowledge production mode 1 as a homogenous practice characterized as 'disciplinary', 'hierarchical', 'conservative' and carried out in the context of a purely academic community. By contrast, mode 2 of knowledge production is claimed to arise from rapid changes in Western societies, one of which is globalization, and is characterized by being 'transdisciplinary', 'heterogeneous', 'heterarchical', 'transient' and carried out in the context of application (Gibbons et al. 1994: 3). The narrative is one of progress. Mode 2 is identified as a new way of doing science and research, where the so-called producers of knowledge work more closely with the so-called consumers of knowledge, making knowledge production more 'socially accountable', 'reflexive' (Gibbons et al. 1994) or 'robust' (Nowotny et al. 2011, Nowotny 2003). *The New Production of Knowledge* received critique for showing a notable lack of empirical evidence for its claims (Shinn 2002), and for contradicting the history of science which shows little or no documentation for the existence of a past where the pure mode 1 university had a monopoly on knowledge production (Etzkowitz and Leydesdorff 2000, Shapin 2008). Despite this, the step1/step2 narrative which forms the core claim of the book has shown strong argumentative powers not just in terms of its solidifying and historicizing effects but also for its effectiveness as a political strategy (Gorm Hansen 2011, Wright and Ørberg 2011). This idea of a progressive shift away from an outdated academic mode 1 university to towards a more agile and competitive mode 2 university also had an enormous impact on research policy in Europe, Asia and North America, and played an important role in how academic universities were governed, funded and managed from the end of the 1990s and onwards (Godin 1998, Hessels and Van Lente 2008, Shinn 2002). To some Danish research policy makers in the late 1990s and early 2000s, the purported change to mode 2 knowledge production was referred to as an actual historical event with almost the same level of facticity as the fall of the Berlin wall

(Gorm Hansen 2011). It seems the hope invested in replacing the mode 1 university with a more competitive, interactive and institutionally distributed knowledge production rested on the assumption that it would also make academic science more agile and capable of competing on a global market (Government of Denmark 2003, 2006). In Denmark, policy makers readily adopted one of the core arguments from *The New Production of Knowledge*, resulting in a performative 'looping effect' where the step1/step2 narrative, rather than describing a development in the university sector, became a predictor of its reform (Gorm Hansen 2011). Echoing both the OECD and *The New Production of Knowledge*, a series of reforms in how Danish universities were governed, funded and managed were slowly initiated from the end of the 1990s and continued well beyond the next decade (Andersen 2006).

These changes were often announced precisely as a response to a perceived need to move Denmark out of an outdated era of the isolated, mono-disciplinary ivory tower research and into a new era in which university and society were imagined as separate spheres of reality in acute need of bridging or 'interacting' by way of commercialization, interdisciplinarity and restructuring (Government of Denmark 2003, Gorm Hansen 2011, Wright and Ørberg 2011).[4]

In 2006 this intensification of the interaction-agenda in Danish research policy resulted in new strategies to give Denmark a more competitive edge on the global market. A 'programme for user driven innovation' was initiated with the purpose of making Danish companies and public institutions more innovative and ultimately able to compete more effectively in a global economy (L.R. Pedersen 2018: 61; The Danish Business and Construction Authority 2007). Danish anthropologists responded: a specialized master's programme in Business and Organizational Anthropology was launched at the Department of Anthropology in Copenhagen in 2009, partly funded by a special scheme from the Ministry of Education and Research.

Consequently, on the one hand anthropologists felt that their research integrity and future existence was being threatened by the mantra of 'insight to invoice', and had difficulty seeing themselves as producers of research results that could feed directly into the design of commercial products. On the other hand, the rise of neoliberalism led to the widespread marketization of cultural and human domains, with regard to which anthropology was increasingly valued as an instrument for growth (L.R. Pedersen 2018: 60). While anthropologists thus felt politically threatened by the 'knowledge economy', neoliberal reforms also created new possibilities and contributed to a growth of the discipline.

The political culture of the welfare state, with its notions of community, participation and equality (cf. O.K. Pedersen 2011: 177–86), has persisted alongside these waves of neoliberal reforms, the intention of which were never to do away with the welfare state, but simply to render it more cost-efficient. The welfare state and its neoliberal reforms therefore provide an important context for the development of anthropology as a discipline in Denmark, in particular the rise of medical anthropology, design anthropology and business anthropology, as well as an increased focus upon interdisciplinary research in Danish universities, since the 1990s. They also provide part of the explanation behind anthropology's move from academia to the labour market outside of academia in the course of the 1980s and 1990s. Other reasons for this have to do with anthropology being a relatively large discipline in a small country, and the fact that several generations of highly competent students have found their way into the labour market and made anthropology known in Denmark.

The moral economy of anthropology that we discuss in the following chapters does indeed seem to resonate with that of anthropology in other countries, as illustrated by our reference to the opening ceremony of the AAA in 2017. It also resonates with the overall change of focus in anthropology from grand narratives of the mid-twentieth century, as discussed earlier. Still, as we have now shown, the growth of the discipline in Denmark since the 1980s, the recognition of its contributions by various societal actors, and the ways in which the moral economy of anthropology is played out in Denmark, that is, the 'mission' of anthropologists in Denmark, are also a result of political projects that have been set in motion in Denmark in the past decades – political projects that again are specific instances of more general, and at times international, trends.

We will now move on to the analytical framework that allows us to unpack the 'mission' of anthropology and the desire to be a 'moral corrective', namely the concept of moral economy.

Anthropology as a Moral Economy

We know all about the delicate tissue of social norms and reciprocities which regulates the life of Trobriand islanders, and the psychic energies involved in the cargo cults of Melanesia; but at some point this infinitely-complex social creature, Melanesian man, becomes . . . the eighteenth-century English collier who claps his hand spasmodically upon his stomach, and responds to elementary economic stimuli . . . [In] my view, these men and women in the crowd were informed by the belief that they were defending traditional rights or customs; and, in general, that they were supported by the wider consensus of the community ... [a] consistent traditional view of social norms and obligations, of the proper economic functions of several parties within the community, which, taken together, can be said to constitute the moral economy of the poor. (Thompson 1971: 78, 188)

Thus goes one snippet from the British historian E.P. Thompson's diatribe against his colleagues from economic history and sociology, who from his humanist-Marxist perspective were scandalously ignorant and presupposed about the lifeways of their countrymen [*sic*] from working class and peasant backgrounds. His now famous concept of 'moral economy' was an attempt to mitigate this lack by homing in on the distinct social, economic and ethical values, which – in his view – were shared by groups and communities belonging to lower socioeconomic strata in Britain and elsewhere. In the decade following the publication of Thompson's essay, a number of leftist historians, sociologists and anthropologists began using the concept, including Raymond Williams (of whose work Thompson was very critical), Eric Hobsbawm and, above all, James Scott, whose *The Moral Economy of the Peasant: Rebellion and Subsistence in Southeast Asia* became a modern classic among political theorists and anthropologists. Following Thompson, Scott used the concept of moral economies to assess and analyse the motivation and the potential for societal uprisings: 'If we understand the indignation and rage which prompted [Burmese peasants] to risk everything, we can grasp what I have chosen to call their moral economy: their notion of economic justice and their working definition of exploitation' (1977: 4). As such, the concept provided radical/activist students and scholars of politically and economically marginal groups with a new conceptual language for theorizing ideas, values and practices that would otherwise be deemed as backward, primitive or irrational from the vantage of neoclassical economy and modernization theory. Thus, as Fassin (2009) explains, the 'concept of moral economy ... refers to two very distinct levels of analysis. . . First, the moral economy corresponds to a system of exchange of goods and services and characterizes pre-market societies . . . Secondly, the moral economy also corresponds to a system of norms and obligations . . . More than a set of economic rules, these norms are principles of good character, justice, dignity, and respect' (2009: 11). What is more, as Fassin also points out, the concept of moral economy can be applied to two scales of investigation: 'On the one hand, we can consider the moral economies of a society (or group of societies) in a given historical moment. On the other hand, we can focus more specifically on moral economies of certain social realms or segments of society . . . at the global, national, or local level' (2009: 47).

Now, the question that we would like to ask here is: might (Danish) anthropology itself also be described as a moral economy in the sense theorized by Thompson and other Marxists? And if so, what might be the analytical purpose of making this move, both in relation to the specific purposes of this volume, and with respect to the wider discussion concerning anthropology's role in the world? At first glance, the community of (mostly middle-class, white) Danish anthropologists hardly meets the criteria of a moral economy in the most common anthropological understanding of this term. As one of our colleagues objected when we presented an early version of these thoughts at a seminar, the community of Danish anthropology and anthropologists are part and parcel of a broader neoliberal political economy, whose hegemonic logic of self-control and optimization permeates virtually all professional (and personal) relationships in the Danish private and public sector, including universities. Clearly, to assert that the members of this community partake in a 'system of exchange of goods and services [that] characterizes pre-market societies' (cf. Fassin 2009: 47) would not just be imprecise if not inaccurate, but also frivolous and privilege-blind.

However, there are versions of the concept of moral economy that offer a better match with the case of anthropology and anthropologists. Let us briefly consider two of these in turn. In 1995, Chicago historian of science, Lorraine Daston, published a now classic paper, which both extended the empirical scope of the moral economy concept to a community of (natural) scientists, but also represented a theoretical break from the version discussed above. A 'moral economy', Daston writes,

> is a web of affect-saturated values that stand and function in well-defined relationship to one another. In this usage, 'moral' . . . refers at once to the psychological and to the normative . . . Although it is a contingent, malleable thing of no necessity, a moral economy has a certain logic to its composition and operations . . . Although moral economies are about mental states, these are the mental states of collectives, in this case collectives of scientists, not of lone individuals . . . [It is] a gradual shaping of a collective personality akin (and . . . sometimes identical) to Norbert Elias's 'civilizing process'. (1995: 4–5)

As Fassin points out in his critical remarks on Daston's work (Fassin 2009: 28–35), this definition is old-school Durkheimian (and, as Daston herself also implies, classic Weberian). Gone is Thompson's historical-materialist focus on exploitation, resistance and revolution, and in comes instead a socially constituted and morally sanctioned subculture of shared meanings, symbols and values of the sort so well-known from the anthropological canon. And much like in the case of Scott's extension of Thompson's concept of moral economy to non-Western peasant contexts, it is not difficult to see why Daston's widening of the concept of moral economies gained traction, at least among historians and sociologists of science, who have generally tended to study communities (viz. Western natural scientists) who are not as socially and economically marginal as Thompson's 'workman' [*sic*] or Scott's peasants, but who nevertheless often harbour moral ideals which are in direct opposition to dominant economic logics. Indeed, Daston asserts,

> [m]oral economies . . . are integral to science: to its sources of inspiration, its choice of subject matter and procedures, its sifting of evidence, and its standards of explanation . . . Insofar as the study of moral economies in science is about power, it is power of the microscopic, internalized Foucaultian sort, rather than of the political (or martial), externalized kind. In other words, the moral economy of science is more about self-discipline than coercion. (1995: 6)

Evidently, it would seem to make a good deal of sense to conceive of anthropology as a scientific moral economy in Daston's Durkheimian/Weberian sense. To be sure, one would be hard pressed to identity 'quantification, empiricism and objectivity' (1995: xx) as the dominant values in the moral economy of anthropology, but then again, anthropologists hardly consider themselves to be 'scientists' in Daston's narrow sense. Nevertheless, it seems to us that Daston's generic definition of the moral economy of science as a 'web of affect-saturated values that stand and function in well-defined relationship to one another' applies well to anthropology, including her observation that this involves the shaping of a 'collective personality akin to . . . [a] civilizing process'. Indeed, this emphasis on the cultivation of a particular scientific disciplinary self, and indeed a certain self-disciplining, might be said to apply particularly well to the modern Danish context, where students and scholars of anthropology tend to identity very strongly with their discipline and to spend considerable time and energy on maintaining and patrolling boundaries towards other professions inside and outside the academy.

Still, it is hard to disagree with critics of Daston, like Fassin, that her notion of moral economies as (sub)cultures is too watered down and too generic (as well as overly culturalist and bourgeois, in a critical theory sense). Ideally, we are looking for a version of the concept that is not as empirically restricted as Thompson's, and to a lesser extent Scott's and Fassin's, but one that is still sufficiently narrow and analytically precise to capture what could be thought to be characteristic of self-acclaimed and aggrandized 'moral' academic groupings like anthropologists. And fortunately, we have stumbled across a good candidate for just such a concept in our oftentimes meandering and sometimes desperate sifting through multiple partly overlapping anthropological literatures:

> The moral economy of capitalism is based on the separation of two spheres, the market and home, which represent ideally impersonal and personal social life. The payment of money for labour marks the first and unpaid, especially female labour the second. People are expected to divide themselves daily between public production and private consumption, to submit to impersonal rules outside the home and to express themselves as persons within it. This division has never been actually achieved, but a huge cultural effort goes into generating it. (Hart 2011)

The subtlety and the sharpness of this definition from the noted economic anthropologist Keith Hart is significant. Notwithstanding its merits for the anthropological study of capitalism (a question that is beyond the scope of this discussion), Hart's notion of capitalism as moral economy provides us with what we have been looking for: a reconceptualization of this concept that significantly widens its analytical purchase to ethnographic contexts beyond 'workers' and 'peasants' and other economically and culturally marginalized groups, while retaining the original concept's degree of sharpness.

In fact, we would go so far as to suggest that the passage above contains the potential to pin down the content as well as the form of the moral economy of anthropology with almost surgical precision. All that we need to do is to substitute 'capitalism' with 'anthropology'. Before we make this attempt, let us have a look at what kinds of divisions we have seen anthropologists make when it comes to making sense of their own practice. Accordingly, in what follows, we return to some of our key findings from the joint research project on which most chapters in this book are based.

The Moral Economy of Danish Anthropologists

During our fieldwork we all independently discovered that a large part of the conversations we had with anthropologists, as well as a large part of the decisions they made at work, revolved around an ongoing concern for the moral value as well as the authenticity of their work. For many of our interlocutors, it seemed like their identification with the discipline of anthropology came with implicit moral imperatives. Sentences starting with 'as an anthropologist I must', 'as an anthropologist I will have to' or 'as an anthropologist I could never' frequently appeared in our material. Reading our fieldwork material together, we started to wonder why our interlocutors were so concerned with assessing whether or not their work would be helpful in creating a 'better world', while their concrete vision of this world differed so enormously between them. Most of our interlocutors were concerned with not compromising on their own moral standards, and others saw themselves as defending a set of moral values against all odds, sometimes to the point of seeing themselves in opposition to the very organizations they work for or with.

Our collective fieldwork experience shows anthropologists putting much effort into thinking critically about the moral landscape they work in and expressing a need to change things for the better, often in opposition to the logic of the systems they work within, and with a great deal of ambivalence towards occupying a formal position of power or becoming part of the establishment. Medical anthropologists divide their world up into two spheres. On one side is a world of real, embodied people whose experience, suffering, everyday life and practices they feel obliged to faithfully represent. On the other side is a world of abstract and calculative logic created by medical or natural scientists, managers and state bureaucrats, whom they feel obliged to critically challenge in order to be helpful in the long run (Chapter 1). In the three other fields we cover in this book we saw similar ambitions: anthropologists working in the (profit-led) field of business distanced themselves from the logic of capitalism and did not see profit accumulation as a morally justifiable goal (Chapter 2). Anthropologists in leadership positions seemed to distance themselves from their formal roles as managers, or at least attempted to become another kind of manager, one who understands the organization as a complex set of human social practices rather than in terms of bottom line numbers, budgets or business fads (Chapter 3). Academic anthropologists working in interdisciplinary projects often distanced themselves from the logics they encountered in other disciplines and found it morally questionable to compromise their affiliation to anthropological epistemology, methods and ethics when engaging in cross-disciplinary collaborations, as this in itself felt reductionist and immoral to them (Chapter 4).

It seems that providing results in management, interdisciplinary research, healthcare or business consulting was more a means to an end than a goal in itself for our interlocutors. Key Performance Indicators or core tasks in their job had to provide the world with something more, something better. Looking at our materials across field sites, it seems that interlocutors assessed this 'more' or 'better' by plotting their own work in relationship to morally charged spheres that were often put in opposition to one another. Thus, we found it fruitful to try to understand our interlocutors' incessant moral self-assessment by thinking of it as a moral economy. An absolute division of spheres was never actually achieved but, as Hart says in relation to the moral economy of capitalism, a huge cultural effort went into generating it.

Many of the anthropologists we worked with told us they did not feel that they were 'real' or 'true' anthropologists and we often heard them say that compromising with the demands of 'real anthropology' was a moral challenge to them. Is there something inherently moral about being a real anthropologist? Do anthropologists share a common code for what constitutes moral integrity?

The answer is a resounding no! Our individual interlocutors' moral values themselves seem rather fluid and dependent on context. In fact, our interlocutors show very little coherence when it comes to the specific content of their individual moral values and visions for a better world. One anthropologist's moral high ground may be another anthropologist's moral defeat, and moral values can, moreover, change in the course of a career.

What we do see across fields, however, is the ongoing preoccupation with juxtaposing one's work with a more or less specific moral ideal as well as juxtaposing it with the work of others in relationship to this ideal. Across fields, our interlocutors were engaged in a process of plotting their work within what we have chosen to call a moral economy, the world being constantly divided into spheres that the anthropologist will find more or less aligned with what they find just, good or right.

Allow us to stress here, that we do not see the moral economy of anthropology as a description of some pre-existing and fixed entity, such as a common set of moral guidelines that apply to all anthropologists. Our use of the concept is analytical and in that sense predominantly heuristic. The concept of moral economy helps us to ask questions about what kinds of spheres anthropologists divide their world into and how these spheres are given different moral values in relation to each other. It makes us interested in the way in which interlocutors position their work and that of others in an economy of moral value assessment.

What we refer to here as a moral economy of anthropology, then, may be conceived of as a sort of coordinate system within which a given anthropologist positions him- or herself in relation to two axes or scales of moral value.

We have identified two overall axes that seem to govern the way in which anthropologists assess the moral value of their work. The vertical axis makes a distinction between what our interlocutors see as 'things as they are' versus 'things as they seem'. The horizontal axis makes a distinction between what we choose to call 'anthropology as an identity' and 'anthropology as a tool'. Together, the two axes form a matrix that can be loaded with moral value and used in a process of assessment of one's own work – and that of colleagues or co-workers inside and outside the discipline.

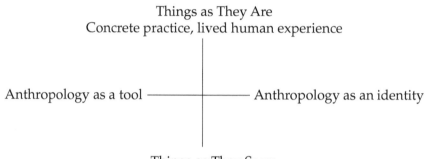

Things as They Are
Concrete practice, lived human experience

Anthropology as a tool ——————— Anthropology as an identity

Things as They Seem
Abstractions, numbers calculative logic, bureaucratic systems

Figure 0.1 The horizontal and vertical axes of the moral economy of anthropology

The Vertical Axis: Metaphysics

The vertical axis is metaphysical in nature, in that it divides the world into two poles – or spheres – that we could pragmatically call 'things as they are' and 'things as they seem'. The highest value of this axis points towards what the anthropologist perceives to be a real world of concrete, lived human experience, a world whose richness and complexity testifies to its reality. The lowest value points towards a world of abstraction where numbers, concepts, graphic representations, calculative logic and bureaucratic systems reign. The lower part of the scale on this axis points to a world that is merely an abstraction of the real (things as they seem) rather than being the real itself (things as they are). Dividing the world up according to these two spheres is in no way unique to anthropologists. Most professional groups can be said to subscribe to metaphysical assumptions about what constitutes the real and what does not. In fact, we can hardly think of a human society that does not divide up the world in terms of different levels of reality. What seems unique to the anthropologists we meet in this book is not the poles of this metaphysical axis but rather the way in which this axis is moralized.

According to our interlocutors, anthropological practice and the kind of knowledge it generates cannot be presented in abstract and simple terms such as graphs, numbers, Excel sheets or bullet-point executive summaries without some kind of moral compromise. Something more is going on, something thicker and richer and less explicable that eschews abstract or numerical representation. Functioning as a spokesperson for this 'more', however it is defined, seems to be vital to the anthropologists' sense of moral high ground.

It became interesting to us, that while anthropologists associated the lower part of this scale with things as they seem, their colleagues from other professional groups would almost certainly express the opposite view. Whereas mathematicians and economists (Barany and MacKenzie 2014), physicists (Knorr-Cetina 1999), engineers (Latour 1996), accountants (Boll 2014) or biologists (Gorm Hansen 2011) base many of their decisions on abstract representations and strongly believe in their own ability to speak for reality by way of these, our interlocutors tend to have it precisely the other way around. They seemed to attribute not only a higher level of reality but also a higher level of moral value to a concrete, lived human practice, which they claim cannot be explicated in abstract, graphical or numerical representations without making/ causing a dangerous slippage from representing 'things as they are' to merely representing them 'as they seem'. Thus, the higher we go on this axis towards things as they are, the closer the anthropologist is to positioning him- or herself as a spokesperson for the concrete, real, embodied and lived experience of people whose practice they manage, represent in academic publications, or develop healthcare or provide other assistance for by way of consultancy services or design. In contrast, the lower we go on the scale of this axis, the further away we move from representing the real, and thus the more likely anthropologists are to assess their own work (and that of others) as superficial, reductionist or simply misguided. Consequently, the anthropologist becomes less trustworthy as a spokesperson for what is 'real' and 'true' and, more importantly, therefore less morally justified in the work they do.

Again, our interlocutors may differ greatly when it comes to their view of what constitutes reality, their ontology, so to speak. But across fields we see a shared metaphysics: an attempt to divide the world into these two spheres. The moralization of this axis makes our interlocutors align with whatever they individually perceive to be most concrete, real and empirically grounded, striving for the high end of the scale on this axis. At the same time, we see, across fields, an ongoing attempt by our interlocutors to negatively define the lower scale on this axis and to self-represent in a way that clearly disassociates their professional identity from the negative pole of this axis. The two end points of this axis will, however, be defined very differently depending on the context in which the interlocutor is doing their work, as well as the current expression of their personal moral values.

The Horizonal Axis: Identity

Shifting position in our coordinate system, the horizontal axis is stretched out between a position at one end of the axis in which there is a conflation between personal identity and academic discipline, and a position at the other end where anthropology is used as a tool to obtain a different goal than the one of doing 'real anthropology'. Like the moralization of the vertical axis, the identity/tool axis is at times also loaded with moral value in the sense that anthropological knowledge often stands for authenticity when anthropologists talk about their contributions to a workplace. Perhaps that is part of the context for the concern many of our interlocutors' express about being 'real anthropologists' and their striving towards (or idealization of) high value positions on the horizontal axis. Anthropological authenticity, many of our interlocutors imagine, will strengthen their sense of being entitled to speak on behalf of a human reality and make them less doubtful about their own ability to do so. In fact, when studying anthropologists ethnographically, we would at times find ourselves negotiating (and in some cases competing) for anthropological authenticity with our interlocutors in a way that gave rise to a subtle pecking order revolving around who gets to turn the other into 'data' (Chapter 5). In other cases, our interlocutors would be primarily invested in a different project, the one of the organization that they worked for, and only be concerned about their position on the vertical axis, feeling that the higher they were on the vertical axis, the better they could contribute to their goals of their organization (Chapter 1). Again, the values themselves are fluid and context-dependent. There is no agreement between interlocutors about what constitutes 'real anthropology', and the high end of this axis is almost exclusively negatively defined. It seems that across fields, a real anthropologist is defined by their distance to the non-anthropological. Our interlocutors are quite clear in labelling work in their field as non-anthropological, but their specific reasons for doing so may vary greatly across fields. For some, being a real anthropologist would require them to have spent a year doing fieldwork in a specific setting (which the majority of our interlocutors lament not having done). Others seem to subscribe to the idea that being a real anthropologist is determined by one's proximity to university life and academic research. Others, still, define real anthropology as taking place outside university 'ivory towers' where anthropologists can use anthropology as a tool in ways that directly address the key issue for their employer, client or customer.

Taken together, these two axes form the basis for a moral economy of anthropology. In this moral economy, some anthropologist will be called to strive for a position in the upper right 'magic quadrant' of our coordinate system (Barany and MacKenzie 2014). Others will be more interested in positioning themselves in the upper left corner. However, none of our interlocutors identify with the two quadrants below the horizontal line in our coordinate system. As the division between a real human reality and its opposite as well as the division between real anthropology and its opposite remain fluid and context-dependent, the magic quadrant is often negatively defined in terms of what one is not really achieving. Thus, there is an immanent sense of needing to enquire into whether one's work is in fact in danger of slipping into the wrong side of these divisions. Thus, in the words of Hart, a 'huge cultural effort' goes into generating these divisions again and again and positioning oneself correctly in relationship to them in every new work relationship. In sum, we will argue in this book that the moral values of anthropologists are in no way absolute. Indeed, they are relative and negotiable. What we will show in chapters 1–5 is not where in the coordinate system particular anthropologists are positioned. Rather, we will show the ongoing re-enactment of the above distinctions and the constant effort to position themselves and the people they work with in relation to these spheres, marked by their two axes. This continuous effort we will call the moral work of anthropology.

So, to paraphrase Hart's definition of the moral economy of capitalism by substituting 'capitalism' with 'anthropology':

> The moral economy of anthropology is based on the separation of two spheres, things as they seem and things as they are, which represent, ideally, abstraction into dead numbers and concrete and lived everyday life, respectively. Explications of all kinds, especially for bureaucratic, commercial or otherwise hegemonic (capitalist, hetero-normative and patriarchal)

purposes, mark the former, and long-term (or permanent!) fieldwork, especially of an inter-subjective, caring sort, aspiring to gain access to otherwise tacit norms undergirding peoples' experiences, marks the latter. Anthropologists are expected to divide their work between meaningless labour that reduces complexity by representing and reproducing things as they seem on the one hand, and meaningful work that retains complexity and reduces suffering on the other hand, and to express themselves amorally by reductionist explicitness outside the sphere of anthropological integrity and express themselves as moral embodiment inside it. This division has never been actually achieved, but a huge cultural effort goes into generating it.

In the chapters that follow we will present the studies and collaborations from which we generated the above analytical framework. The chapters in the book explore anthropologists at different points in their career and in different kinds of working conditions. Some added anthropological training to their skills after years on the labour market; some majored in anthropology at the university but had many years of work experience in non-academic organizations like the healthcare system when we met them, and had less difficulty realizing their moral project while at the same time identifying with their workplace and job function (Chapter 1). Others have been at their workplace for many years but continue to identify strongly with anthropology, and feel called to do things differently due to this identification. We also encountered anthropologists who were at the beginning of their career and still struggled to dissociate themselves from anthropology as an identity project and/ or work with the production and selling of anthropological methods and knowledge, and who thus continuously faced dilemmas and questions concerning the authenticity of the way in which they did anthropology (Chapter 2 and Chapter 5). Finally, we have encountered anthropologists who work in interdisciplinary settings within academia where the personal and the disciplinary identity remain indistinguishable (Chapter 4). In the conclusion of the book we tie the chapters together through a return to the framework presented here in the Introduction.

We hope that the book will contribute to an awareness and debate of what happens to anthropology as it moves in and out of academia and into new arenas, and that future research will explore yet other arenas in Denmark as well as in other countries, and follow up on how the moral project of anthropology evolves over time and space.

Hanne Overgaard Mogensen is associate professor at the Department of Anthropology, University of Copenhagen. Her main topic of research is medical anthropology and international health, primarily in Africa. She has also published literary anthropology based on her research. She teaches medical anthropology at the University of Copenhagen.

Birgitte Gorm Hansen is an independent consultant and researcher. She is trained as a psychologist from the University of Copenhagen and received her PhD in science studies and management from Copenhagen Business School in 2011. Her postdoctoral research on anthropologists working in leadership positions formed one of the four sub-studies conducted in the Department of Anthropology at the University of Copenhagen.

Morten Axel Pedersen is a Professor at the Department of Anthropology and Director of SODAS. After having spent two decades doing anthropological research in and on Inner Asia, he has for the last eight years been working on political forms and digital economies in Denmark.

NOTES

We gratefully acknowledge the 'Danish Council for Independent Research, Culture and Communication' for funding the research project on which this book is based, the Department of Anthropology, University of Copenhagen for hosting the project, and all our colleagues at the department for their comments, ideas, critical thoughts and interest in the project.
  1. It would indeed have been relevant to include global development in the discussion of anthropology's moral project, but morality was not the object of the study from the outset of the project.
  2. In Aarhus, the other major Department of Anthropology in Denmark, it is still based at the Faculty of Humanities.
  3. In 2007 the book had received over 1000 citations in academic journals and the number still increases (Hessels and Van Lente 2008). Shinn (2002) investigates the impressive impact of *The New Production of Knowledge* from its publication in 1994 and detects a marked increase in citations around the end of the 1990s: 'For the period of 1995 to June 1999 a total of 98 references were made to the book ... The number of references for the first six months of 1999 already equals those for 1998; the total (not including self-citations) from 1995 to July 2002 is 266 citations' (Shinn 2002: 601). Education reviews in particular are abundant in citations but citations are also found in the field of science policy, sociology of science and technology, psychology, sociology and social psychology. Citations are mainly found in Western Europe but also in the United States and Canada. The concept of mode 2 knowledge production has been found in policy documents in Europe, Canada and the United States (Hessels

and van Lente 2008; Godin 1998). Interestingly, a very steep increase in citations occurs around 1999 and rapidly climbing upwards from there to 2011,
coinciding with the period in which the push for a radical reform of Danish
university management and the need to embrace industrial interests began to
pick up speed (Andersen,2006). Today a general Google search on the full title
of the book will give 34.,00,000 results while keywords like 'mode 2 knowledge' will give 1,370,000 hits.

4. See Jensen (2010) and Godin (1998) for similar performative readings of the
mode 2 concept.

REFERENCES

American Anthropological Association. 2012. *Code of Ethics of the American Anthropological Association*. Retrieved 14 January 2021 from https://www.american
anthro.org/LearnAndTeach/Content.aspx?ItemNumber=22869&navItem
Number=652.

Andersen, P.B. 2006. *An Insight into Ideas Surrounding the 2003 University Law –
Development Contracts and Management Reforms*. Working Paper 4 on the University Reform. Published online by the Danish University of Education.
Retrieved 14 January 2021 from https://dpu.au.dk/fileadmin/www.dpu.dk/
forskning/forskningsprogrammer/epoke/workingpapers/Working_Paper_
4__An_Insight_into_Ideas_Surrounding.pdf0.pdf.

Baba, M.L. 2006. 'Anthropology and Business', in H.J. Birx (ed.), *Encyclopedia of
Anthropology*. Thousand Oaks, CA: Sage Publications, pp. 83–117.

———. 2014. 'De-Anthropologizing Ethnography: A Historical Perspective on the
Commodification of Ethnography as a Business Service', in R.M. Denny and
P.L. Sunderland (eds), *Handbook of Anthropology in Business*. Walnut Creek:
Left Coast Press Inc., pp. 43–68.

Barany, M.J. and D. MacKenzie. 2014. 'Chalk: Materials and Concepts in Mathematics Research', in C. Coopman, J. Vertesi, M. Lynch and S. Woolgar (eds),
Representation in Scientific Practice Revisited. MIT Press Scholarship Online.

Beck, S. and C.A. Maida (eds). 2015. *Public Anthropology in a Borderless World*. Oxford, New York: Berghahn Books.

Benson, Peter. 2014. 'Year in Review, Public Anthropology, 2013: Webs of Meaning,
Critical Interventions', *American Anthropologist* 116(2): 379–89.

Boll, K. 2014. 'Representing and Performing Businesses', *Journal of Cultural Economy* 7(2): 226–44.

Campbell, I. 2014. 'Radcliffe-Brown and "Applied Anthropology" in Cape Town
and Sydney', in R. Darnell and F. Gleach (eds), *Anthropologists and Their Traditions across National Borders*. Lincoln: University of Nebraska Press, pp. 111–40.

Capacent. 2009. *Beskæftigelsenundersøgelse 2009*, Department of Antrrhopology,
University of Copenhagen. Retrieved 20 September 2019 from http://antro
pologi.ku.dk/uddannelser/soegende/beskaeftigelse/.

Cefkin, M. 2009. 'Introduction: Business, Anthropology, and the Growth of Corporate Ethnography', in M. Cefkin (ed.), *Ethnography and the Corporate Encoun-*

ter: Reflections on Research in and of Corporations. Oxford, New York: Berghahn Books, pp. 1–37.

Clifford, J. and G.E. Marcus (eds). 1986. *Writing Culture: The Poetics and Politics of Ethnography*. Berkeley: University of California Press.

Das, V. 2012. 'Ordinary Ethics', in D. Fassin (ed.), *A Companion to Moral Anthropology*. London: John Wiley & Sons, pp. 133–49.

Daston, Lorraine. 1995. 'The Moral Economy of Science', *Osiris* 10: 2–24.

Etzkowitz, H. and L. Leydesdorff. 2000. 'The Dynamics of Innovation: From National Systems and "Mode2" to a Triple Helix of University-Industry-Government Relations'. Research Policy 29: 109-12.

Fassin, Didier. 2009. 'Les économies morales revisitées', *Annales. Histoire, Sciences Sociales* 24(6): 1237–66.

Faubion, J.D. 2011. *An Anthropology of Ethics*. Cambridge, UK: Cambridge University Press.

Friedman, J. 1994. *Cultural Identity and Global Process*. London: Sage.

Gibbons, M., C. Limoges, H. Nowotny, S. Schwarzman, P. Scott and M. Trow. 1994. *The New Production of Knowledge: The Dynamics of Science and Research in Contemporary Societies*. London: Sage.

Godin, B. 1998. 'Writing Performative History: The New Atlantis?', *Social Studies of Science* 28(3): 465–83.

———. 2006. 'The Knowledge-Based Economy: Conceptual Framework or Buzzword?', *Journal of Technology Transfer* 31(1): 17–30.

Gorm Hansen, B. 2011. 'Adapting in the Knowledge Economy: Lateral Strategies for Scientists and Those Who Study Them', PhD thesis. Copenhagen: Copenhagen Business School, University of Copenhagen.

Government of Denmark. 2003. *Nye veje mellem forskning og erhverv – fra tanke til faktura*. Retrieved 20 September 2019 from http://vtu.dk/publikationer/20 03/nye-veje-mellem-forskningog-erhverv-fra-tanke-til-faktura/.

———. 2006. *Fremgang, Fornyelse og Tryghed – strategi for Danmark i den globale økonomi*. Albertslund: Statsministeriet, Schultz Information.

Hansen, Anne-Louise L. and Steffen Jöhncke. 2013. *Omsat antropologi: En undersøgelse af det antropologiske arbejdsmarked i Danmark* [Realized Anthropology: A Study of the Anthropological Labour Market in Denmark]. Copenhagen: AnthroAnalysis, Department of Anthropology, University of Copenhagen.

Hart, Keith. 2011. 'Commentary to the Blogpost "Defining Capitalism"', *The Open Anthropology Cooperative*. Retrieved 15 August 2019 from http://open anthcoop.ning.com/group/economicanthropology/forum/topics/defining-capitalism?commentId=3404290%3AComment%3A114742&groupId=34042 90%3AGroup%3A785#sthash.DLzwlGD7.dpbs.

Hessels, L. and H. van Lente. 2008. 'Re-thinking New Knowledge Production: A Literature Review and a Research Agenda', *Research Policy* 37: 740–60.

Hill, C.E. and M.L. Baba. 1997. *The Global Practice of Anthropology*. Virginia: College of Williamsburg.

Holbraad, Martin and Morten Axel Pedersen. 2017. *The Ontological Turn: An Anthropological Exposition*. Cambridge: Cambridge University Press.

Iphofen, Ron. 2013. *Research Ethics in Ethnography/Anthropology*. European Commission. Retrieved 14 January 2021 from http://ec.europa.eu/research/participants/data/ref/h2020/other/hi/ethics-guide-ethnog-anthrop_en.pdf.

Jensen, C.B. 2010. *Ontologies for Developing Things: Making Health Care Futures Through Technology*. Rotterdam: Sense.

Jordan, A.T. (ed.). 1994. *Practicing Anthropology in Corporate America: Consulting on Organizational Culture. NAPA Bulletin* 14.

———. 2003. *Business Anthropology*. Long Grove, Illinois: Waveland Press, Inc.

Josephides, L. and A.S. Grønseth (eds). 2017. *The Ethics of Knowledge Creation*. New York: Berghahn Books.

Kapferer, B. and M. Gold. 2018. 'Introduction: Reconceptualizing the Discipline', in B. Kapferer and M. Gold (eds), *Moral Anthropology: A Critique*. Oxford, New York: Berghahn Books, pp. 1–24.

Kaspersen, L.B. and J. Nørgaard. 2015. *Ledelseskrise i konkurrencestaten*. Copenhagen: Hans Reitzels Forlag.

Knorr-Cetina, K. 1999. *Epistemic Cultures: How the Sciences Make Knowledge*. Cambridge, MA: Harvard University Press.

Laidlaw, J. 2014. *The Subject of Virtue: An Anthropology of Ethics and Freedom*. Cambridge: Cambridge University Press.

Lambek, M. (ed.). 2010. *Ordinary Ethics: Anthropology, Language, and Action*. New York: Fordham University Press.

Lassiter, L.E. (ed.). 2005. *The Chicago Guide to Collaborative Ethnography*. Chicago: Chicago University Press.

Latour, B. 1996. *Aramis, Or the Love of Technology*. Cambridge, MA: Harvard University Press.

Lewis, D. 2012. 'Anthropology and Development: The Uneasy Relationship', in James G. Carrier (ed.), *Handbook of Economic Anthropology*. Cheltenham: Edward Elgar Publishing Limited,

Low, S.M and S.E. Merry. 2010. 'Engaged Anthropology: Diversity and Dilemmas', *Current Anthropology* 51(2): 203–26.

MacClancy, J. (ed.). 2017. *Anthropology and Public Service: The UK Experience*. Oxford, New York: Berghahn Books.

MacIntyre, A. 1981. 'The Nature of the Virtues', *The Hastings Center Report* 11(2): 27–34.

Marcus, G.E. 2005. 'The Passion of Anthropology in the U.S, Circa 2004', *Anthropological Quarterly* 78(3): 673–95.

———. 2008. 'The End(s) of Ethnography: Social/Cultural Anthropology's Signature Form of Producing Knowledge in Transition', *Cultural Anthropology* 23(1): 1–14.

Marcus, G.E. and M.F. Fischer. 1986. *Anthropology as Cultural Critique: An Experimental Moment in the Human Sciences*. Chicago: University of Chicago Press.

Matsutake Worlds Research Group. 2009. 'A New Form of Collaboration in Cultural Anthropology: Matsutake Worlds', *American Ethnologist* 2: 380–403.

Mattingly, C. and J. Throop. 2018. 'The Anthropology of Ethics and Morality', *Annual Review of Anthropology* 47: 475–92.

Mills, D. 2003. 'Professionalizing or Popularizing Anthropology? A Brief History of Anthropology's Scholarly Associations in the UK', *Anthropology Today* 19(5): 8–13.

———. 2006. 'Dinner at Claridges? Anthropology and the Captains of Industry, 1947-1955', in S. Pink (ed.), *Applications of Anthropology: Professional Anthropology in the Twenty-First Century*. Oxford, New York: Berghahn Books, pp. 55–70.

Mosse, D. (ed.). 2011. *Adventures in Aidland: The Anthropology of Professionals in International Development*. Oxford, New York: Berghahn Books.

———. 2013. 'The Anthropology of International Development', *Annual Review of Anthropology* 42: 227–46.

Niehaus, I. 2018. 'Anthropology at the Dawn of Apartheid: Radcliffe-Brown and Malinowski's South African Engagements, 1919–34', in L. Chua and M. Nayanika (eds), *Who are 'We'? Reimagining Alterity and Affinity in Anthropology*. New York, Oxford: Berghahn, pp. 37–59.

Nolan, R.W. 2003. *Anthropology in Practice: Building a Career Outside the Academy*. London: Lynne Rienner Publishers.

———. (ed.). 2013. *A Handbook of Practicing Anthropology*. Hoboken, NJ: Wiley Blackwell.

———. 2017. *Using Anthropology in the World: A Guide to Becoming an Anthropologist Practitioner*. New York: Routledge.

Nowotny, H. 2003. 'Dilemma of Expertise – Democratising Expertise and Socially Robust Knowledge', *Science and Public Policy* 30(3): 151–56.

Nowotny, H., P. Scott and M. Gibbons. 2001. *Re-thinking Science – Knowledge and the Public in an Age of Uncertainty*. Malden: Blackwell Publishers Ltd.

Pedersen, L.R. 2018. 'Fact Finders: Knowledge Aesthetics and the Business of Human Science in a Danish Consultancy', PhD thesis. Copenhagen: Department of Anthropology, University of Copenhagen.

Pedersen, O.K. 2011. *Konkurrencestaten*. Copenhagen: Hans Reitzels Forlag.

———. 2013. 'Political Globalization and the Competition State', in B. Brincker (ed.), *Introduction to Political Sociology*. Copenhagen: Hans Reitzels Forlag, pp. 281–98.

Pink, S. (ed.). 2006. *Applications of Anthropology: Professional Anthropology in the Twenty-First Century*. Oxford, New York: Berghahn Books.

Pink, S., V. Fors and T. O'Dell (eds). 2017. *Theoretical Scholarship and Applied Practice*. Oxford, New York: Berghahn Books.

Radcliffe-Brown, A.R. and F. Eggan. 1957. *A Natural Science of Society*. Glencoe: Free Press and the Falcon's Wing Press.

Robbins, J. 2004. *Becoming Sinners: Christianity and Moral Torment in a Papua New Guinea Society*. Berkeley: University of California Press.

Schwartzman, H.B. 1993. *Ethnography in Organizations: Qualitative Research Methods*. London: Sage Publications.

Scott, James E. 1977. *The Moral Economy of the Peasant: Rebellion and Subsistence in Southeast Asia*. New Haven, CT: Yale University Press.

Shapin, S. 2008. *The Scientific Life – a Moral History of a Late-modern Vocation*. London: University of Chicago Press.

Shinn, T. 2002. 'The Triple Helix and the New Production of Knowledge: Prepackaged Thinking on Science and Technology', *Social Studies of Science* 32(4).

Shore, C. and S. Wright. 1997. 'Towards an Anthropology of Policy: Morality, Power and the Art of Government', *Anthropology in Action* 2(2): 27–31.

Strang, V. 2009. *What Anthropologists Do*. Oxford: Berg.

The Danish Business and Construction Authority. 2007. *Brugerdreven innovation, Årsrapport 2007*. Retrieved 14 January 2021 from http://www.ft.dk/saml ing/20072/almdel/eru/bilag/142/544278.pdf.

Thompson, E.P. 1971. 'The Moral Economy of the English Crowd in the Eighteenth Century', *Past & Present* 50: 76–136.

Throop, C.J. 2014. 'Moral Moods', *Ethos* 42(1): 65–83.

Wright, S. 2006. 'Machetes into a Jungle? A History of Anthropology in Policy and Practice, 1981-2000', in S. Pink (ed.), *Applications of Anthropology: Professional Anthropology in the Twenty-First Century*. Oxford, New York: Berghahn Books, pp. 27–54.

Wright, S. and J.S. Ørberg. 2011. 'The Double Shuffle of University Reform – the OECD/Denmark Policy Interface', in A. Nyhagen and T. Halvorsen (eds), *Academic Identities – Academic Challenges? American and European Experience of the Transformation of Higher Education and Research*. Newcastle upon Tyne: Cambridge Scholar Press, pp. 269–93.

Zigon, J. 2007. 'Moral Breakdown and the Ethical Demand: A Theoretical Framework for an Anthropology of Moralities', *Anthropological Theory* 7(2): 131–50.

CHAPTER 1

Caring for Others
Moral Health Care in
the Company of Anthropology

Hanne Overgaard Mogensen

W hy do health workers care so much for anthropology – and anthropologists for healthcare? Medical anthropology is an en-
ergetic and successful subfield of anthropology that has expanded
considerably since the 1980s, internationally as well as in Denmark,
inside as well as outside of academia. When I embarked upon a search
for medical anthropologists all over Denmark I found them in remote
corners of the country as well as in central positions in the welfare and
healthcare system. They received me with open arms, delighted to see
one of their former teachers from the Department of Anthropology,
delighted to get a chance to discuss anthropology with me and to let
me know what a big difference anthropology had made to their professional as well as their personal lives. It had been 'eye-opening' and
'life-changing', they said, and useful indeed in their daily work.

At first sight it seemed to me that these anthropologists-cum-
health-workers and health-workers-cum-anthropologists were drawn
to anthropology by what Kleinman has referred to as the 'caregiving
paradox', that is, the fact that medicine is becoming increasingly technical and is in many ways enabling health workers as technical experts
while disabling them as caregivers (Kleinman 2008: 23). Anthropological texts and concepts, it seemed, gave health workers a language for
dealing with the tension between healthcare as a profession and a call
and the healthcare system gave anthropologists a place to do good
with anthropology. But when looking more closely at what they told
me, it becomes clear that something changed in their move from the

university to the workplace. They now positioned themselves differently in relation to biomedicine, physicians and the healthcare system than what is implicitly assumed to be the case in medical anthropological literature. Their enemy had become their ally, or, in less dramatic words, medicine and anthropology were perceived to be on a shared moral quest and a new 'other' had been identified.

In this chapter I discuss anthropology at work in the healthcare system through an attempt to conceptualize this sense of commonality, this feeling of shared aims and values between anthropologists and health workers. In other words: I try to get at what it means to them 'to do good' with anthropology.

Medical Anthropology: A Thriving Sub-Discipline

Both disciplinary and societal factors have contributed to the establishment and growth of medical anthropology. The crisis of representation in the 1980s led anthropologists to seek their object in new professional arenas; as a result, anthropology now gains much of its vitality from what happens on the margins of the discipline and in collaboration with other academic communities (Marcus 2005: 682, 687). Medical anthropology, according to Marcus, has been one of the most successful subfields of anthropology, thriving within interdisciplinary constituencies and enjoying a derived prestige in anthropology by dint of this participation (Marcus 2005: 681).

Arthur Kleinman's book, *Patients and Healers in the Context of Culture* (1980), is often referred to as a mission statement for medical anthropology. As Kleinman and his colleagues started developing programmes in the US, medical anthropology also found its way to departments of anthropology in Denmark, at first because they were approached by patient organizations and the Danish Development Aid, requesting insights into patients' behaviour and experience (see Steffen and Samuelsen 1992, and Whyte and Mogensen 2005 for descriptions of the early years of medical anthropology in Denmark). International health has played a significant role in the expansion of medical anthropology in Denmark, due to generous financing by the Danish Development Aid that allowed for long-term collaborations with universities in developing countries. International health still constitutes a significant proportion of the research, but funding of areas of political priority within Denmark, such as chronic diseases, healthy ageing and technologies of health and welfare, has increased considerably in recent years.

Political and societal changes in Denmark in the 1980s and 1990s contributed to creating space for the growth of medical anthropology.

A political debate about the fast-growing welfare state – including the extensive and free healthcare system – started to appear in Denmark in the 1970s (O.K. Pedersen 2013), a critique that was further intensified in the course of the 1980s and 1990s. This resulted in a wave of financial cuts and the introduction of new management tools in the public sector (Kaspersen and Nørgaard 2015: 74–86). The ideology of the welfare state as such was not questioned, the purpose of organizational rationalization being to render the welfare state more cost-efficient. The introduction of new public management tools in Denmark is commonly referred to as the 'djøfisering' of society, 'Djøf' being the name of the trade union for people with a background in economy, political science and law, the vast majority of public administrators. 'Djøfer' (the person) and 'djøfisering' (the process) are now used in everyday language to refer to the massive influx of new public management tools in the public sector since the 1990s.[1]

It may be argued that financial cuts, demands for cost-effectiveness and the decrease in public employees' time and resources ended up nourishing the need for more knowledge about people's (here patients') perspectives and behaviour, which created a space for anthropology outside of academia. In the early days of medical anthropology, it was, as mentioned, the healthcare system and development agencies that approached anthropology – not the other way around.

Medical anthropology continues to take up a relatively large proportion of externally financed research at the university departments in Denmark, to attract students and to give job opportunities to anthropologists outside of academia. Graduates from the two departments of anthropology in the country have BAs as well as Masters of Philosophy (MPhils) in anthropology (i.e. a five-year-long degree in anthropology). Many of them specialize in medical anthropology and find work within the healthcare system or in public administration of health and welfare. In addition, a professional master's degree in Anthropology of Health, designed for health workers, was launched in 2003 and has since then attracted health workers to the study of anthropology. The participants in this programme are primarily nurses, midwives, physiotherapists, nutritionists and others with professional bachelor's degrees in health, but also medical doctors and pharmacists and others with more advanced degrees.[2]

The Study

Anthropology is well-known among health workers, and even more importantly, when one moves around in the healthcare and welfare system in Denmark, one senses an awareness of anthropology as something that may be useful, even though people often have no clear picture of what it is that anthropology can do. As a part of the research project 'The Practice of Anthropology: People and Ideas in Action' on which this book is based,[3] I went on a search for medical anthropologists at their workplaces, those with a MPhil as well as those with a professional master's degree in Anthropology of Health. I asked them what their work involved and what their anthropological training had turned into in their everyday work practices. They were eager to collaborate with me on finding out what anthropology is all about and had become in their lives. I had taught some of them myself, and my discussions with them were in many ways a continuation of a dialogue that had started in the classroom.

It was striking how positive they were about their anthropological training. I was there to discuss a degree with them that they had invested a lot of time in, and in the case of those with a professional master's degree, they or their employer had also invested resources in it.[4] The narrative about anthropology that was told to me was a positive one, partly due to who and what I represented. Their enthusiasm may diminish with time and depend on their working situation. The ones who agreed to be interviewed perhaps did so exactly because of their positive experience with anthropology. Participation in their daily work would maybe have revealed more dilemmas than the interviews did. What I discuss in this chapter is their self-representation of their moral work and their continuous effort to position themselves as anthropologists in the health care system.

Health workers with a professional master's degree have anthropology added to their previous training and work experience. It provides them with extra skills without devaluing the ones they already have, and their master's degree often helps them advance in their career within the healthcare system or public administration. However, those with a MPhil in anthropology who leave university while in their twenties, having studied nothing but anthropology since secondary school, experience having to 'de-anthropologize' and learn other kinds of skills required at their new workplace.[5] They are in the process of changing from being first and foremost 'anthropologists', to being professionals with particular responsibilities *and* anthropological training. Those with a professional master's degree often emerged during fieldwork as being more explicit on what they can do with anthropology in addition to what they already did before, as compared to those with a longer training who were in the process of 'de-anthropologizing'. The latter were more concerned with questions of 'how to do good – or proper – anthropology' than were those with a shorter training. They saw anthropology as a set of added skills but were less preoccupied with questions of doing 'good anthropology'. However, when it comes to questions concerning 'how to do good in the world *with* anthropology' and what it is that makes anthropology – and their work – meaningful to them, then they were on an equal footing, in the sense of being preoccupied with the same questions.

There are of course branches of biomedicine and parts of the healthcare system with no or little room for anthropologists, but my field was delimited by people and encounters in the healthcare system where a space had been carved out for medical anthropologists. Most of those interviewed were public employees, with the exception of two who worked for NGOs and one physiotherapist working in a private clinic. Healthcare is financed by general taxation and is, generally speaking, free in Denmark, the private sector playing an insignificant role, though some services, such as physiotherapy and dental services for adults, are offered by private clinics that are partly supported by public financing. The interlocutors in this study worked as primary healthcare nurses paying home visits to families with new-born babies, physiotherapists or nurses making preventive visits to the homes of elderly people. They were responsible for communication (or lack of communication) between the University Teaching Hospital and local authorities. They were managing directors of health and welfare in municipalities or clinical nurses and midwives in hospital wards. Many worked in primary healthcare, for instance with rehabilitation, chronic disease or healthy ageing in municipality health centres. There was an occupational therapist working with homeless people; a director of welfare in a rural municipality; a project manager in a patient organization for people with dementia and their relatives; one in an NGO working with socially deprived young adults; a risk manager in the board of health services in the city of Copenhagen; a quality assurance expert at one of the major hospitals in Denmark; and the senior dentist in the school dental services of a municipality in the northern part of the country.

In total I interviewed thirty anthropologists (from 2015 to 2018) working with healthcare and welfare in the primary healthcare system, regional and national hospitals, the administration of the healthcare system and NGOs. We always met at their workplace. The interviews had their work experience as a starting point but they usually developed into mutual reflections over anthropology. I had follow-up exchanges with most of them, sometimes by email. I participated in annual meetings of the alumni network of those with a professional master's degree in Anthropology of Health and network meetings of anthropologists who are employed in the civil service. I followed some of them for some hours or a full workday, but I do not claim to present what they actually do in their daily work and whether they do things differently after having studied anthropology, or do things differently from their colleagues with a different professional training. My aim in this chapter is to understand what they say they do and to elicit the moral quest revealed through their laying out of the role of anthropology in their work life.

What Was Missing: An Anthropological Version of Humanism

Well, you know, we are always debating this and that new kind of initiative at the labour-ward that can maybe save one more child one day in the future, but it has been very safe to give birth in Denmark for a very long time and I was kind of dying for the obstetricians to take seriously questions about what it actually feels like to give birth. What it feels like for the women to be told to follow our procedures and what it does to their experience of giving birth that we make our decisions based on the opening of the mouth of their uterus. (Midwife with a professional master's degree in Anthropology of Health)

Anthropology is just more sympathetic. The thing is, if you know what is at stake between people and how they do things, then it is also easier to make them change their behaviour. That doesn't sound right, I know, but still, it just is a more sympathetic way to change things if you take your starting point in people. Anthropologists are not observing bacteria, dogs or the stock exchange. They observe people. We try to understand people and that just is more sympathetic, isn't it? (Nurse with a professional master's degree in Anthropology of Health)

After graduating I was offered a job as a consultant, due to my knowledge of qualitative methods. I had worked a bit for the consulting company while studying, but it just didn't seem meaningful to me to use my skills to sell ryebread and liver pate. I felt somehow ashamed that I wasn't grateful to be offered a job, but it just didn't have that element of benefitting others. You can do so many good things with anthropology. I really had this feeling that I had studied anthropology to do good for others. After secondary school I had been a volunteer with an NGO working with refugees, and that had made me feel that I made a difference for others. During my studies I also had an internship at a Danish embassy in Africa, working with development aid. Then we had courses in applied anthropology and medical anthropology and they made so much sense to me. So after graduating I took this job with the patient organization which at first sounded a bit boring, but I took it because I knew that their work benefitted other people. And then the job also turned out to be really interesting. (MPhil in Anthropology)

Whether they started out as health workers or not, my interlocutors gave me the impression that anthropology not only helped them get a job, but also to do good in the world, to make work meaningful, to fill up an empty space and give them a language for what had been missing in their work life. They would say: 'I always sensed that something more was at stake'. 'I always suspected that people have a reason to do what they do. But I failed to get at what it was that was missing'. A nurse who had worked within various specializations over the years explained why she had chosen anthropology: 'I was surprised that so many of our interventions didn't work and how hard it was to change people's lifestyle. I needed to understand more about people'. Health workers were, as mentioned above, drawn towards anthropology by what Kleinman refers to as the 'caregiving paradox', the fact that medicine as practised today had disabled health workers as caregivers (Kleinman 2008: 23). But people with a MPhil, who had not started their work life as health workers, also expressed a desire to be 'caregivers', to do work that benefits others, that makes a difference for refugees, patients and other vulnerable people. Whether they started out as health workers or not, anthropology was perceived by my interlocutors as something that could help them to do good in the world. People also choose other disciplines and professions for that reason – to make the world a better place, to make a difference for others – and I do not intend to launch a discussion of healthcare and anthropology as vocations rather than professions (though we will in the concluding chapter of the book return to a discussion of anthropological identity). I wish, rather, to get a better understanding of the implicit understanding of 'good' in anthropology and why it fits so well with health workers' perception of 'doing good'.

After having studied anthropology, they can never let go of it again, they say. They can switch this new view of the world on and off, depending on the situation, but never let go of that constant voice in their head reminding them that they now know of a 'new angle' from which to look at the world. Like the medical students Byron Good (1994a: 73–74) writes about, they have experienced a perceptual shift, learned an alternative way of seeing. Medicine is a symbolic form, through which reality is formulated and organized in a distinctive manner, Good argues (ibid. 68), and I will show that my interlocutors also experienced a perceptual shift and have been taught a particular symbolic form with which to formulate reality. They describe how the world now appears to them through what we may refer to as an 'anthropological gaze'.

Some said that they regretted not having the possibility to use anthropology even more than they did, that they would have liked to 'do more projects', by which they meant using qualitative methods to evaluate new initiatives and procedures. But they often added: 'In a sense I do fieldwork all the time'. One person gave the example of doing fieldwork whenever she was in a staff meeting: 'When my colleagues discuss whether to introduce time recording sheets or not, and I see some of them rolling their eyes, then I start thinking about forms and diagrams as exotic objects. I wonder where my colleagues each come from and what is at stake for them. I cannot just be at the meeting anymore without having that constant voice in my head'. An occupational therapist explained that negotiating access to a homeless person is like doing a stint of fieldwork each time, and a visiting nurse said: 'Each time I enter a new home of a family it is as if I start a new fieldwork. I am only there for an hour, but I see things I used not to see when I was in people's homes'.

'Being on fieldwork all the time' has come to epitomize their anthropological gaze and the ongoing oscillation between participation and observation, engagement and distance or, in other words, the omnipresent reflective state of mind that studying anthropology has given them. The medical students studied by Good were taught how to catch sight of a world filled with objects that most of us cannot see: the intricate structure and anatomical features of the human body and of pathology (1994a: 73). I will now turn to my interlocutors' description of what they learned to see with anthropology.

People, Positions and Perspectives

I don't do fieldwork as such, but I think that I am often present in a different way. When I am with nursing students I am much more tolerant about their way of approaching patients. I now understand that they come from very different backgrounds, both socially and culturally, and that this has an impact on how you approach other people, also how you approach patients. I used to have a voice in my head saying: 'Why don't they understand what it is that I ask them to do?' But I now have this voice saying: 'I wonder how this student understands the situation we are in right now and what it is that makes her respond to the patient the way she does?' So yes, I am kind of analysing the situation while I am in it, and I hope that it has made me a better supervisor to the nursing students. (Clinical Nurse

with a professional master's degree in Anthropology of Health, working in
the Department of Respiratory Medicine at a regional hospital)

The nurse cited above went on to explain that she also felt that she
responded differently to patients after having studied anthropology,
that she has a better understanding of why it is, for instance, that they
don't just stop smoking even though they have chronic obstructive
pulmonary disease or lung cancer:

> When Peter goes home to visit his friends who sit on the bench outside
> the supermarket, smoking a cigarette, then they will tell him to stop being
> a saint and have a smoke with them. If one of our patients with an aca-
> demic background goes home to his friends and family, then they will tell
> him to stop smoking. But who am I to judge what is a good life for Peter?
> Why shouldn't he spend time on the bench with his friends rather than live
> two months longer without friends? My discussions with patients about
> what it is that matters to them have become very different after studying
> anthropology.

Anthropology helps this person to take people and their perspective
as her starting point. Getting closer to the other person's perspective
simultaneously creates a distance to, and raises questions about, her
own previous practice: is it better to smoke and have friends or to live
longer without friends? Anthropology, we could say, helps her take a
more 'humanistic' stance, if we understand humanism as the ethical
stance that emphasizes the value and agency of human beings, the
stance that takes its starting point in the person, rather than in the biomedical diagnosis. She also makes it clear that it is the person as a social
being that is now her starting point. She focuses on people's social and
cultural background, that is, the logic that shapes the ways in which
they speak and act: whether the patients' friends are the kind of people
who sit on the bench and smoke or not matters, it affects the way they
end up responding to their disease. In other words, it is her ability to
see their social positioning – and not just their individual perspective –
that gives her a sense of seeing things from a new angle. While anthropological debates have always been preoccupied with the balance and
interaction between the individual and the social, and in recent decades
with questions of how to transcend this dichotomy, then anthropology
clearly comes across in these interviews as the discipline that studies
people as part of cultural patterns, social contexts, structures and systems – as opposed to, for example, medicine and psychology:

> I always had a feeling that there was somehow more to it . . . that we as
> health workers and social workers are too caught up in our own under-

standing of things. I sensed a need to go deeper into what people's challenges are really about but I absolutely did not need the psychological angle. I had no desire to try to get deeper into people's heads. My colleagues say things like: 'Why don't they just. . .', and 'the family should get its act together and do so and so . . .', and I was always kind of thinking: 'Well, but what kind of family is it? What can we expect family members to do for each other? What if the members of the family do not get along?' I always felt that there was something at stake that did not fit into the box that the system had provided us with and I needed help to find answers to those kinds of questions. (Occupational therapist with a professional master's degree in Anthropology of Health, working with homeless people)

Psychology used within the publicly financed healthcare system is primarily cognitive psychology and cognitive psychology has, for health workers, come to epitomize an approach to the individual where limited or no attention is paid to his or her social surroundings. What the above cited occupational therapist was looking for was a discipline that supported her gut feeling that people do what they do as a result of the kind of relationships they have with each other, and anthropology has served that purpose for her.

Finally, to round out the point that anthropology teaches students how to take a starting point in people as social and cultural beings, I will quote a Director of Health and Welfare in a rural municipality who emphasizes that anthropology has helped her to include power relations in her analysis of a situation:

In a political organization like this one it is *so* useful to be able to somehow put oneself in an outside position and look at the culture that dominates our organization. It already brings something new to public administration to say that we need to listen to what people understand their problems to be. But then what anthropology also does for me is to help me understand the structures that people are subjected to. Why does the public administration have the kind of expectations that it has of people? What does the law say – and what does the system look like from the point of view of those on social benefits, sitting all day on a bench in the town square? Anthropology helps me put myself in an outside position, but I actually do it in order to get closer to understanding what it is like to be an object of the system that I myself am administrating. I have always tried to understand what is best for the citizens, the children, the patients, and that is maybe why I became interested in anthropology in the first place. But I used to not really include the people in power in my analysis: politicians, associations, patient organizations, parents, relatives, and so on. All the kinds of power structures that shape people's experience. Anthropology helps me dissect the many layers of a complex problem. A dissection that is basically about understanding the many different social actors involved and how they are positioned in relation to each other. I am always in the midst of that kind of analysis. I am on fieldwork every day when trying to communicate with differently positioned social actors who are all part of the problem I have to solve and who are all necessary for the solution to the problem. (Director of Health and Welfare in a municipality with a professional master's degree in Anthropology of Health)

What runs through the above quotations is the idea that anthropology helps them to get closer to people's experience and the way in which this experience is shaped by and positioned in larger social and cultural patterns. Anthropologists in the healthcare and welfare system thus use anthropology to position themselves as people whose job it is to infuse humanism into their workplace by having the experience of people as social beings as their starting point, and thereby provide an alternative to the biomedical approach as well as to a political science perspective on societal structures and a (cognitive) psychological understanding of what constitutes a person.

Practice

A nurse with a professional master's degree in Anthropology of Health, who is employed as a risk manager in a large municipality, is responsible for a database containing information about what is referred to as 'unintended incidents' in primary healthcare units all over the city (such as council home help, visiting nurses, nursing homes, general practitioners, physiotherapists and occupational therapists; that is, about 5,000 health workers in total). In her account of what this work entails, she brings to the forefront a recurring point made by my interlocutors, namely that an anthropologist has an eye to practice, to what is 'actually happening on the ground' as opposed to what people say is happening.

A health worker who has witnessed a mistake can report it in the database, and the report is then forwarded to the local risk manager at the unit where it happened, whose responsibility it is that the staff there learns from it. About 8,000 such incidents are reported each year. Her responsibility as a risk manager in the central administration is to identify patterns and issues that the central administration should do something about, and also to assist the local units in developing action plans that prevent incidents of the same kind in the future.

To explain her work to me, she relates an incident at a nursing home where an elderly woman suffering from dementia ended up dying from a urinary tract infection due to a series of delays and misunderstandings. For days the staff at the nursing home failed to do a urine stick test, and this for multiple reasons: because the woman was not able to say that she needed to urinate; the general practitioner delayed in sending them the result before the weekend; the woman at first refused to take the tablets, for days; after completing the treatment they again delayed doing another urine stick test; and so on. One evening the woman seemed uncomfortable and the night shift was asked to keep an eye on her. It was not documented whether they actually remembered to do so or not. Maybe they did. Maybe they did notice that the blood pressure was low and the pulse high, but thought that she had a good complexion and decided to let her sleep and wait for the day shift to decide what to do. Nobody knows what actually happened. The next day the woman was doing badly. The staff called the emergency number and had her admitted, but she died of septicaemia the following day. The nurse-cum-anthropologist, now risk manager in the central administration of a large municipality, explained the incident to me while drawing the timeline on the whiteboard in her office:

> So you see, we try to look at what happened over time and what could have been done differently at different moments, without blaming anybody. It is so easy to sit here in the central administration and say: 'Why didn't they just do so and so. Why didn't they follow the guidelines?' But there are, of course, damn good reasons why things happen the way they do. And nobody goes to work to do a bad job. They all do their best. But it matters that information has to be communicated from one shift to the next, that it is difficult to know when a person with dementia needs to pee, that the general practitioner is not always available, and that when you call the emergency number you need to persuade them to come even though you have a patient who is not able to say herself how she is doing. And maybe the one who was on night shift was alone due to sickness among staff, etc. . . . . If we do not go out there and look at how things actually work in this unit then we will never learn from it. If we don't look at the complexity of practices behind the numbers in the database, then we have not understood anything about what actually happened. We have this huge database and everybody here in the administration wants me to pull out numbers from it to support one argument or the other. But I first and foremost see this database as a qualitative tool, because every single time a nurse fails to do a urine stick test or has dosed someone with the wrong medicine, there is a whole story behind the incident. I see myself as the one whose job it is to constantly vouch for the qualitative aspect of these numbers, for the story behind them, for what actually happened and resulted in the nurse failing to do the urine stick test. There may be 8,000 unintended incidents reported to the data base every year, but they are all cases, not numbers.

'Practice' is a recurring concept, or we may say, one of the recurrent symbolic forms with which my interlocutors now see the world. Practice takes precedence over numbers, the nurse-cum-anthropologist cited above explained. Anthropology has taught her to look for the 'qualitative aspects' of the numbers, 'the story behind them', what 'actually happened'. Her interlinking of 'practice' and 'the story' behind the number is not coincidental. By 'practice' she does not attempt to make a distinction between 'doing' and reflective action, but to state that if we know how to look, then we see that many actors were involved and that what happened was a result of their interaction with each other as well as with their surroundings, objects at hand, working conditions, etc. People and events are linked over time and her 'anthropological gaze' allows her to catch sight of this interlinking – of what 'actually happened' – as opposed to descriptions of what ought to have happened.

Participation

Me, I was drawn to anthropology because of this feeling that human beings are influenced by others all the time. I chose anthropology because I had an urge to acknowledge this in my work. After studying anthropology, I don't think of occupational therapy as holistic at all. I now see that we need to make room for how people think about things themselves. We need to look at them from the outside, see them in relation to their surroundings, in order to understand what is important to them. That kind of fiddles with the psychological focus on the individual, which is usually the frame within which we work. And that has been *so* liberating to me. . . But anthropology has also taught me that we need to be less scared to participate, to go into their world together with them. As health workers we are constantly being reminded about the need for professional distance. And yes, professional distance needs to somehow be there, but now I think more in terms of using both observation and participation in my work. (Occupational therapist with a professional master's degree in Anthropology of Health, working with the rehabilitation of elderly people)

Anthropology, we are told by the above interlocutor, 'fiddles with' both the 'psychological approach' and the call for 'professional distance' that health workers are taught to respect in their daily work. It provides the occupational therapist cited above with a different perception of closeness and distance and impels her to try to understand people by participating in their world. As a consequence, she now approaches people in a different way than her colleagues do: 'I now ask people about their relationships to others before I even ask them how they are doing', she says. And this approach, she insists is 'more holistic'. It gives a more complete picture of the person because it allows her to see the person in relation to his or her surroundings.

We already heard above that anthropology helps health workers take their starting point in people and their perspectives; what is added here is that participation helps them to do so. You learn about a person by engaging with them, not just through distanced observations.

The Open-Ended Fieldwork

Finally, I wish to draw attention to their reference to 'fieldwork' as a state of 'openness' and 'exploration'. The occupational therapist working with rehabilitation, who was cited above, explains that anthropology has given her the ability and confidence to let things happen and unfold by themselves. She spends much of her time making preventive health visits to elderly people's homes, and she says that with the help of anthropology she approaches people in a different and more open way. She trusts that this will help her to understand the home she has entered:

> Doing fieldwork, for me that means being more open to what it is that matters in this situation, this home, for this person. But the thing is that I do so by paying attention to those small details in their home that I would have maybe never noticed if I did not know about doing fieldwork. I have an agenda, of course, when I visit the elderly people. I am there on behalf of the civil service in order to identify whether they have any needs or are coping alright by themselves. In a sense it is very patronizing, so it is very useful for me to know how to go there with an open approach, to let them talk, let them show me what their life is like without asking too many questions. I take my time to look and sense whether this is a home where a compliment on the garden would be a good thing, what is the policy about shoes, and what kind of photos are on the wall. The confidence with which I go into a home without having any idea what is there, but trusting that I will be able to find out what is at stake in their lives, what are the important questions to ask – that confidence comes from having studied anthropology and learned how to do fieldwork. It also has something to do with experience, of course. I have made many home visits by now. But anthropology has helped me understand what it is I do and how to use openness more systematically.

This ability to contain 'openness' and to trust that it will take you somewhere brings a more 'questioning mind' with it, which is often pointed out as one of the skills noticed by colleagues.

'My boss, she calls on me to be the "disturbing element"', said a nurse working in a health centre in the western part of the country. 'She tells me to be part of this or that committee because I usually come up with questions that make things happen. I think she means that I am out of sync with the others – in a good way'. This nurse-cum-anthropologist went on to tell about a situation where she and her boss were invited by the politicians to discuss what to do about demographic differences in the utilization of health services in western Jutland (the western part of Denmark). Everybody in the room seemed to agree that people in remote rural areas of the municipality, whose health condition and ed-ucational level are below average, also use health services more than people in town do:

> I just listened for a long time, sensing that something wasn't right. And then I put up my hand. I felt a bit intimidated with thirty clever heads around the table, but then I asked: 'Do we actually know whether they are a burden to the healthcare system? Do we know how much they use it? It is my impression from working with chronically ill people out there that the problem is rather that they do not use the healthcare system'. Then the room got quiet for a moment before they hesitantly started discussing whether I was right. My boss likes to bring me along to stir up things a bit that way.

What these two health workers-cum-anthropologists remind us is that the explorative approach, and the attention to what Margaret Mead (1928) would have called 'a negative instance', a single case that disproves the general axiom, bring with it a state of openness that can be used to challenge pre-existing ideas and dogmas, and once more, therefore, get closer to people and their particular perspectives of the world.

The Anthropological Version of Humanism

What is being said about anthropology in the above quotations may come as no surprise to scholars acquainted with the curriculum in an-thropology at the University of Copenhagen. Their ability to convert anthropology into useful tools in settings with very different agendas than in academia may be more surprising. This conversion, in itself fascinating, is, however, not the object of this chapter and will be dis-cussed elsewhere (Mogensen and Jöhncke 2021). The point I wish to make here is that a particular version of humanism is being culled by the students from the texts they read.

A very rudimentary overview of what they are taught could go as follows: already during the first weeks of their studies, students are being introduced to Durkheim's notion of the social being greater than the sum of its parts and 'the collective consciousness' formed through social interaction (2017 [1895]); to Malinowski's iconic fieldwork and its open-endedness (1922); to the role of kinships studies in anthropology (e.g. Evans-Pritchard 1976 [1937]; Carsten 1995). They are being introduced to functionalist, structuralist and symbolic approaches and the shift towards practice theory that happened in the 1970s and 1980s, spearheaded by scholars like Bourdieu (1972, 1990) and Ortner (1984, 2006), and elaborated in opposition to the dominant, essentially Durkheimian view of the world as ordered by rules and norms. They read a series of fieldwork accounts, many from an edited collection by Hastrup (2003), in which fieldwork is discussed as a process of stepping into social life as it comes into being through people's practices and where the fieldworker is understood as being her/his own tool, learning through engagement with people in the field.

Both those with an MPhil and those with a professional master's degree are being taken through a general introduction to the history of anthropology from its early days to the present, before moving on to medical anthropology, and learn that the healthcare system includes the popular and the alternative sector in addition to the professional sector (cf. Kleinman 1980), and that illness and health are socially and culturally shaped (e.g. Foster 1976; B. Good 1977; Nichter 1981; Janzen 1978). They are being taken through the shift in focus from healthcare systems to the phenomenologically inspired work on experience and narratives (e.g. M.D. Good 1992; B. Good 1994b; Mattingly 1994; Desjarlais 1997) and they learn about the importance of paying attention to 'what matters' and is 'at stake' in people's daily lives (Kleinman and Kleinman 1995; Kleinman 2006) and read about the concept of social suffering (e.g. Kleinman, Das and Lock 1997; Kleinman 2016).

They are also introduced to the explicit criticism of biomedicine and medicalization by scholars like Scheper-Hughes who has shown how hunger and poverty are translated into a discourse on sickness and treated with tablets (1992), and Kleinman's move from the meaning centred approach to discussions of biomedicine as a leading institution of industrialized society's management of social reality through which various forms of human misery are constructed as health problems (1995: 38). They read texts which, inspired by Foucault and others, discuss the ways in which the subject is shaped by health policies and by biomedicine, but also how people act and create their world, not in spite of but through biomedicine (e.g. Lock and Kaufert 1998). They read about bio-sociality and biological citizenship, and how biomedicine can be used to claim identity and rights (e.g. Gibbon and Novas 2008, Petryna 2013), and about the interaction of humans and technology (e.g. Mol 2008).

Many leading voices in the early years of medical anthropology were highly critical of the continued growth of the biomedical sector and insisted on the importance of a discipline like anthropology to bring humanism into the healthcare system and challenge the biomedical view of the person: people and their experience matter and suffering is as important as biological pathology. 'Who am I to judge what is a good life for Peter?', as the nurse said above after having learned, through her anthropological training, that something more is at stake in people's lives than a diagnosis, as fatal as it may be. It is noteworthy that there is little talk of 'cultural difference' and immigrants in the interviews. Literature on 'the culturally different patient' in Denmark does exist and is part of the curriculum (e.g. Johansen 2007) but the relevance of 'cultural difference' is often challenged in these texts and replaced with discussions of social conditions, and this tendency is reflected in the interlocutors' description of the anthropological gaze that they bring with them to their workplace.

Again, this overview of the curriculum at the University of Copenhagen is rudimentary indeed, and my presentation of it is furthermore shaped by the analysis of the interviews presented above, i.e. by what my interlocutors said they carried with them from their anthropological training into their workplace. The point is that they have extracted from these texts – and from discussions of them in class – something that we may call a particular 'anthropological version of humanism'.

Humanism as a philosophical and ethical stance emphasizing human beings over pre-existing ideas and dogmas has had many shapes over the years, depending on the intellectual movements that have identified with it. I will argue that the health workers-cum-anthropologists and anthropologists-cum-health workers cited above hint at a version of humanism that takes its starting point in the person as a social (more than a cultural) being, in people's experience, and in practices and interactions rather than knowledge and abstractions, and which argues that an engagement with the person is a precondition for the ability to challenge existing ideas and dogmas. What students of anthropology are taught, and what makes the most lasting impression on them, it appears, is an a version of humanism that is closely tied to the way in which the ethnographic method of participant observation has been presented to them – hence the feeling that they 'do fieldwork all the time'.[6]

What Things Are Really Like:
An Anthropological Version of Reality

Anthropology prides itself on always having been a discipline that questions pre-conceived ideas about the world. Since the crisis of representation of the 1980s, anthropologists have furthermore known that the empirical and the analytical are inseparable in fieldwork as well as in writing. The insight that there is no field without the researcher, and that being researched has consequences for the field, is maybe one of the most influential contributions that anthropology has made to other disciplines.

Still, it seems from my encounter with anthropologists in the health-care system that they claim to have a particularly privileged access to a more 'true' or 'real' reality, to 'things as they really are' than do their non-anthropological colleagues. They notice people, their perspective and position, they say, because what anthropology – and more specifically participant observation – gives them access to is 'practice' and 'people's experience': to what people do as opposed to what they say they do or ought to do. Paying attention to practice and experience gives them access to what is 'really' happening, what logic is 'really' at stake when an elderly woman dies of a urinary tract infection, a therapeutic plan has not been made or a waiting room is full of people.

I thus suggest that some of the most predominant 'symbolic forms' – as Good (1994a: 73) would have called them – which they use to formulate and organize reality in a distinctive manner are on the one hand 'practice', and on the other hand concepts derived from phenomenologically inspired anthropology like 'experience', 'what matters', 'what is at stake for people', and 'things as they are'.[7]

An anthropologist with a MPhil in anthropology and twenty years of work experience in public administration, now working as a quality assurance specialist in one of the major hospitals in Denmark, was particularly explicit about the ways in which his awareness of practice and people's experience set him apart from his colleagues with a different professional background and I therefore quote him at some length:

> There are some [quality assurance specialists with a different professional training than anthropology] who go to the wards and say: 'Do you manage to live up to your therapeutic plans within 48 hours of admitting a patient?' And then there are others like me who go out there and say: 'I have heard that there is something called therapeutic plans. Can you tell me about that?' 'Yes', the staff at the ward will then answer, 'let me explain

it to you, it has to do with. . .'. Then maybe I go on, asking them: 'What are the steps you take in order to realize these therapeutic plans?' They will then answer: 'Well, we do like this and like that. . .'. The thing is, I inquire into their practice, and that just is a different approach. Because if I go out there and say: 'Please let me know whether you have made your therapeutic plans or not', then they see it as an attempt to control them. Instead I use my fieldwork methods to ask them about their actual practice. I am on fieldwork all the time . . . It is about having a particular view on the world, a particular view on where to start: do we start with the indicators and organizational issues – or with the actual practices. I am a soft 'djøfer'. I don't judge anybody. [As explained earlier, a 'djøfer' is an academic with a degree in law, economy or political science, the professional background of the vast majority of academics in public administration.]

'Do "djøfers" judge other people?' I then asked him.

I don't know . . . But I don't judge people. I ask them what things are really like. For the moment, I am in the emergency ward. I go and sit in the waiting room with the patients and say: 'Hi, I am so and so and I would really like to know what we can do better', and then people immediately start talking: 'Well, listen, let me tell you that so and so. . .'. And it is the same with the clinicians. They are also happy to talk when you ask them openly about their actual practices . . . One of the targets we have had to live up to for years is that every patient who is admitted for more than 24 hours has to have a contact person who can guide them through the system when being moved between wards, in order not to feel lost. One of the indicators used is that a certain percentage of the patients have been assigned a contact person and given the business card of that person within the first 24 hours. All wards have failed to live up to this year after year, but then I heard of a ward that suddenly succeeded and went there to hear what they had done. They had decided to name the head nurse as the contact person of all patients and hand the patients her business card though in reality they would never be able to get hold of her and she would know nothing about their particular case. That is one of the ways that clinicians survive a work life full of targets, indicators and political agendas. And that is perverted, isn't it? But it is not practice that is perverted. It is the targets that are perverted . . . I have a deep, deep respect for practice. There are always reasons why practice develops the way it does. If we try to understand practice and write instructions for the clinicians so that they correspond to their existing practices, instead of inventing new practices on their behalf, then we spare ourselves a great deal of work.

This quality assurance specialist sounds as if he is quoting Bourdieu that there is a difference between the logic of theory and the logic of practice, between the spectator's point of view and the actor's point of view (Bourdieu 1990: 82). Do you write instructions and then ask people to follow them, or do you find out what practice is like and write instructions in accordance with the existing practice? The 'djøfer' who is writing instructions is a spectator. Anthropologists taking their starting point in practice are actors and hence they have access to a different kind of logic than do 'djøfers'. This quality assurance specialist spent time in the wards in order to understand the reasons that practice there developed the way it did, the ways in which indicators made people behave in certain ways and develop certain – at times unintended – practices: unintended from the point of view of those who had defined the indicators, and with no beneficial consequences for the suffering of the patient. What he found was in his own words what things were 'really' like, a truer and 'less perverted' version of reality. He and the risk manager cited above thus both suggest that guidelines and indicators have estranging effects and that we should instead pay attention to how life is lived and experienced in wards or nursing homes, including how guidelines and indicators are used there and with what consequences.

Bourdieu's criticism of and relationship to phenomenology, and whether his understanding of practice is deterministic and deprived of human agency and subjectivity or not, are issues that have been discussed elsewhere (e.g. Throop and Murphy 2002) but they are not a concern of my interlocutors. While I do not intend to conflate practice theory with phenomenology, I do suggest that their respective contributions to anthropological debates merge in my interlocutors' attempt to lay out their 'anthropological gaze' and their claim to 'reality'. What the risk manager, quality assurance specialist and others describe is that by paying attention to the logic of practice, by entering into social interactions and also asking people to explain what things are like from their perspective, they gain access to people's practical and participatory experience (cf. Jackson 1989: 2) and that this 'anthropological gaze' sets them apart from their colleagues with a different professional training. When talking about their ability to provide an alternative to the perverted version of reality staged by guidelines and indicators, they are in line with Jackson's claim that 'descriptions of lived reality help us restrict the estranging effects of conceptual models and systematic explanations which, when pushed too far, isolate us from the life we live' (1996: 2). Inspired by Husserl's discussion of 'things themselves' and how things are actually given to experience, one of Jackson's volumes has been entitled, *Things as They Are* (1996). This title was often cited by my interlocutors, whether they had actually read the volume, read texts by scholars inspired by the contributors to this volume or simply heard of the title. They used phrases like: 'As anthropologists we can see things as they are' [in Danish: *'tingene som de er'*], 'we are able to get closer to what is "actually there"'. In other words, they were implicitly stating that a phenomenologically inspired anthropology helped them to get closer to 'reality' than others were able to.

Phenomenology has had a significant influence on medical anthropology (and on anthropology in general) since the 1980s and 1990s (see Desjarlais and Throop 2011 for a review of phenomenological approaches in anthropology), and maybe even more so at the Department of Anthropology in Copenhagen than in, for example, the US and other places (Robert Desjarlais, personal communication). The phenomenological method involves 'setting aside' or 'bracketing' questions concerning the rational and objective status of ideas to do justice to the ways in which people live, experience and use them (Jackson 1996: 10). We may argue that it has always been the ambition of anthropology to 'bracket' or to 'question' taken for granted assumptions about the world. Even though the anthropological method differs from philosophical phenomenology because of its participatory, situational and intersubjective underpinnings then, there are also points in which they intersect and mutually illuminate one another (Throop 2018). Whether phenomenologically inspired anthropology has been more successful than previous anthropology in moving beyond preconceived ideas and concepts, or whether it has, as others have argued (e.g. Pedersen 2020), failed to bracket its own key concepts, such as 'experience', 'suffering', the 'human' and 'humanism' or indeed been able to make a critical analysis of these concepts (e.g. Desjarlais 1994 on the concept of experience), is not the object of the present argument. I do, however, wish to point out that I do not intend to align phenomenology with humanism. Attempts are indeed made by critical phenomenologists to bracket the category and discursive space of 'the human' as well as categories like 'experience', 'the subject' and 'agency' (Desjarlais, personal communication). But in spite of anthropological attempts to bracket phenomenological concepts of 'the human' and 'experience', and in spite of the influence in recent decades of post-humanist approaches of, for example, Science and Technology Studies on medical anthropology, I suggest that anthropology in general, and practice theory and phenomenologically inspired anthropology in particular, have provided anthropologists-cum-health-workers and health-workers-cum-anthropologists with a sense of having a privileged access to reality, and it has given them a language with which to argue for what they consider to be a more humanistic approach to healthcare, an approach that takes its starting point in the person rather than the disease, in practical experience rather than guidelines.

I furthermore suggest that the interest of phenomenologically inspired anthropology in social suffering has made anthropology appealing – and useful – to health workers. The subject living in pain, poverty or under conditions of violence or oppression has become an important object of anthropological inquiry. Two decades after his first publication in medical anthropology Kleinman discusses his own shift from symbolic anthropology and medical systems to the lived experience of suffering, and argues that if you strive to understand everyday life, then you have to take suffering as your object. Suffering is more real, closer to 'things as they are', than are disease categories (1995: 6–7).

Robbins (2013) suggests that this interest in the suffering subject is related to anthropology's loss of 'the savage' as its 'radical other' in the course of the 1980s. One way in which anthropologists responded to the criticism of anthropological 'othering' was to shift attention from critical comparison focused on difference to empathetic connection and moral witnessing of human unity (ibid.: 453). Because of its universalistic quality, the suffering subject appeared to anthropologists not just as something new to study, but as a solution to the problem of anthropology's loss of the 'radical other' as its object (ibid.: 454) and as a way to respond to the criticism that anthropology, through its 'othering' of people, had helped to foster their domination and exploitation (ibid.: 449). Kleinman's growing interest in the suffering subject cannot be seen independently from his attempt to respond to the criticism of the 'meaning centred approach' in medical anthropology, that it had failed to pay attention to political economy and exploitation.

It is striking that many of my interlocutors mention their interest in 'cultural differences among patients' as one of things that made them aware of anthropology as a discipline in the first place, but cultural difference plays a limited role in their accounts of how they use anthropology once back at their workplace. They instead tell about ways in which they use anthropology to bring people and their experience of suffering on the agenda. This shift in anthropology from studying the 'other' to studying the universal category of the suffering subject, from studying difference to working against oppression and marginalization, has – even more than 'cultural difference' – helped to make anthropology immediately recognizable and appealing to health workers.

In sum I thus suggest that one of the things that students of anthropology carry with them into their workplaces is a sense that anthropology in general, and practice theory and the phenomenological approach in particular, bring them closer to 'reality', to 'things as they are', than other approaches do. It gives them a sense of having a privileged access to reality. Other disciplines also make a distinction between the empirical and the theoretical, between 'the world as it is' and 'researchers' representation of the world', so what is noteworthy is not that anthropologists also end up doing so, in spite of anthropological (and phenomenological) claims that it is indeed possible to transcend the distinction between reality and abstractions over reality. Rather, what is interesting for the present argument is the mandate these anthropologists invoke based on their way of making this distinction. They use this mandate to act in what they perceive to be more 'humanistic' and 'morally defensible' ways.

The Moral Economy of Medical Anthropology

As noted above, many anthropologists see anthropology as something that can help them do good for others. Implicit in the many quotations presented in this chapter is a drive towards 'being a spokesperson' for people's experience, in particular the experience of those who are not doing well (who are sick, homeless, in labour, overworked, culturally different and so on), and at times even a moral obligation to 'do good with anthropology'. In addition, hints are made at the ways in which anthropology makes people better persons, make them act in more sympathetic ways, more tolerant, less judgmental. 'I am a soft "djøfer". I don't judge other people', the quality assurance specialist said above, and the nurse who is a risk manager in the central administration of a municipality explained that anthropology has made her more tolerant, also in the eyes of others:

> Some of the people involved in these unintended incidents have made quite serious mistakes, but I always insist on looking at the context in which they worked – and that makes my colleagues here at the central administration think that I am good at handling conflicts. They think it is because of the kind of person I am. But I think it is because of anthropology. All those texts I have read where you start out thinking that you will never understand why people do like this or that and then after five pages you anyway sit there and think, well, okay, there really always is a good reason why people do what they do. . . When I tell a potential employer what it is I can do, then I talk about qualitative methods, analytical competences, being able to translate large amounts of data into concrete products, to connect small things to larger questions, etc. In a sense, many of these are general academic competences, but then I have this secret anthropological competence

of mine which I know that I use all the time: tolerance. (Nurse and risk manager in the central administration with a professional master's degree in Anthropology of Health)

As noted in the Introduction to this book, the merging of medical activism and anthropology is not new to medical anthropology. Prominent scholars like Paul Farmer have long argued for the ability and responsibility of anthropology to make the world a better place, but what is meant by 'better' is usually not elaborated in these texts beyond the call for 'health for all' (Farmer 1999). I will now attempt a more nuanced definition of what anthropologists implicitly say when they say that they 'can do good in the world' with anthropology.

In the Introduction of this book, we referred to Keith Hart's (2011) definition of moral economy of capitalism as an inspiration for our definition of the moral economy of anthropology. We suggested that the moral economy of anthropology is based on a division of the world into two spheres: things as they seem and things as they are, abstractions over life and concrete everyday life.

I now suggest that we may also talk about a more specific moral economy of medical anthropology, or a moral economy of anthropologists working in the healthcare system and public administration in Denmark. In other words, we may talk about the particular way in which they divide the world into two spheres, into abstract and concrete: medical anthropologists try to do good by morally defending experience and empathy (the understanding of people's perspectives) as opposed to diagnoses, numbers, spreadsheets and budgetary bottom lines; they take their starting point in people and their practical experience as opposed to indicators, guidelines, political agendas and bureaucratic procedures, and in social positioning and intersubjectivity as opposed to individualizing and psychologizing. They defend holism as opposed to the reduction of a problem's complexity to single factors. They value openness and a reflective mind against fixed categories and pre-defined solutions. This is not an absolute division of the world into good and bad. Rather, we need to understand their moral quest as an ongoing effort to position themselves and the people they work with in relation to these spheres.

The New Other: Scales of Objectification

I am not interested in writing instructions and guidelines. I can do that. I know that world by now, but I am not here to satisfy a political agenda or a bureaucratic procedure . . . What interests me is practice and that behind each practice there is a patient needing our help. I am here for the patient. If I can make things just a little bit better for the patients today than they were yesterday, then my life is meaningful. That is my deep motivation, and it is a motivation that I share with the clinicians . . . I am not here to satisfy the civil service and a political agenda. I know that politicians will also say that they are here for people, but what separates the sheep from the goats is whether we take our starting point in guidelines and indicators or in people and everyday practice. (MPhil in Anthropology and quality assurance specialist in a major Danish hospital)

The quality assurance specialist once more quoted above makes it clear that the 'other' to whom he opposes himself is not the clinician, with whom he shares his deep motivation to help the patients, but the dehumanizing approach of 'djøfers' – those who turn people and reality into indicators and guidelines. In other words, he and the clinicians are of one kind, the kind that are there to improve the health of the patients. The others are of a different species, for whom the end goal is a number, a budgetary bottom line or a political agenda rather than the alleviation of suffering.

I rarely heard my interlocutors invoke their version of humanism and their privileged access to reality in order to position themselves in opposition to the claim made by physicians and biomedicine to objective truths. Disease categories, diagnoses and technical aspects of care may at times divert the attention away from practice and patients' experience of suffering, but not as much, it seems, as do spreadsheets and indicators. It is not medicine, or the physicians, that anthropologists see themselves as acting in counterbalance to. It is not the individualizing approach of the psychologist that is in focus either, but the bureaucratic and potentially de-humanizing approach of 'djøfers', the bureaucrats who have little sense of 'what is actually happening' and who reduce the world to abstractions with their indicators, targets, political agendas and administrative steering tools. Why has this apparent shift in alliance taken place? And is it a shift at all?

Many of the health workers with a professional master's degree in the Anthropology of Health reflect on the fact that, in a sense, the anthropologist in them was always there:

Anthropology gives me a more systematic way of making use of what I always sensed. I always had some kind of sense that people mattered. That there was something about people that mattered in relation to health. Now I know that it was not just a feeling. That there is a science for it. A science about people mattering. I am better at arguing for the importance of taking people into consideration. I don't necessarily mention anthropology when I do so. But I am better at arguing that I think it matters to ask people what they think and how they experience giving birth. (Midwife working in a regional hospital)

Anthropology was an eye-opener for them, but what was eye-opening was not only the discipline's particular perspective on the world, but also that it fitted so well with a sense that they had always had of what was important in their professional lives. One primary healthcare nurse visiting families with new-born children explained that she had always had this curiosity, wondering who would open the door when she rang the bell, and what kind of life was lived behind that door, and that when she found out about anthropology she realized that she had always been an anthropologist at heart. Another nurse went even further when trying to explain her sense of commonality between anthropology and healthcare: 'There is something about the same values being at stake, the same view on human nature, something about all stories and perspectives being equally important in anthropology and everybody having the right to treatment. And if you don't have a set of values guiding you then your work doesn't feel meaningful'.

Based on statements like these, I suggest that anthropology elicits practices and values in a heightened form which are already present in healthcare settings. We may say that there are interweaving threads that link anthropology and healthcare, or, inspired by Gammeltoft (2008), we may talk of 'figures of transversality', that is, emotionally dense realms of sentiments and practices that blur the boundaries between the two (ibid.: 571). Gammeltoft draws on this mathematical notion of lines that intersect other lines, in her attempt to trace the diffusion of culturally powerful figures across spaces that are otherwise kept conceptually separate (ibid.: 573). I suggest that empathy and ethical demands to help suffering others – or 'to care' – are such culturally powerful figures cutting across healthcare and much of anthropology, spheres that are otherwise often thought of as separate. During their studies of medical anthropology, the health workers become acquainted with Kleinman's concern with the lack of care in the highly technical and bureaucratic environment of present-day healthcare (Kleinman 1995). They have read about his call for care as a social, emotional and moral activity (e.g. Kleinman 2008, 2012; Kleinman and van der Geest 2009). They have read about care as a practical response to specific needs, and a sensitivity to 'what matters' and 'what is at stake' for people in their everyday lives. They have read about anthropology's obligation to inquire into social suffering. And that is what makes anthropology immediately recognizable to many health workers. Anthropology, it seems, gives health workers a language for what they already sense and what they cherish in their profession. They sense that the call to care and to do good is also what drives many anthropologists. Getting a language for it makes their work (once again) meaningful despite the absurdities and pressures of the system (and particularly of new public management).[8]

This does not mean that there are never any tensions between the lived experience of patients versus the increasingly technical and medicalized care. Smoking continues to kill, even if quality of life also matters. At times this tension is manifested as tensions between different categories of health workers (e.g. midwives and nurses vs. physicians) and in other situations the tension is played out within the health worker him or herself, no matter his or her training.

Health workers studying anthropology, as well as other anthropologists getting a job in the healthcare system, often start out thinking that their role is to deal with this tension between patients and the medicalization of their suffering, and they are drawn to anthropology by a sense of being morally obliged to speak for the lived experience and suffering of patients. However, it seems that once back at their workplace this tension has been replaced by another one. The role of the anthropologist then becomes one of speaking for both patients and health workers, who both experience themselves as being constrained by (abstract) administrative procedures. At this point in history the most tenacious tension in their work life is not the one between anthropology and medicine, but between the experience and practices of health workers and patients vs. new public management and its various kinds of (abstract) administrative technologies – epitomized by the 'djøfer'. In the attempt to deal with this new tension, anthropologists and health workers have become allies and end up speaking with one voice about their shared cultural figure of 'humanism': of people as social beings with many things at stake in their lives, and of every person's right to care and treatment, to the alleviation of suffering.

'I know that the politicians will also say that they are here for the people', noted the quality assurance specialist above, and it is not only anthropologists who believe that they are there to do good for other people. 'Some "djøfers" are good', said the risk manager in the municipality. Her immediate manager was a particularly competent 'djøfer' who knew how to translate clinical and anthropological insights into 'djøf' language and hence get decisions passed by the politicians who, according to her, know very little about what happens on the ground.

In other words, it is not only anthropologists and health workers who are on a moral quest. 'Djøfers' and politicians are likely to be so too. What I have been trying to get at is how anthropologists and health workers-cum-anthropologists re-enact their distinction between 'good' and 'bad' within the health care and welfare system. I suggest that we may understand their 'moral quest' in terms of what I choose to call 'scales of objectification', i.e. a scale of interaction on which positioning is determined by power relations and which, in turn, determines who is objectifying and who is being objectified/ dehumanized.

While phenomenological anthropology and practice theory have pushed anthropology even further towards humanism and towards the subject in the past decades, 'djøfisering' has pushed society even further away from the subject. At an intersubjective scale, health workers and biomedicine do at times objectify the patient through diagnoses and technical measures of treatment. But at this scale of objectification, health workers still remain closer to the concrete person and his or her suffering than the 'djøfer' who operates according to indicators. And yet, 'djøfers' remain closer to the realities of public health than do politicians and they can at times become allies of health practitioners and patients against politicians who are even further away from the concrete practices on the ground. Medical doctors still have power in the healthcare system, but health workers on all levels in the healthcare system experience that 'djøfers' now have more power than they do; and above the 'djøfer' you find the politicians. Put more generally, the more power the person has, the further he or she is from the concrete human subject.

Anthropology provides health workers with a sense of definitional power. They can now define 'doing good for others' as a way of paying attention to what it is that 'really matters' to people and what things are 'really like in practice'. They may not always succeed in changing things, but they feel more confident that it is possible, and they have come to see it as their moral obligation to give voice to what matters to concrete suffering persons, who are being objectified, dehumanized and suppressed by abstractions employed by people above them in the organizational hierarchy, be they patients in their interactions with health workers, or health workers in their bureaucratic negotiations with 'djøfers', or even a 'soft djøfer' trying to resist dogmatic policies and politicians. Who is above, and who is below, depends on the situation.

Engagement: Anthropology as a Tool and Healthcare as an Identity

There is this idea within the public administrative system, this thing about humanism, that humanism is something the health workers represent. And well yes, health workers do have these ideals about caring, about self-less devotion, they have a large sense of responsibility for others. There is something about recognition of others in this and in a sense this recognition of others is also found in anthropology. Anthropology supports this idea among health workers that everybody has a perspective that matters, we all have particular life stories. In the healthcare system it is understood as seeing the person as a whole person and [the idea] that everybody should be given treatment when needed... But I absolutely do not think that anthropologists can in any way speak from some kind of higher moral ground. On the contrary, I sometimes feel that I am being unethical because I observe what people do all the time, and behave as if I have the right to speak about them from a different position outside of this organization – an organization that we all have a responsibility towards. As if I am looking at them like ants in a theatre performance rather than working together with them. I try very hard to always combine my analytical gaze with my re-sponsibility to act on behalf of the organization that I work for . . . But well, yes, many health workers are shrouded in some kind of Florence Nightin-gale myth, while they also feel that in practice, and in the public debate, they are not being taken seriously. And then suddenly, with the help of an-thropology, they get some kind of authority with which to speak about the importance of care and their devotion to the patient and to the alleviation of suffering. (Midwife with a MPhil in Anthropology and the Director of Health in a municipality)

Anthropology is an unethical practice if observation stands alone, says the midwife-cum-anthropologist quoted above.[9] An engagement with the person is at the foundation of ethical practices and thus a precondition for helping someone, says Bauman (1998), and while ac-ademics often debate whether their primary obligation is to critical analysis or to engagement, this question is not raised at all by the anthropologists I have interviewed. They agree with Bauman. These are people who engage in improving things for other people on an everyday basis, and 'doing fieldwork' all the time helps them feel that they do so in 'more ethical' ways and at the same time get better results. Their work feels 'more ethical' because anthropology helps them to be 'more humanistic', that is, get closer to and engage with the concrete person. A consequence of getting closer to people's expe-rience is, in turn, that they obtain an outside perspective on their own previous practice, which also (at times at least, they say) helps them to change their practice and to achieve the goals they work for more successfully.

One could argue that they do not really have any other choice. They cannot choose not to collaborate with other health workers or stop being health workers while working in the healthcare system. Maybe they could be more critical of biomedicine and of medicalization, if they listened more carefully to 'that constant analytical and critical voice' in their head. We could argue indeed that it is a pragmatic choice to focus on lines of transversality cutting across anthropology and healthcare, rather than on differences between the two.

What makes them different from anthropologists in academia, though, is that their personal and professional identity is no longer (or never was) closely tied to anthropology as a discipline, no matter how life-changing it felt to be studying anthropology. It is tied to the organization that they work for. Anthropology becomes a tool towards the realization of the goal of that organization. Their overall ambition is not to realize what we may refer to as the 'moral project of anthropology', but to realize the project of the healthcare and welfare system. They seek to provide health care and they use the particular anthropological way of dividing the world into 'things as they are' and 'things as they seem' to do so.

What has become clear from the discussion in this chapter is that aligning themselves with health workers is relatively uncomplicated for anthropologists. Anthropologists, whether first trained as health workers or not, experience being on the same moral quest as health workers; they share the same ethical demand to care for others and to give voice to those suffering. They manage to use the anthropological division of the world into 'things as they are' and 'things as they seem' to position themselves on a 'scale of objectification' and to give voice to and morally defend those who are being objectified by others, and ultimately to provide what they perceive of as better health care. At a micro-scale of analysis, anthropologists side with the patient whose suffering is being objectified by biomedicine. At a meso-scale of analysis, they side with the health worker whose healthcare practices are being objectified by the 'djøfer'. And sometimes, at a macro-scale of analysis, anthropologists side with 'djøfers', whose work is objectified by politicians. No one is an ally or enemy per se; positioning is determined by power relations within a specific scale of interaction which, in turn, determines who is objectifying and who is being objectified/dehumanized.

Conclusion

Anthropology provides health practitioners with tools that help them to see the concrete person embedded in complex social interactions, and it provides them with tools for participation and engagement in people's lives and problems. Participating in other people's lives and realities triggers a kind of 'Copernician revolution', a paradigmatic shift, allowing practitioners to understand things from the point of view of those who bear the consequences of their treatment or policies, and hence, potentially change these.

Anthropological tools, and the humanist values perceived to come along with them, can be applied at a variety of scales, and the same actor may objectify people below them while criticizing people above them in the organization hierarchy for objectification, depending on the situation.

Anthropologists discussed in this chapter work within a field that does not ask them to compromise the way in which anthropology has taught them to think of good and bad, real and less real. In their experience, both anthropologists and health workers (with or without anthropological training) strive to be spokespersons or caretakers of those who are suffering and are being objectified by others, rather than to be spokespersons for the budgetary bottom line and political agendas. They are therefore not necessarily faced with the same challenges and moral dilemmas as anthropologists working in, for example, the corporate world (see Chapter 2 and 3, this volume). Budget lines also matter in the healthcare system – but budget lines are more easily configured as one of those 'evil others' that outsiders impose on them than in the corporate world. Budget lines are not what gives purpose and meaningfulness to the organization and their work.

Anthropology gives health workers a language and a mandate for their moral project, and healthcare gives anthropologists an organization through which they can realize their moral project and do good with anthropology. It is no wonder, then, that health workers care for anthropology and anthropologists care for health work!

Hanne Overgaard Mogensen is associate professor at the Department of Anthropology, University of Copenhagen. Her main topic of research is medical anthropology and international health, primarily in Africa. She has also published literary anthropology based on her research. She teaches medical anthropology at the University of Copenhagen.

NOTES

I gratefully acknowledge the 'Danish Council for Independent Research, Culture and Communication' for funding the research, my interlocutors and students for their time and interest in the project, and Quentin Gausset, Susan Reynolds Whyte and Robert Desjarlais and the project team for their comments on drafts of the chapter.

1. See the Introduction of the book for more detail on political and societal changes in Denmark and internationally.

2. The professional master's degree in Anthropology of Health is conducted in collaboration between Århus University and the University of Copenhagen. Students on the two-year-long professional master's degree are first introduced to classical anthropological texts and learn about fieldwork, participant observation, positioning and perspectives. During the second semester they move on to an introduction to medical anthropology and in the third and fourth semesters they specialize and carry out a small fieldwork project on which their master's thesis is based.

3. See the Introduction of the book for more information about the project

4. Paying for a degree is an exception in the otherwise free educational system in Denmark, where only certain kinds of supplementary training are paid for by the individual, and even then, it is often paid for by the employer.

5. We know from another study on anthropologists (MPhil) entering the labour market that many of them are critical of their degree, and especially of the ways in which they are prepared for the labour market and their lack of ability to explicate to future employers what it is that anthropologists can do (Hansen and Jöhncke 2013). One of the motivations for the research project 'The Practice of Anthropology' was exactly to become better at explicating anthropological competences and discussing them with the students.

6. Anthropology is not the only discipline used by health workers to deal with the 'caregiving paradox' and infuse their work with humanism, but the study on which this chapter is based focused on the ways in which anthropology travels from academia to the health care system. The University of Århus in Denmark offers a professional master's programme in 'humanistic health sciences' which draws on philosophy but also on ethnology, sociology and psychology, and which is likely to serve a similar purposes for health workers joining this programme, though the particular appeal of anthropology, compared to related disciplines, seems to be exactly its focus on practice, empiricism and fieldwork.

7. They rarely use the words 'lifeworld' and 'subjective experience', but I suggest that phrases like 'what matters to people' and 'what is at stake for people' are more easily translated into everyday language in Danish and that they are inspired by phenomenological discussions of lifeworld when they use them.

8. Another point of commonality between anthropology and health work is gender. The vast majority of students of anthropology as well as medicine and other health sciences are now female in Denmark. The relationship between gender, ethics and care calls for further exploration, and it has no doubt also

shaped the development of anthropology and of medical anthropology in Denmark and elsewhere.

9. See Chapter 3 for a discussion of the anthropologist's dilemma when having to deal with hierarchical differences while at the same time feeling obliged to defend people below oneself.

REFERENCES

Bauman, Z. 1998. 'On Universal Morality and the Morality of Universalism', *European Journal of Development Research* 10(2): 7–18.

Bourdieu, P. 1972. *Outline of a Theory of Practice*. Cambridge: Cambridge University Press.

———. 1990. *The Logic of Practice*. Cambridge: Polity Press.

Carsten, J. 1995. 'The Substance of Kinship and the Heat of the Hearth: Feeding, Personhood, and Relatedness among Malays in Pulau Langkwai', *American Ethnologist* 22(2): 223–41.

Desjarlais, R. 1994. 'Struggling Along: The Possibilities for Experience Among the Homeless Mentally Ill', *American Anthropologist* 96(4): 886–901.

———. 1997. *Shelter Blues: Sanity and Selfhood Among the Homeless*. Philadelphia: University of Pennsylvania Press.

Desjarlais, R. and J. Throop. 2011. 'Phenomenological Approaches in Anthropology', *Annual Review of Anthropology* 40: 87–102.

Durkheim, É. 2017 [1895]. 'What is a Social Fact?' in R.J. McGee and R.L. Warms (eds), *Anthropological Theory: An Introductory History*. London: Mayfield Publishing Company, pp. 86–93.

Evans-Pritchard, E.E. 1976 [1937]). *Witchcraft, Oracles and Magic among the Azande*. Oxford: Clarendon Press.

Farmer, P. 1999. 'Pathologies of Power: Rethinking Health and Human Rights', *American Journal of Public Health* 89(10): 1486–96.

Foster, G. 1976. 'Disease Etiologies in non-Western Medical Systems', *American Anthropologist* 78: 773–83.

Gammeltoft, T. 2008. 'Figures of Transversality: State Power and Prenatal Screening in Contemporary Vietnam', *American Ethnologist* 35(4): 570–87.

Gibbon, S. and C. Novas (eds). 2008. *Biosocialities, Genetics and the Social Sciences: Making Biologies and Identities*. London: Routledge.

Good, B. 1977. 'The Heart of What's the Matter: The Semantics of Illness in Iran', *Culture, Medicine and Psychiatry* 1: 25–58.

———. 1994a. 'How Medicine Constructs its Object', in *Medicine, Rationality, and Experience*. Cambridge: Cambridge University Press, pp. 65–87.

———. 1994b. 'The Narrative Representation of Illness', in *Medicine, Rationality, and Experience*. Cambridge: Cambridge University Press, pp. 135–65.

Good, M.D. (ed.). 1992. *Pain as Human Experience: An Anthropological Perspective*. Berkeley: University of California Press.

Hansen, Anne-Louise L. and Steffen Jöhncke. 2013. *Omsat antropologi: En undersøgelse af det antropologiske arbejdsmarked i Danmark* [Realized Anthropology:

A Study of the Anthropological Labour Market in Denmark]. Copenhagen: AnthroAnalysis, Department of Anthropology, University of Copenhagen.

Hart, K. 2011. 'Commentary to the Blogpost "Defining Capitalism"', *The Open Anthropology Cooperative*. Retrieved 20 September 2019 from http://open anthcoop.ning.com/group/economicanthropology/forum/topics/defining-capitalism?commentId=3404290%3AComment%3A114742&groupId=340429 0%3AGroup%3A785#sthash.DLzwlGD7.dpbs.

Hastrup, K. 2003. *Ind i verden. En grundbog i antropologisk metode*. Copenhagen: Hans Reitzels Forlag.

Jackson, M. 1989. *Paths Toward a Clearing: Radical Empiricism and Ethnographic Inquiry*. Bloomington and Indianapolis: Indiana University Press.

—— (ed.). 1996. *Things as They Are: New Directions in Phenomenological Anthropology*. Bloomington and Indianapolis: Indiana University Press.

Janzen, J.M. 1978. *The Quest for Therapy in Lower Zaire*. Berkeley and London: University of California Press.

Johansen, K.S. 2007. 'Kategorisering i psykiatrien: Patienter med anden etnisk baggrund end dansk' [Categorizing in the Psychiatry: Patients with Another Ethnic Backgrounds than Danish], in K.F. Olwig and K. Pærregaard (eds), *Integration – antropologiske perspektiver* [Integration – Anthropological Perspectives]. Copenhagen: Museum Tusculanums Forlag, pp. 155–73.

Jöhncke, S. and H.O. Mogensen. 2021. *Antropologer på Arbejde*. Copenhagen: Forlaget Samfundslitteratur.

Kaspersen, L.B. and J. Nørgaard. 2015. *Ledelseskrise i konkurrencestaten*. Copenhagen: Hans Reitzels Forlag.

Kleinman, A. 1980. *Patients and Healers in the Context of Culture: An Exploration of the Borderland between Anthropology, Medicine and Psychiatry*. Berkeley: University of California Press.

———. 1995. *Writing at the Margin: Discourse between Anthropology and Medicine*. Berkeley: University of California Press.

———. 2006. *What Really Matters: Living a Moral Life amidst Uncertainty and Danger*. Oxford: Oxford University Press.

———. 2008. 'Catastrophe and Caregiving: The Failure of Medicine as an Art', *The Lancet* 371: 22–23.

———. 2012. 'Caregiving as Moral Experience', *The Lancet* 380: 1550–51.

———. 2016. *A Passion for Society: How We Think About Human Suffering*. Berkeley: California University Press.

Kleinman, A., V. Das and M. Lock (eds). 1997. *Social Suffering*. Berkeley: University of California Press.

Kleinman, A. and J. Kleinman. 1995. 'Suffering and its Professional Transformation: Towards an Ethnography of Interpersonal Experience', in A. Kleinman, *Writing at the Margin: Discourse Between Anthropology and Medicine*. Berkeley: University of California Press, pp. 95–119.

Kleinman, A. and S. van der Geest. 2009. '"Care" in Healthcare: Remaking the Moral World of Medicine', *Medische Antropologie* 21(1): 159–79.

Lock, M. and P.A. Kaufert. 1998. *Pragmatic Women and Body Politics*. Cambridge: Cambridge University Press.

Malchau, S. 1998. 'Kaldet – et ophøjet ord for lidenskab', *Sygeplejersken* 47: 34–50.

Malinowski, B. 1922. *Argonauts of the Western Pacific*. London: Routledge and Kegan Paul.

Marcus, G.E. 2005. 'The Passion of Anthropology in the U.S, Circa 2004', *Anthropological Quarterly* 78(3): 673–95.

Mattingly, C. 1994. 'The Concept of Therapeutic "Emplotment"', *Social Science and Medicine* 38(6): 811–22.

Mead, M. 1928. *Coming of Age in Samoa: A Psychological Study of Primitive Youth for Western Civilization*. New York: William Morrow & Company.

Mol, A. 2008. *The Logic of Care : Health and the Problem of Patient Choice*. London: Routledge.

Nichter, M. 1981. 'Idioms of Distress: Alternatives in the Expression of Psychosocial Distress: A Case Study from South India', *Culture, Medicine and Psychiatry* 12: 379–408.

Ortner, S.B. 1984. 'Theory in Anthropology since the Sixties', *Comparative Studies in Society and History* 26(1): 126–66.

———. 2006. *Anthropology and Social Theory: Culture, Power, and the Acting Subject*. Durham, NC: Duke University Press.

Pedersen, M.A. 2020. 'Anthropological Epochés: Phenomenology and the Ontological Turn', in *Philosophy of the Social Sciences* (June 2020). doi:10.1177/0048393120917969.

Pedersen, O.K. 2013. 'Political Globalization and the Competition State', in B. Brincker (ed.), *Introduction to Political Sociology*. Copenhagen: Hans Reitzels Forlag, pp. 281–98.

Petryna, A. 2013. *Life Exposed: Biological Citizens after Chernobyl*. Princeton: Princeton University Press.

Robbins, J. 2013. 'Beyond the Suffering Subject: Toward an Anthropology of the Good', *Journal of the Royal Anthropological Institute* 19: 447–62.

Scheper-Hughes, N. 1992. *Death Without Weeping*. Berkeley: University of California Press.

Steffen, V. and H. Samuelsen. 1992. 'Fra Sygdom til Sundhet – Snvendt Medicinsk Antropologi i Danmark', *Socialmedicinsk tidsskrift* 9–10: 425–34.

Throop, J. 2018. 'Toward a New Humanism: Being Open to the World', *Hau: Journal of Ethnographic Theory* 8(1/2): 197–210.

Throop, C.J. and K.M. Murphy. 2002. 'Bourdieu and Phenomenology: A Critical Assessment', *Anthropological Theory* 2(2): 185–207.

Whyte, S.R. and H.O. Mogensen. 2005. 'Susan Reynolds Whyte: Redigeret Interview ved Hanne Mogensen', *Tidsskrift for Forskning i Sygdom og Samfund* 1: 39–58.

CHAPTER 2

Doing Morally Acceptable Business
Anthropologists in the World of Consultants

Jazmin Mølgaard Cullen

Anthropology has, in the last couple of decades, become something of a 'brand' and, as a result, a rising number of anthropologists are being employed in as diverse settings as innovation, commercial research, marketing and design, and in an array of consultancy companies. This chapter investigates the moral conflicts experienced by anthropologists working in consultancies. It shows their moral conflict in, on the one hand, needing to take a stand against what they feel is a logic of pure profit maximization, while at the same time being deeply engaged in helping companies increase their revenue by making better products and services.

In the following I will show how my interlocutors justify their affiliation to their clients by making sense of their work as a way to move 'beyond capitalism'. Their work is, they state, 'for the people', not for the profit alone. Sometimes 'the people' refers to the clients who hire the anthropologists, sometimes the term refers to their customers or employees. In this chapter I show how the anthropologists I met in the field position themselves in relation to negative and positive 'ideal types', against which they attempt to evaluate the moral value of their own work. This is done by vilifying imagined types of companies and consultants – thereby allowing the anthropologist to position themselves as the 'lesser evil'. In effect, this activity of self-scrutiny allows my interlocutors to come to terms with the moral dilemma of working for profit while distancing themselves from the logic of profit maximization that constitutes a basic condition for their services. These ideal types, however, remain ephemeral or imagined forms that never really materialize in the lives of the business anthropologists themselves. On the one hand, my interlocutors imagine a sphere of organizations and people that are engaged in ruthless profit maximization, and on the opposite end of this, a sphere of people and organizations who are engaged in empathic listening to and speaking for real, human lives whose conditions can and should be improved by the consultants. It goes without saying that my interlocutors strive to dissociate their own work from the former and strive towards identifying with the latter. In other words, the anthropologists discussed in this chapter feel morally obligated to create what they believe to be more meaningful and helpful encounters between companies and 'the people' who are their employees and customers. They take it upon themselves to be empathetic towards the people affected by their client's strategic decisions. However, as the nature of their work is for-profit, they are constantly thrown back into doubt about the moral value of their work.

During fieldwork, I observed that my interlocutors frequently gravitated towards lengthy discursive attempts to assess the moral value of their own work, as well as that of others. Our interactions revolved around mutual and repetitive self-scrutiny and collective reflections around moral conflicts to the extent that this became a topic in and of itself in my fieldwork. As the chapter unpacks the way in which these business anthropologists reflect on and evaluate the moral value of their own work, I have selected citations from both formal interview situations and impromptu conversations arising during our working day in the consultancies or at a conference, moments where we get caught up in collective reflection around this topic or where I return to the topic to get a better sense of what is at stake for them.

The material for this chapter was collected among business anthropologists, most of whom had a five-year long degree in anthropology from a university in Denmark, though some of them were trained in other countries. The study was conducted in consultancies that worked primarily with anthropological approaches, as well as in various networks and conferences on the anthropology of business and organizations.

Fieldwork was carried out for twelve months in four consultancies (three in Denmark and one in New Zealand) that are comparable in size and in the services they offer. They all had between seven and fifteen employees, and all of them provided a variety of solutions in terms of creating change in organizations, co-creation, new internal procedures, new products and the engagement of citizens. They did at times work for private clients and NGOs, but all of them primarily worked for the public sector. I took part in everyday work in the respective offices: client meetings; data collection/fieldworks carried out for their clients; and workshops. The professional yet to some extent friendly relationship I had with my informants was often challenging to navigate. I encountered multiple and wide-ranging difficulties in relation to the positioning of myself in the field. Such difficulties spanned feeling alienated to being appointed unofficial mentor and peer. There were no clear boundaries between me as the observer and my informants as the observed. As Krause-Jensen and Cefkin suggest, methodological encounters studying peers and other academics can be seen as a 'walk down an infinite hall of mirrors' (Krause-Jensen 2017, Cefkin 2017: 3).

Prior to this fieldwork, I had myself been employed as a business anthropologist working for a Danish organization, and in the discursive exchanges that form the main material for this chapter, I am conversing and questioning in a way that reflects this double position. I will show how my interlocutors position themselves in relationship to me as a fellow anthropologist and as an academic researcher. I am aware that my interlocutors were in many ways very much like myself, also in terms of the kind of companies they worked for and that I had previously worked for. Anthropologists working in different kinds of companies and organizations may define the ideal types of 'good' and 'evil' differently and their self-scrutiny may take a different form and play a different role in their working life than what was the case for my interlocutors. But as my material from EPIC (Ethnographic Practice in Industry Conference) shows, business anthropologists working in other kinds of (larger) companies, not defining themselves as working with anthropological approaches, as did the consultancies in my study, were also preoccupied with the need to position themselves in relation to an imaginary 'evil other'.

Most of the material presented here is based on recorded and transcribed conversations that took place as part of my fieldwork, and some is drawn from field notes. I will occasionally compare my interlocutors' reflections to those found in the published writings of leading business anthropologists who have had an impact in the field where my interlocutors work, thus using these texts as part of my material too.

I have observed situations in which my interlocutors were confronted with ethical dilemmas – i.e. problems of how to be the spokesperson of 'the little man'– and the feelings of unease this sparked. Usually they did not make it explicit, during their interaction with the clients or their colleagues, that they argued as they did due to their anthropological training. This was, however, what they themselves suggested in my discussions with them about their work.

Moral Economy

Let us begin with a discussion of moral economy as presented in the introduction to this book to stimulate a reflection of what a 'moral economy of business anthropology' could look like in this material. Referring back to Keith Hart's definition of capitalism, which was discussed in the introduction to the book:

> The moral economy of capitalism is based on the separation of two spheres, the market and home, which represent ideally impersonal and personal social life. The payment of money for labour marks the first and unpaid, especially female labour the second. People are expected to divide themselves daily between public production and private consumption, to submit to impersonal rules outside the home and to express themselves as persons within it. This division has never been actually achieved, but a huge cultural effort goes into generating it. (Hart 2011)

What could be the two spheres on which the moral economy of business anthropology is based? How are these spheres generated in my interlocutors' self-reflexive considerations of the moral value of their work and that of others? What function does this separation have in the working lives of the business anthropologist? What happens when my interlocutors attempt to achieve this division in practice through their work as business consultants? Our inquiry begins with an evening of drinks with a group of international anthropologists gathered in South America.

The Philip Morris Ghost: Pointing to the Evil Other

EPIC was one of my field sites, which I attended in 2015 in Sao Paulo and in 2016 in Minneapolis. These conferences bring together anthropologists, ethnographers and interested others in industry/business from around the world. Represented industries include Fortune-500 companies, technology giants such as Intel and Microsoft, management consultancies, design studios, NGOs, public policy organizations and think tanks. Apart from serving as a 'nest for business anthropologists', EPIC is a conference where several of my primary interlocutors have presented papers and taken part in discussions about how to apply anthropology and ethnography in industry.

On the first day of the conference, a group of us were heading to a high-end restaurant in the shopping district in Sao Paolo for the con-

ference dinner party. As we walked to the restaurant from the 5-star
conference hotel, I chatted with a French woman I had only just met. I
mentioned how weird I found it that money and having to earn money
was like an elephant in the EPIC room that no one cared to mention.
In the same breath I said, 'But well, I wouldn't go around bragging
too much about having gone over to the dark side as an anthropologist either'. I didn't pay much attention to her response and continued
talking, 'But then again, I am also privileged to not have to make a profit
for the University', referring to my employment at the Department
of Anthropology at the University of Copenhagen. I finally stopped
to look at the woman. Her facial expression conveyed a big question
mark. Obviously, what I was saying made no sense to her at all. I back-
tracked to regain the connection with her and asked what her work
involved, back in France. She told me she was attending EPIC to learn
how to use anthropology in the consultancy at which she worked. She
was a consultant working for a company doing user-surveys. I had
failed to recognize that this woman was not an anthropologist.

This encounter from one of the first days on my fieldwork was probably the first time it dawned on me that my own and other anthropologist's moral dilemmas around profit-maximation and the way we tend
to speak about it as a 'necessary evil' was perhaps not as self-evident as
I had thought it to be. In fact, it made me realize that this type of moral
dilemma may not be shared with colleagues from other professions
and disciplines and perhaps had more to do with my identification
with anthropology than with the nature of the work my interlocutors
and I did in business consultancy.

At the dinner party that night I met some anthropologists from the
US, one with a master's degree and the other with a PhD; both worked
for big corporations in Silicon Valley. The two had known each other
for quite a while. Luckily, we had just the right amount of drinks to
remember each other the following day when the two Americans and I
gathered again by the pool for more of those dangerous, delicious caip-
irinhas. We were in the midst of chatting, getting to know each other
a bit more, when one of them, Justin, suddenly exclaimed, laughing:
'Have you heard about the guy from Philip Morris[1] who's attending
the conference?' We were shocked, and it showed. This was brand-
new, jaw-dropping information. Immediately and simultaneously we
barraged Justin with questions: 'Have you seen him? Have you talked
to him? Does he have to present a paper? Why is he here?'

Justin had not seen him. He had just seen his name on the conference programme, which listed the names and professional affiliations
of all EPIC attendees and presenters. This list was available to all of

us, but only Justin had studied it closely. We never did track down the Phillip Morris representative, and he did not present a paper at EPIC that year. Perhaps for this reason, he became a near-mythical character for us throughout the rest of the conference. We continued to speculate about his identity, his reasons for coming there and his relationship to his employer in the days to come. However, our desire to meet this person whom we had already personified as some sort of Devil never materialized. He remained a ghost.

The above anecdote demonstrates how my interlocutors and I rank the moral value of our colleagues and the work they do in the industry. I did not notice it then, but as I worked through my material in the months to come with the rest of the group of researchers behind this book, it started to dawn on me that my interlocutors and I would continuously evaluate the moral value of our own work and make moral judgements about the people affiliated with our discipline, as if the moral divisions between right and wrong in business anthropology were self-evident to all of us. To explore this dynamic, we will now turn to one of the consultancies I studied in my fieldwork and examine how my primary interlocutors would take for granted whom one could engage with professionally, and whom one could not.

Claude is the owner of a consultancy company that has based its services on anthropological methods and theory. He is himself an anthropologist by training and always impeccably dressed. In one of our introductory conversations, he described to me the company's business model, the vision and overall strategy, as well as the kinds of projects they take on. 'Of course, there are the ethical aspects, right?', he said. Even though he had posed this as a rhetorical 'you-know-what-I-mean' statement, I did ask him to elaborate on 'ethical aspects' a bit more. He then continued, 'Well, we don't want to just do any assignment, like any other consultancy, and take on whatever project comes along'. At this point, one of the other consultant-anthropologists steps into the room. Overhearing our conversation, he eagerly chimed in: 'No, we would not do anything for Philip Morris'. Claude looked at him, then back at me, and nodded eagerly.

The function of Phillip Morris in these two episodes is interesting. There seems to be an implicit agreement among my interlocutors that this particular company name represents everything that they do not want to be associated with. My interlocutors (and to a great extent myself) seem to construct the same ghost here as Justin, the other anthropologists and I did at EPIC. The function of this particular tobacco company in my interlocuters' accounts seems to be the imaginary other who is unequivocally immoral and in opposition to the kind of work one would like to identify with as an anthropologist. The ghost of Phillip Morris becomes the negative definition or the ground upon which the moral value of the business anthropologist's best work stands out as figure. I propose that Philip Morris here serves the function of the 'evil other' that my interlocutors and I can dissociate from and thereby understand ourselves as an alternative to: an alternative that is not just 'better' than but one that allows us to plot a position on the right side of a foundational moral fault line. Most of the anthropologists I met in the field would agree that Phillip Morris was a 'no-go' employer, at least not if you were a self-respecting anthropologist who still had a shred of moral decency left. Claude, however, was far from being the only interlocutor who continuously compared the moral value of his own anthropological practice to that of other businesses and attempted to rescue a sense of being on the right side of a moral fault line.

Working for the People – Not the Company, Not the System

It was a recurring theme throughout my fieldwork that my interlocutors would point at their practices as something other, something different and even something better than 'business as usual'. For them, business as usual was represented by what they imagined as an uncompromising, hard core, capitalist drive toward profit maximization and an unshakeable faith in the free market. In contrast, my interlocutors saw their own mode of business as moving beyond capitalism as we know it. Their businesses, they would tell me, were for the 'the people' or the 'little man', not for the capitalists, the shareholders or the investors. Here, 'the little man' often referred to consumers who bought the products made by, for example, large multinational companies. Alternatively, it could refer to the people who were affected by public policy, or who were the imagined target groups for the many different projects that my interlocutors worked on.

Sometimes they would have a hard time solving the tasks they were given, because they were morally dubious or, rather, they represented two fundamentally incompatible spheres of the moral economy, and they then tried to take action to support the separation of the two spheres. I observed how during a series of interviews made for a client, one of my interlocutors was repeatedly being told by the informants that there were no specific plans, hopes or dreams behind the application they made to the Ministry of Innovation for financial support to spark innovation through their new or existing business ideas. They simply needed money and saw it as one way of getting access to money. When I later overheard this interlocutor present her 'insights' from the interviews to one of the partners in the consultancy firm, she downplayed the informants' insistence that they did it for the sake of money. She made an effort to create a narrative about why these people needed the money, which as far as I could see was not based on the interviews I had observed her make. In other words, she struggled hard to keep people on the ground, 'the little man', and financial logic in two different spheres.

I describe below an example of how one of my interlocutors explicitly formulates moral obligations and duties as anthropologists as if they were self-evident. The passage derives from a full-day discussion I had with five interlocutors about anthropological competences. I asked them to quickly jot down (on post-it notes) what they believed to be the core anthropological competences based on their experiences and current work in consultancy, and then present what they had written. Carina, an anthropologist in her thirties, shared one of her post-its:

> Well, I have written that it is something idealistic. I have also written that it is to fight for the little man [*sic*]. They sort of go together. Then I've written curiosity. . . one is curious. . . So, yes, that is similar as well, you know, having an interest in other people. But also, you know, you can make people speak and reflect. And also, I think, it is like having an overview. There's also this [post-it] of doing some generalizations. And like more general academic competences, there is analysis. But I believe there's something anthropological about that as well, but it is probably hard to argue that we are the only ones analysing. The same goes for project coordination. And empathy, something that is really re-occurring in anthropology. . . Holistic, I believe.

As this excerpt shows, Carina sees being an anthropologist as a calling that involves quite a wide range of competences. It is also a calling that involves having high expectations of her own capabilities as an anthropologist. She opens with the statement that fighting for the 'little man' is a core anthropological competence. For Carina, this anthropological endeavour clearly goes hand in hand with values like idealism, empathy, being holistic and having an overview. Carina seemed to valorize her own work and obligations, perhaps in opposition to an implicit, but unnamed other. What kind of division is she making here? What would my interlocutors consider to be in opposition to this definition of anthropological competences?

The following excerpt is from a conversation I had with Summer, a junior heading straight to senior consultant. Summer is an anthropologist by training and had worked for her present consultancy company for a couple of years when I met her as part of my fieldwork. In the beginning of our relationship, she seemed a bit nervous around me, but during this particular conversation, taking place one day after work, this no longer seemed to be the case. We were sitting outside a café, enjoying some beverages on a sunny afternoon, and our conversation turned to the subject of the kind of work that would not be morally acceptable to us. Summer told me that she was constantly evaluating whether she would continue in the consultancy and stressed that she wanted to make sure that she was working for clients whom she actually wanted to work for. I asked if she could give me some examples of which companies she would not want to work for. She could not come up with concrete names from the top of her head so, based on previous experience, I suggested a by now familiar one: 'Phillip Morris?' I asked (somewhat leading the witness). 'What?' Summer replied. I repeated: 'Philip Morris?' Summer laughed and I continued: 'A company that produces cigarettes. Would you work for them?' At this point Summer gave an unexpected reply: 'I don't know, at this rate'. 'Really?' I said, somewhat surprised; this was new.

Summer seemed to know where I was coming from and continued: 'It would have been a really clear-cut call even before I started working [at the consultancy]. I would have been like "No! Not doing that!"' We continued talking about Philip Morris. I described how representatives from another cigarette company would wait outside schools in developing countries in order to offer kids free cigarette samples. The cigarette company did this because smoking has become less popular in wealthier societies, so they were looking for a new market to get hooked on tobacco/nicotine. In recalling this conversation with Summer, it is clear to what extent I took for granted that Summer would not want to associate with Big Tobacco. But instead, Summer said to me, 'Two years ago, I would have been right there with you, and it's not that I'm not with you right now. It's that I've become weaker in my views because I've become more aware of my hypocrisy'. She laughed and made me laugh at myself as I leaned forward and grabbed a smoke from my pack, lit it, and said: 'Yeah, I'm a total hypocrite'. Summer continued:

> Also, because I've started wondering where the good intentions are. Right? In your example [about the company handing over free samples to kids], clearly bullshit. Right? Right now, I can't see good intentions through that. But If you were to say: 'Hey, there's a team in Philip Morris that are looking at how we might let people have the same experience as smoking, but without having to smoke a cigarette . . .' Then you are like, 'Oh, OK.' . . . Don't

want to work for Philip Morris, because they're assholes, but that's a really interesting project. It seems like they've got good intentions, so maybe I do [want to work for them]. Maybe you could really do something quite useful, but maybe it's just a band-aid, and you're not solving the actual problem. Maybe you're just creating a different crutch for people. Maybe it's just a marketing scheme, so now they get the smokers and they get the non-smokers. Philip Morris is still a dickhead company. But then isn't the point that I'm in business because I'm supposed to be growing businesses, so why wouldn't I want Philip Morris' business to grow? . . . Ah, because actually part of me still thinks they're dickheads. . . . Then if I'm going to work for them because I think this project is interesting, but I think they're dickheads, what does that say about me? What am I really doing with my ideals and my ethics? Where am I really drawing the line? It's all of that. It's that dynamic.

'Where am I really drawing the line?' Summer asks rhetorically. This question epitomizes the reflections she puts forward. Summer walks us through a meditation on the moral conflict in being both an anthropologist and a business consultant, identities that seemed to both of us to be somewhat irreconcilable. She considers herself a hypocrite for taking on tasks for a business whose intentions are to create a 'crutch' or a dependency on nicotine, to put a band-aid on a fundamental moral problem rather than helping 'the people' to kick their addictive and lethal habits. At the same time, she knows that her work involves helping companies grow. Her strong self-reflexive skills do not spare her from this somewhat paradoxical recognition. She says she struggles to identify the truly good intentions in Philip Morris' business model, understanding clearly that her stated responsibility as an anthropologist is to do exactly this, to help the company grow according to its own agenda; yet she does reach the conclusion that she essentially thinks Phillip Morris is a 'dickhead' company, regardless of their stated intentions, as their main incentive is to sell tobacco. However, this moral dilemma between being a consultant who helps companies grow, and the fact that there are 'dickhead' companies out there that she may or may not work for in the future, makes Summer feel 'weakened' in her own position. Not only does she question the moral justifications of the imagined evil other, she simultaneously questions the moral justifications for her own work. This seems to provoke doubt in her own sense of having a position or following a moral compass inherent to her identity as an anthropologist ('what does that say about me? What am I really doing with my ideals and my ethics? Where am I really drawing the line?'). On the one hand, it seems that Summer's obligations as a business consultant gives her a sense of obligation to fulfil the task she has accepted as her work. The entire exercise takes form as a repetitive process of questioning and self-scrutiny where Summer questions the moral value of her present and imagined future work. As a side effect, this has the potential to position her in opposition to the core product and purpose of the organization she works for as a consultant (helping companies grow).

What is interesting is that both Summer and I seemed to take for granted that we can evaluate the moral value of a big company we have never worked for or even known anyone who did. Phillip Morris is, in essence, a 'dickhead company' to both of us and neither of us thinks to question this sweeping moral judgement or explore its basis further. We both see this company as a symbol for something that directly clashes with our worldviews. At the time, this did not strike us as odd. In fact, the conversation turned to my asking Summer to elaborate further on her views on business ethics and in this conversation more 'evil others' came up. Such as the Coca Cola Company:

> I wouldn't want to work for Coca Cola, because sugar is one of the most evil and unhealthy things around. It [sugar] has a relatively good reputation, it's perceived as fine, and it's sold in major quantities to children. You're just creating thousands and thousands of obese people and diabetics. You're putting it in all your products just because it's more addictive that way and people will keep buying your products. That's terrible . . . Then you think, oh, Coca Cola as the design-led company that it is, and you see some of its initiatives, and you go, 'That's really cool.' They're one of the companies that has more clearly epitomized for me that companies should be ethical. Companies should be looking at sustainability issues, because it's a business concern. . . Not many other businesses out there can have that clear vision of 'I need to be doing something about these wicked problems for my own business to be sustainable'.

Again, we see the confidence with which Summer sums up the moral value of a huge company that neither of us have worked for or interacted with. Summer uses the Coca Cola brand to elaborate her points about businesses that may have good intentions, but when looking further into their motivations for doing good, the fact that they still do bad things cannot be ignored, such as causing sugar dependency, obesity and diabetes among children. Setting up this simple formula, Summer continued to propose to me that Coca Cola could become a frontrunner for sustainability by creating a better environment for the agriculture on which their business relies. In other words, it makes good business sense for Coca Cola to do good, as she explains below:

It's really simple. If climate change is affecting how things grow and weather patterns and water and dry seasons, then it's affecting how many oranges you have. If it's affecting how many oranges you have, then it's affecting how much juice you can sell as Coke, so it's really clear-cut . . . For most businesses, it's a question of 'I need to be seen to be doing good' or 'it's not my problem'. I don't know what it is for Coca Cola, but I have at least seen them articulate it in such a way: 'It's wicked problems that we should be solving for the world. Actually, it just makes good business sense for us, so we need to be doing it and all businesses should be doing it' . . . At the same time, I can't get over the fact that you're still selling sugar to children who don't need the sugar.

The moral conflict for Summer is that she sees Coca Cola as a company that is 'doing good' in the projects they outline but this is just not 'good enough' for her. Below, Summer again presents her capacity to evaluate Coca Cola's business ethics as self-evident: 'Right? It's something that lots of businesses are grappling with – both the ones with good intentions and the ones with bad intentions, because even the ones with really good intentions have unintended negative impacts in the world. Right? I mean, I do, too'. Summer and I continue our conversation in a way that shows that at the time it was self-evident to us that we can evaluate, from the top of our head, which businesses have 'good intentions' and which have 'bad intentions'. What enables us to do that? Below we move closer to an understanding of how Summer evaluates the moral output of different businesses more specifically. I asked her to tell me more about how she proposed that one might lose sight of the issue of having a bad or a good impact in the world:

It's always that play. The consultancy has its own set of values originally defined by the managing team in terms of what they will do and what they won't do. They're quite clear on that, which means that, for the most part, it's been OK. But as we grow and have more options and are getting more ambitious and competitive and going into [private markets], I can see some from management really clearly drawing the line on things that they don't agree with. But I can also see others just getting really passionate and attracted to the idea of doing things for major companies, because it'll be a really fascinating project, a concept, whatever it is. No bad intention behind it, but perhaps less awareness over what's going on systemically and what are the other negative impacts of it. That's where I start wondering at what point will our values no longer overlap and start departing from each other.

What is worth noting here is how Summer evaluates the moral compromise, or lack of it, of the organization she works for, by speculating about whether the management team has a broader 'awareness of what´s going on systemically' or not. To her, the moral compromise occurs the moment her management team, or she herself for that matter, loses sight of the broader context and impacts of the companies they work for. She suggests that she may have to leave the job if they reach a point where senior consultants entertain the possibility of working for large corporations whose overall project may not be morally defensible to them, but who may have interesting and 'morally defensible' projects within the company. She continues:

> I've got more of a sense of. . . I don't know. Capitalism and business growth is not sustainable. I mean, you can't just grow. There are finite and limited resources, so therefore the answer is not 'let's grow business'. I think that some of the people in the management team probably still come with the background of 'let's grow business' and 'let's do an awesome job for our clients'. So yeah, that's always a bar. Yeah, it's kind of that play. I find it fascinating, because I think a lot of people go into anthropology with good intentions and with the idea – 'I'm fascinated by humans and I want to do good' and blah, blah, blah. When you end up in the business world, it's a little bit of 'How do you come to terms with what you're doing in the business world?' And you might find a way that you're comfortable with ethically or you might not.

Here we encounter the core of the moral dilemma for Summer as a trained anthropologist. 'Capitalism and business growth is not sustainable', she says, yet she needs to come to terms with 'what she is doing in the business world'. Summer identifies as an anthropologist, something that she here connotes with having 'good intentions', being 'fascinated by humans' and wanting to 'do good'. It is as if she perceives the calling of an anthropologist as an inherent moral obligation to go 'beyond capitalism'. The academic skills of being able to see the broader context (cultural, economic, environmental) of the companies she works for is perceived as something that comes with a (moral) obligation of some sort. She is therefore constantly occupied with how to navigate in the ethical dimensions of their work. She naturalizes the ostensible 'badness' of particular businesses or products and she simultaneously naturalizes anthropology as a calling that, by definition, compels one to 'do good' and thus stands in direct opposition to the 'evil other' symbolized by certain businesses, by the unrealistic idea of endless economic growth or simply by capitalism as a whole.

Throughout my fieldwork, I directly and indirectly encountered the idea that anthropologists understand 'the system' better than their non-anthropological colleagues, that anthropological training allowed for a somewhat broader analytical vantage point, a less clouded judgement due to a training in considering a relationship in a more encompassing whole. Interlocutors would, for example, tell me that others (especially stakeholders) would only focus on 'money' while they themselves focused on saving the world or creating real impact and change for people. However, this way of scrutinizing and continuously evaluating the moral implications of taking on the role of a business anthropologist is not limited to the anthropologists I encountered during fieldwork. We also find it in the literature on business and organizational anthropology. Anthropologist Ann Jordan expresses a similar view in her book, *Ethical Concerns*:

> In some cases, consumer research seems clearly ethical. If an anthropologist is asked to provide design guidance for a new software package intended for a particular market niche, chemists, for example, and having such a package makes the chemists' job easier, then studying chemists' research behaviour in order to design the package effectively seems harmless. In other areas the harmless factor is less clear. Improving marketing strategies for a product people do not really need may seem less desirable. Are the purchasers who are the subjects of the study harmed if they are convinced to buy a product when they never knew they needed it before? This simply increases corporate profit at the expense of the little guy, does it not? Are consumers all that easily brainwashed into buying things they do not need, and if so, is it the anthropologist's responsibility to protect consumers from themselves? Is it patronizing of the anthropologist to decide for others what they do and do not need? These are all questions each anthropologist must answer on a case-by-case basis. The primary responsibility is clear enough: anthropologists should not cause harm to those who are the subjects of their studies. In real life, however, applying this ethical rule is difficult. Each anthropologist must think through the issues in each case and reject those projects she feels are harmful. (Jordan 2003)

Jordan, like Summer and several of my interlocutors, expects anthropologists to reject projects that they feel could be 'harmful', and proposes that continuous and rigorous self-evaluation is simply part of the job. As in the conversations I had with my interlocutors cited above, this ongoing moral evaluation is taken for granted as an activity that comes with the profession, not only of being a business consultant but of coming into this line of work from a background in anthropology. Jordan proposes, however, that the parameters of this responsibility fall upon each anthropologist to continuously and subjectively evaluate the broader consequences of their work in relation to the project at hand. Sarah Pink (2006), who has written extensively about applied anthropology, makes a similar point. Applied anthropology inevitably constitutes a social intervention, she argues, in whatever context one is working, be it commercial, public sector or for another independent organization. Ethical questions not only apply to the choice of who to work with/for, but also to the question of to whom one is responsible when involved in an applied project.

This difficult task of ethical and moral evaluation seems to be considered by both to be intrinsic to identifying as an anthropologist. It makes sense that my interlocutors who have been subjected to anthropological training, and are likely to have been exposed to the kind of literature cited above, take it for granted that they can, and should, embark on the abstract and difficult task of constant moral evaluation and ranking of the kinds of projects they may choose to work on.

On the one hand, my interlocutors, who are all highly invested in anthropology as their main professional identity, are continuously preoccupied with evaluating and weighing whether they are significantly distinguishable from an imagined 'evil other' that is sometimes personified by large, multinational companies with profit as their only objective and sometimes more vaguely defined as organizations or groups that are blinded by capitalist logic, by delusions of endless growth or by greed to the extent that they have lost sight of the bigger picture or the system-effects of their actions. In other words, they respond to 'things as they seem' to them, but are either not willing or not able to see the larger context or understand what is going on systemically. It then falls on the anthropologist to become a voice for 'things as they are', for considering the broader context of one's actions and work to make their more systemic overview heard. It seems, from reading our conversations so far, that both my interlocutors and I expect, in line with the prescriptions of Ann Jordan, to not take on a job that conflicts with the identity project of the anthropologist as someone who can understand the system or foresee the larger consequences of the projects they engage in.

This moral obligation seems at times to trump the professional identity they have simultaneously accepted as consultants. Contrary to the expectations of some of their non-anthropological colleagues or some of their management teams, my interlocutors seem to expect of themselves that they should reject jobs that are not in accordance with the moral values associated with identifying as an anthropologist. Since the colleagues, managers, stakeholders and others working in the industry alongside my interlocutors are not necessarily equipped with the anthropological tools to see the wider scope of things, it falls upon the business anthropologist to make the right choices for herself and, whenever possible, make those moral distinctions visible to others.

It would, however, be a mistake to conclude that interlocutors like Summer, Justin, Claude and others presented themselves as the ones with both feet on the moral high ground of business anthropology. As already hinted by Summer above, it is quite the opposite. The enquiry into optimizing the moral value of one's work, the desire to work for 'the people' or 'the little guy', or the aim to 'do good', seem to require a process of constant ethical self-evaluation. Claude introduces me to his company by telling me, first off, that of course there are ethical concerns. Summer explicitly speaks to the danger of becoming 'weak' in her moral stance, thus losing sight of 'where to draw the line'. It is as if without this constant concern they could unknowingly wake up one morning on the wrong side of the moral divisions that seem to come naturally with their identity as anthropologist. Rather than a final and attainable status as someone who 'does good', we see an effort to distance oneself from the ghost of 'the evil other'. And the image of running away from a ghost is in fact quite apt to describe this activity. The people or organizations my interlocutors imagine as personifying the wrong side of the moral division remain without material substance in their narratives. 'They' become mythical figures, much like the anthropologist from Phillip Morris haunting the EPIC conference. Their imaginary qualities in the narratives of our conversations make them capable of haunting the self-reflections and self-presentations of my interlocutors. In what I will below refer to as a moral economy of anthropology, this haunting sense of 'badness' seems to drive my interlocutors to constantly question the moral value of their work. Allow me to elaborate on the concept of a moral economy before returning to the moral dilemmas of my interlocutors.

The Self-Scrutinizing Anthropologist

Didier Fassin has argued elsewhere:

> Considering the relationships anthropologists had with colonization in the case of Europe or with imperialism in the case of the United States, as well as, symmetrically and more recently, their stance against the oppression of people or in favour of human rights suggests that their axiological neutrality has often been an ideal or even an illusion rather than a faithful representation of their activity. Histories of the discipline often retain the scandals that have marked its development, such as involvement with the military or the intelligence, which is often represented as the 'dark side' of anthropology, but they have been less attentive to its 'bright side', that of the denunciation of evil in the world and of the defence of the wretched

and the dominated, which are no less revealing of their taking sides on moral grounds and no less problematic precisely because they generally remain unquestioned. (Fassin 2012)

Drawing on this observation we could ask: why is it that the 'bright side' of anthropology remains unquestioned, not just in the history of anthropology as a discipline, but also in the self-reflections of the business anthropologists I met in the field? And what impact does this lack of engagement with questioning the value of 'denouncing evil' have on my interlocutor's reflections on the moral value of their work? For several of my interlocutors, and in the literature on business anthropology, the 'wretched and the dominated' are vaguely personified as 'the people' or 'the little guy', but how is it that it remains unclear to the anthropologists we have met in this chapter whether they are really serving the people or whether their work as consultants is in fact doing the opposite? Why does this remain an ongoing case-by-case-evaluation that, in practice, never reaches a sure footing on some moral high ground?

Before moving on to my interlocutors, I would like to pay close attention to the narrative of anthropologist Kathi R. Kitner who, in 'The Good Anthropologist: Questioning Ethics in the Workplace' (2014), reflects on her decision to leave the fishing industry, where she was asked to write a more positive report about the prospective social impact she had investigated. She found this impossible to execute without losing her 'self-respect as an anthropologist and as a human being'. As a consequence, she quit her job and took on a new one at Intel. What is interesting is not so much Kitner's story, as the way she has written the text. Kitner moves between reflecting critically on how anthropologists have this 'we have to save the world thing' (the unquestioned 'bright side') and uncritically investigating 'the dark side' by pointing out who is the 'enemy of the people' (ibid.: 314). Kitner, like my interlocutors, thus compares her work at Intel with more 'evil' work, and so identifies the positive moral outputs of her endeavours by way of keeping a distance from the negatively defined evil other. It seems the function of the evil other is to allow business anthropologists to come to terms with the inevitable pro-profit conditions of their practices by reassuring themselves that they are indeed 'the lesser evil'. In this operation, the 'bright side' of anthropology as inherently 'good work' remains unquestioned, as pointed out by Fassin. Let us return to Summer and hear her reflections on the moral dilemma of being identified as a business anthropologist, which seems to almost be a contradiction in terms for her and her colleagues. On the same sunny afternoon, a bit further into our conversation she tells me:

You've got Richard [an attendee at one of the EPICs] going: 'We love our jobs' and 'we live a thousand lives through our jobs' and all these really strong emotional messages that really tied to either let's do good in the world or look at the emotional connections that we're establishing that are a lot more personal. On the other side, you've got people going, yeah, but remember we're here for business and our job is to improve business. Why are we being so shy about talking about the money and talking about our business goals? It does sometimes feel even. . . I don't know how much of it I'm projecting, but even in the community [anthropological and EPIC community] . . . that there's this strong sense of good intentions, but also insecurity, because 'is what I'm doing really what I should be doing?' There's a little bit of guilt. It's like that colonial guilt. . . There's the guilt of, 'ohhh, I'm working for business' sort of guilt.

The positioning of money and business goals here seems fundamentally opposed to anthropology. Summer proposes that 'the EPIC community and other anthropologists' have some form of guilt about working for a business, and makes an analogy to 'colonial guilt', in that there is a disowned relationship to the 'business' in business anthropology: they work for businesses yet refrain from speaking about money or economic goals. In other conversations I have had with her she also speaks more specifically about 'privilege guilt'. By using this analogy of colonial guilt or privilege guilt, she manages to distance herself from both the bright and the dark side of anthropology. She is deliberately not presenting herself to me as a 'save the world' kind of anthropologist (like Richard), but she is not really presenting herself as an 'enemy of the people' either. In fact, quite a bit of effort goes into neither coming off as 'the good anthropologist' nor as the 'evil other' in her narrative. She presents to me her sense of guilt or self-doubt, yet it would be quite a leap from there and into displaying any kind of willingness to strive explicitly for a career within the 'dark side' of anthropology. This leap seems to be a no-go for Summer and for my other interlocutors too.

Another example of this phenomenon is the way my interlocutors feel about sales. I attended a business fair with Britt, another anthropologist working in one of the consultancies, whose job it was to promote the consultancy and sell their services. Beforehand, Britt had emailed me about a project she had to pitch. At the fair I asked her about the email and she said:

I feel a bit uncomfortable having to sell things. I'm not that good at it. But as I wrote in the mail to you, I just put on the anthropologist-hat when I have to sell. [What do you mean, I asked? Britt elaborated:] Well, instead of selling it directly, I would do it more anthropologically by asking: 'What are you guys doing now? How is that working for you?' You know. . . asking about their needs and then pitching.

According to Britt, selling 'anthropologically' involves first asking the customer about their needs, showing an interest in their perspective, listening. The direct, raw and purely instrumental sales pitch makes her feel too uncomfortable. Of course, Britt did give a presentation at the fair in which she provided an overview of the consultancy's projects and their impacts. It was followed, as is usually the case at the end of conference presentations, by her being approached by colleagues and invited to engage in further conversations ending in, of course, the exchange of business cards. We met for lunch shortly thereafter. Britt was relieved to finally have finished the promotion speech. She told me about a woman she had spoken with who had made her uncomfortable: 'She came there, and I just felt she was trying to sell me something. I don't like it, you know. . . it's like. . . there she comes wanting to make money, while I just want to save the world', Summer said. We both laughed. None of us were comfortable with pitching to people who had not given us the go-ahead in terms of expressing a need for our reflections or services. None of us liked it when this was being done to us either. Both of us felt the need to express this in our conversation, thus distancing ourselves from this type of instrumental behaviour. What is interesting is the way in which Britt and Summer, and myself for that matter, accept the negative definitions when trying to perform the moral sentiments that we feel obligated towards. We are clear about what kind of professional we do not want to be and keep this identity at bay despite the fact that it haunts our conversations again and again.

But it also seems as though it is not only the dark side of anthropology that is personified as a kind of ghost that never really materializes and that we never fully embody ourselves. The 'bright side' or the unequivocally 'good anthropologist' is equally elusive in our narratives. When touching on what kind of work my interlocutors do feel comfortable about taking on, it remains an unattainable goal. Rather than working to arrive on the moral high ground and close the door on the 'evil other', Summer here explains to us how the sense of doing good anthropology is never fully realized:

> When I was younger, I used to see it as – I'm in a position where I can play with the system and be an advocate and a champion within the system and be someone who's savvy enough and capable enough of working with the system, but also to change the system for our own gains. Some of those less

privileged people might not understand how the system works, might not have the networks. They might have heaps of wherewithal. They might be extremely capable, and they might also be incredibly angry. They might be resentful. They might not want to work with the system. I'm in a privileged position. I'm in the position to work with the system to enable the change that they need to do to blah, blah, blah. The more I grow up, the more I think that I'm just becoming part of the system. I'm not doing what I thought I would be doing.

Clearly, becoming part of the system, according to Summer, is a compromise. Summer expresses doubt about whether she has stayed true to the moral standards that guided her entry into business anthropology. Had she seen herself as an unequivocally 'good anthropologist', she would have had to show a career track where she had indeed used her privilege to change the system by way of her services as a business consultant. But how would such a big and elusively defined impact ever be possible in practice? Yet, it is as if Summer continues to frame her identification with anthropology as if it naturally requires her to position herself in opposition to 'the system' that does not afford the same opportunities to 'less privileged people'. In a sense, Summer is saying that she owes it to 'the people' to make the best of her privileges. Carina, whom we met previously at the post-it session, expressed a similar sentiment earlier of the archetypical professional anthropologist: 'Being idealistic, empathic, holistic, and having an overview'. However, as soon as we stop talking about anthropologists and their skills in abstract terms and begin discussing how real anthropologists feel about their actual career trajectory, difficult questions begin to crop up in relation to the 'bright side' of anthropology, questions that, according to Fassin, are not addressed in the more academic reflections within the discipline, questions we seem to forget to problematize and 'bright sides' that do not appear as problematic as long as we are not practicing business anthropology on a day-to-day basis. Let us take a closer look at this. I asked Summer if she had become part of the system by working for the consultancy:

> No, not only because of the consultancy. Just everything. Being a business consultant is one of the things that has been part of life evolving. There's me going: 'I'm kind of not doing what I thought I'd be doing, and I'm kind of more part of the system than I am changing it'. There's another part of me going: 'I'm not sure whether it's about working with the system. I think the system is broken and I think what I've been doing is creating a bunch of band-aids'. If I'm creating band-aids, what I'm doing is I'm enabling it to go on for longer. . . . I'm just being the glue that keeps things going, which means instead of challenging the system, instead of being the person that

understands enough about the system to change it, I'm being one of the en-
ablers of the system. I'm maintaining it, and I'm doing that sort of stuff. . .
I'm. . . because I'm an anthropologist, because I'm empathetic, because
I'm open to considering different options, because I never really think I'm
right, which is a problem sometimes. Sometimes you need to think you're
right to be able to make things happen. But it also means that if you don't
necessarily think you're right and you're not that ego-attached to an idea,
somebody else saying, 'But what about this?', means you go, 'Huh? Yeah,
maybe. What about that?'

Here, Summer spells out her moral conflict: the two parts of her, one
that identifies with being someone (a business consultant) who can
work with the system and change things, and the other part of her who
can see through the system, understand the big picture and knows
the system is broken. This latter part, being an anthropologist, offers
no redemption and cuts through all illusions of being a 'good anthropologist', as business anthropology, in Summer's reflection, involves
becoming a band-aid or, worse, an enabler. What Summer seems to be
communicating to me here is that she does not see herself as a good
anthropologist, that she is not complacent, that she in no way considers herself 'home free'; that distinguishing herself from an imaginary
'evil other' and trying her best to do 'good anthropology' has not been
enough for her to represent herself to me as a good anthropologist; that
being a good anthropologist – both doing anthropology right by also
doing good in the world – means working under the premise that you
will never be 'good enough'.

Wrapping up this conversation (in the above citation), Summer
identifies what may be understood as an epistemological trait of anthropologists mixed with what seems to be a personal trait of her own:
Summer never thinks of herself as being 'right', she says. What function does this statement have in our conversation? Perhaps to ensure
that the bright side of anthropology remains forever unquestioned?
Had Summer boldly claimed that she was indeed a 'good anthropologist' and that her work was in fact helping to save the world one business consultation at a time, she would open herself to the possibility
of being proven wrong in practice: wrong by her own standards as an
anthropologist; wrong, perhaps also, in the eyes of fellow anthropologists discussing her perceived moral compromises over drinks at the
next EPIC; wrong in the eyes of the ex-business anthropologist turned
academic researcher who is currently probing her about her work ethics and moral dilemmas. By telling me: 'I never really think I'm right',
Summer shows both herself and me that she is open to critique, that
she knows there is room for improvement, that she is willing to go

through her entire career doubting the moral value of her work, that she will always feel she owes it to 'the people' to do better than she in fact does today.

Unsurprisingly, this aspiration comes with a price. Firstly, the insurance policy against becoming identified with the evil other, never 'being right', sentences the business anthropologist to a life of constant self-scrutiny and internal moral conflict. This seems to be an acceptable working condition for myself and my interlocutors, even if it may leave a few non-anthropologist consultants puzzled. But, Summer states, it also obstructs the very possibility of fulfilling her ambitions of making the most of her privileges and really 'make things happen' in the world of business.

We have come full circle in my interlocutors' moral self-reflections: the impossibility of convincingly presenting oneself as a good business anthropologist is now apparent. You simply can't win. Summer suspects that if she believed that she was 'right', she would also be able to do more good in the world through her work. Yet feeling you are right is ego-attached. It would make her closed to other ideas and in time she could end up willing to sell her 'right' ideas to the world with instrumental insensitivity, and we know that she feels this is wrong too. It seems that the moment Summer, Britt and most of my other interlocuters close their books, leaving academic anthropology and its unquestioned moral mission to 'do good' behind in an attempt to go put their aspirations into practice in the world of business, they have already renounced the possibility of ever fully embodying the 'bright side' of the discipline. The bright side remains as elusive as its 'evil other' in their narratives, if not a haunting ghost, then an ephemeral angel that dissolves when you climb the career ladder and realize that you have already become part of the system. We cannot, from the material on which this chapter is based, comment on what Summer does or does not 'make happen' in the world. We do know, though, that she has worked as a consultant for years, and continues to do so. We also know that she and other consultants would not take on any job. Every consultancy had both formal and informal guidelines for the choice of businesses to engage with. She and her colleagues continue to act and perform tasks for their clients, in ways which are permeated by these moral enquiries and self-critical reflections.

Before concluding this discussion, I wish to go back to EPIC, where I propose we witness what may be identified as the essence of the moral economy of business anthropology and its inherent confrontations in practice. On the third and last day of the conference, we were already repeating our routines. The first half of the day was all about papers and presentations. But on this day I encountered something different. A man from the UK who worked for a Spanish consultancy said: 'Let us be real about this. I did this for "El Corte Ingles"[2] so they could earn more money'. This was quite a departure from my initial impressions of EPIC. On the first day I had thought about how striking it was that the presenters practically never articulated the main reason for having to redesign televisions or figure out which kinds of cars people prefer; namely, to make money for their clients or employers. On the contrary, presenters would primarily focus on examples of how they had generated empathy for 'the people' or created change, which they construed as beneficial for 'the people'.

During the second half of the day, Justin and his colleague (the two men from the US I had met on the first evening of the conference), some other conference attendees and I again got together for drinks. Justin's colleague, whose trust I seemed to have earned, asked: 'Jazmin, can I ask you a rhetorical question?' Of course he could, I replied. He leaned towards me and lowered his voice: 'Let's say a big corporation like, let's say Facebook or Google, asked you to work for them, would you say yes?' I answered that it depended on what they wanted me to do. He nodded his head and said he sort of felt the same. He lowered his voice even more: 'Justin would never speak to me again if I took a job at, let's say Google or Facebook'.

Such questions, as shown in the material presented in this chapter, are indeed rhetorical. As anthropologists, my interlocutors and I seem to take for granted that we could never work for a tech giant, just like we would not work for Big Tobacco. And if we did, we are quite certain that at least some of our colleagues would never speak to us again. However, there also seems to be a counter-narrative, that allows us to say 'I did this to make money', that allows us to feel comfortable with whispering to each other, that we are not at all the good anthropologists we or our colleagues would like to be. The question remains: why is this quite modest and pragmatic recognition not enough to dispel the haunting sense of moral failure? Why is it not enough to admit to each other that as business anthropologists, we will probably never be able to do much better than our very best in any given moment?

Conclusion

In the first section, I presented empirical material that showed how my interlocutors – business anthropologists – would compare their own moral practices with those of others. My interlocutors assume that as anthropologists they are able to 'see through the system' and that this broader contextual view comes with an obligation to not be myopically blinded by interesting sub-projects and instead continuously work to change the system as a whole by being sensitive to the needs of 'the people'. In this ambition, they continuously need to position themselves in relationship to an imaginary 'evil other' who, on quite a few occasions, was personified by Philip Morris or other multinational, capitalist companies. In relation to this evil other, whose material substance and properties remain forever unfixed, they were occasionally, but not always, able to position themselves as the slightly lesser evil. Exactly where to draw the line and how to define what constitutes the difference between themselves and the evil other was left to an endless process of self-scrutiny, one that, according to Jordan, must take place inside the moral universe of each individual business anthropologist on a case-by-case basis. Listening to my interlocutors when they reflect on the moral value of their work, this seems to indeed be the case. My interlocutors would rehearse their moral obligation to do good and attempt the impossible task of 'drawing the line' by negative definition and comparison.

Academic training in anthropology, affording a broader contextual view and thus an ability to 'see through the system', seems to have a dubious reward here, as it makes the lives of business anthropologists somewhat paradoxical. On one hand, they held strong moral sentiments towards the kind of work they were offered; on the other hand, they were irrevocably involved in making companies grow in a world with finite resources, and selling things to people whose needs could perhaps have been expressed otherwise, had they been more 'anthropological' about it. The logic appears to be thus: as long as we are questioning, we are at least not bad, as long as we are not working for the evil other, we are at least less evil than 'them'. Ideal anthropology and its moral outputs were thus presented as an equally unattainable sphere of goodness, which the anthropologist cannot, in practice, achieve. On one hand, business anthropologists voice their moral obligations, yet on the other, they nonetheless have to work for profit and so alter the 'ideal anthropology', abandoning once again the goal of their moral striving a little further up the ladder of moral value.

Returning to Keith Hart's excellent definition of the moral economy of capitalism, I shall end with an attempt to spell out a definition of the moral economy of business anthropology in a similar vein. The moral economy of business anthropology is based on the separation of two spheres: things as they seem to business stakeholders, and things as they really are on a system-level. These two spheres embody 'the evil other' versus 'the good anthropologist'. The characteristics that mark the first sphere include engaging in highly paid work for multinational capitalist corporations, while the second sphere is characterized by seeing the bigger picture and choosing to uncompromisingly work for the 'the people' even if it means quitting your job. Business anthropologists are expected to successfully divide themselves into, on the one hand, identifying as a business consultant who is willing to compromise on moral values when working for profit to help businesses grow and, on the other hand, identifying as an academically trained anthropologist who sees through the fallacies of 'the system', and therefore one who continuously questions the moral value of one's own work and challenges herself to always do better. This division has never actually been achieved, but a huge cultural effort goes into generating it.

Jazmin Mølgaard Cullen has a PhD in anthropology from The University of Copenhagen. She has studied the practice of anthropologists working as consultants in four different consultancies.

NOTES

A huge and special thanks goes to Hanne Overgaard Mogensen and Birgitte Gorm Hansen for editing this volume, and to Morten Axel Pedersen and the rest of the authors for their great support, and their contributions and discussions throughout the past few years. I also wish to thank the consultancies where I carried out my fieldwork.
 1. Philip Morris is the name of a tobacco company that produces Marlboro, among other cigarette brands.
 2. A department store in Spain.

REFERENCES

Cefkin, M. 2009. *Ethnography and the Corporate Encounter: Reflections on Research in and of Corporations*. New York Oxford, Bergahn Books.
Cullen, J.M. 2019. *The Insight Job: Authenticity and Morality among Anthropological Consultants*, PhD thesis. Copenhagen: Department of Anthropology, University of Copenhagen.
Fassin, D. 2012. 'Introduction: Toward a Critical Moral Anthropology', in D. Fassin (ed.), *A Companion to Moral Anthropology*. Malden, MA: Wiley-Blackwell, pp. 1–17.
Hart, Keith. 2011. Commentary to the blogpost 'Defining Capitalism'. *The Open Anthropology Cooperative*. Retrieved 20 September 2019 from http://open anthcoop.ning.com/group/economicanthropology/forum/topics/defining-

capitalism?commentId=3404290%3AComment%3A114742&groupId=340429
0%3AGroup%3A785#sthash.DLzwlGD7.dpbs.

Jordan, A.T. 2003. 'Ethical Concerns', in *Business Anthropology*. Long Grove, IL:
Waveland Press, Inc., pp. 54–64.

Kitner, R.K. 2014. 'The Good Anthropologist: Questioning Ethics in the Workplace', in R.M. Denny and P.L. Sunderland (eds), *Handbook of Anthropology in
Business*. Walnut Creek, CA: Left Coast Press, Inc., pp. 309–20.

Krause-Jensen, J. 2017. 'Fieldwork in a Hall of Mirrors: An Anthropology of Anthropology in Business', *Journal of Business Anthropology* 6(1) 102–20.

Pink, S. 2006. *Applications of Anthropology: Professional Anthropology in the Twenty-
First Century*. Oxford and New York: Berghahn Books.

Thompson, E. 1994. 'Customs in Common', *Review, Canadian Committee on Labour
History*, 253–62.

CHAPTER 3

Not That Kind of Manager
Moral Work in Anthropological Leadership

Birgitte Gorm Hansen

> It is always possible to bind together a considerable number of
> people in love, so long as there are other people left over
> to receive the manifestations of their aggressiveness.
> —Sigmund Freud, *Civilization and Its Discontents*

Any attempt to study anthropologists ethnographically is likely to generate material primarily revolving around how interlocutors conduct themselves when being acutely aware that they are being watched through the eyes of their own discipline. The primary phenomenon studied would therefore not only be the everyday practice of such anthropologists, but to a very high degree also their practices of self-presentation and its relationship to perceived anthropological norms.

As problematic for a study of everyday management practices of anthropologists as it might seem, this effect of the ethnographer's presence in the field is not a bad vantage point for studying the moral work embedded in this practice. As presentations of self will always to some extent reflect the moral values by which a performer expects to be judged (Goffman 1959), we can look to anthropologists' self-representations for more knowledge about the moral divisions they navigate by when working with management.

This chapter dives into the moral work of one particular anthropologist working as a top manager, a job where self-representation and daily work practices are often closely intertwined. I have selected this anthropologist as the focus of my analysis as she is an especially vivid example of a theme that went across my material from other fieldwork or interviews with anthropologists in leadership positions.[1] After interviewing about a dozen anthropologists working in Denmark, and following two of them more closely in the field, I am left with the impression that there is no single trait that would allow me to write about these people as if they formed some kind of homogenous ethnic group.[2] Not only was there a big gap in levels of management experience in my group of interlocuters, they also differed in nationality, political views, gender and industry. All of my interlocutors had an MA in anthropology, but some were trained decades ago, some recently, some outside Denmark and some in the same department that I worked for in Copenhagen. In addition, they all presented themselves as very different from other kinds of managers and told very similar stories about ending up in management by mere coincidence or in response to external pressure rather than as a result of focused career planning or a desire for power. What seemed to unite them all was in fact this tendency to be different.

The anthropologist V, who I have made the single focus point of this chapter, is an especially representative case of being different or unique. V is an anthropologist working as the editor-in-chief and CEO of a Danish newspaper. I have made her my point of focus here partly because she embodied tendencies I saw across my material, but also because I was allowed to study her daily management practice for an extended period of time and with more context than other anthropologists I have met in the field. V agreed to me following her everyday work activities very closely in a period of almost three months. The material about V is thus richer and more detailed than my other material. This allowed for further insights into the moral work involved in the self-representation, self-reflexivity and managerial work of this particular anthropologist but also helped me to make sense of similar trends I found across my material.

Like most of my interlocutors, V tended to distance herself from other kinds of managers, presenting a 'one of a kind' approach to her work which was often in opposition to mainstream management trends. What she also shared with my other interlocutors was the call to reflect continuously on the moral boundaries of her work and especially her leadership. Whereas my previous fieldwork with academics working in management positions mostly revolved around the content of their work, this study of leadership among anthropologists revealed that they all spent a considerable amount of time self-reflecting on the moral value of their management practice. I'm sure all managers do this to some extent, but the anthropologists I met in the field seemed to do it more, as if exercising executive power was itself a moral problem that the anthropologist must continuously reflect on or attempt to solve. This preoccupation with morality did indeed set my interlocutors apart from other kinds of managers I have studied in the past.

V was no exception. In fact, describing her everyday managerial practice and its associated style of self-presentation makes a great case for studying the moral work involved when anthropologists become managers. V was not alone in expressing feeling morally challenged when filling a role that requires them to exercise executive power and act in accordance with organizational goals they may not feel entirely aligned with. But V was the only anthropologist I worked closely with in the field who managed to share with me not only her reflections on moral concerns she encountered in her work but also her concrete solutions or strategies for navigating perceived moral fault lines without disowning her role as a top manager. This also resulted in ethnographic material that could take the analysis beyond the observation that anthropologists reflect continuously about the moral value of their work and into describing the moral work that they might do as managers.

As it happens, the ability to present oneself as unlike other kinds of managers served as more than just impression management for V. Not only is V very highly skilled in setting herself apart from other kinds of managers, but her ability to become different is also at the very heart of her leadership. What I will show in the following is how the 'not that kind of manager' move was part of V's everyday working life as a strategy to resolve moral conflicts tied to the post-bureaucratic, Danish corporate landscape in which she made her career. This move seems to simultaneously work as a way for V to re-establish a sense of professional integrity or a perception of being on the right side of a perceived moral boundary, while also working as a mechanism for employee commitment via a process of leader-follower identification.

This seems to have been quite a successful strategy for V. She has had the longest career as an editor-in-chief in Danish media history. She kept her position for almost twenty years, which is significantly above the industry standard, and did not retire until 2017, a few weeks after my fieldwork with her had ended. She left behind a legacy of impressive achievements in the world of Danish print media and is widely respected in the media debate as a unique thinker who steered clear of the mainstream and followed her own way, even when controversial (Reseke 2017a, 2017b, 2017c). It is probably no coincidence that her legacy matches the way in which she presents herself on public record to her employees and to me during my fieldwork.

In the following I will show how V's self-presentation as a different kind of manager is intrinsic to the way in which she establishes leader-follower relationships in her managerial practice. This tells us something about what kind of moral divisions and boundaries she navigates by in her work, but also what kind of power she is able to exercise as a manager.

I will also comment on how V's training in anthropology forms an important backdrop to the moral distinctions by which she seems to navigate in her leadership practice: how to act responsibly when managing a group of employees in situations where the distinction between manager and employee can potentially collapse into common points of identification, thus glossing over the power differentials inherent to the formal hierarchy that sets them apart.

The moral conflict inherent to V's managerial practice seems to be how to act as a good and responsible leader when ones' relationship to employees is simultaneously one of identification and common ground and at the same time also separated by the division of labour intrinsic to the formal hierarchy. Where the former charges V with the task of understanding her employees' perspectives and establishing points of identification that allow her and her employees to work towards a common goal, the latter obligates V to commit to the organization's goal even when it conflicts with the interests of her employees. The potential conflict between leader and follower is mitigated by V's ability to disidentify with the kind of managerial practice that could become the target of employee critique and aggression.

The solution seems to be V's continuous ability to show what kind of manager she is not. As we will see, this dissociation with her role helps V to persuade her employees to identify with her as a professional and thereby with the goals she sets for the organization. Paradoxically, V's anthropological sensitivity to the social practice and perspective of her employees seems to play out in two ways: on the one hand, her training enables her to stay within the boundaries of her own moral integrity by representing herself a spokesperson for employees' lived experience in order to establish an organization based on non-exploitative transactions. On the other hand, it enables her to manage her employees with little or no resistance in the context of an industry famous for strikes, conflicts and lack of employee compliance. I will argue that V's ability to become 'one with' the organization in the same breath as dissociating herself from the organization is what allows her to do so. The simultaneous sameness and difference allow her to work around conflicts of interest and deflect employee aggression towards a common enemy whose symbolic sacrifice re-establishes the order of her leadership as well as her own sense of moral integrity.

Being Different – in Similar Ways

We are having lunch again. As always, we are seated at the end of the white, shiny, oval meeting table in my informant V's office. This is the same table where every Friday fifteen to twenty-five of the country's top journalists gather for the weekly editorial meeting at the *Paper*. Dwarfed by the size of the table, the four of us are seated at the end like the last lingering guests from a banquet that ended hours ago. On the table is a copy of last week's newspaper, one section left open, the rest folded and shuffled aside. A pot of coffee has gone cold; a pair of reading glasses are resting next to the paper. The rest of the table is occupied by books, some stacked, some still in boxes from Amazon, some just unwrapped, some with their pages open. A raincoat and a long, woollen cardigan hang over the back of the chair next to V's: a transparent plastic rococo chair whose design goes by the name of 'Ghost'. The chair is accompanied by the ghostly presence of the eleven identical chairs around the table. V is wearing a beige cashmere dress today and the obligatory box of handmade chocolates awaits on an over-filled bookshelf right next to the end of the table where I am seated. When V has finished her home-cooked meal that she brings to the office every day, she will ask me to take the chocolates from the shelf, I will hand them to her, she will take off the lid and offer them to me and to her two colleagues sitting across from her at the table. I decide to take only one piece of chocolate today, not only because I do not want to abuse V's hospitality, but also because I'm busy writing down the details of our conversation. We are talking about the early morning meeting with the top management that V came back from, around 10am. V is about to give her two colleagues a summary of what happened 'upstairs' and I am scribbling like crazy because V's report ties in with something that happened the day before.

It was in the afternoon, in the first week of my fieldwork with V, a stay that ended up lasting close to three months. V had suggested that I use a table in the main editorial area near the water dispenser: a strategically good spot for me, she said. From here I could see everyone who passed through the most central room in the building and, more importantly, everyone going in and out of the door to V's office which was right next to me. If the conversation was confidential, the door would be closed, and she would not invite me to join the meeting. However, the door remained open most of the time and when it was closed, I was often invited to join V along with whoever was on the other side of it. On the few occasions where I had to wait outside, she took care to bring me (and my notebook) to lunch at her table, usually along with her head editor, to hear the summary if it was shareable. When I was not sitting at my own table or the oval table in V's office, I would follow her around the building as she visited employees in their offices and spoke to them about editorials and upcoming stories.

I was at my desk that late afternoon, when V came by me on her way home. It had been a busy day. She had been writing up her weekly editorial and there had been numerous back-and-forth interactions about the front page layout and also a few technical hiccups, before the paper finally went to print as it did every Thursday. This meant V had spent most of the day at her desk and had left me at mine, from where I watched the coming and going between offices. But now that the paper had gone to press, everything had suddenly gone very quiet, the building almost empty. V was on her way home – a little later than usual. She arrived at my desk carrying her handbag, a coat and a piece of paper. After asking about my day and telling me a bit about her own, she handed me the paper: an A3 printed organizational diagram. 'This may help you get a sense of what kind of place this is', she said to me. The *Paper* is part of a larger Danish media company whose history goes back to 1749. Today it is owned by an even larger media giant with headquarters in western Europe. The diagram V handed me showed the organization of the *Paper*, a subsidiary where V is employed as the CEO and Editor-in-Chief. Her name was written at the top of the page on the same level as the names of two middle managers, her head editor and her CFO. From that managerial trinity the diagram proliferated into several arrows pointing to administrative functions, newspaper sections and names of editors and journalists – or 'writers' (*skribenter*) as V likes to call them. As I am soon to realize, not all journalists at this paper are trained as journalists. Quite a few of them are university trained academics, most at MA level but a few of them also at PhD level. Using the term 'writers' seems to make room for more diversity, which is reflected in the quality of the work but also signals that the *Paper* is more than one notch up from ordinary journalism (Reseke 2017a).

The first thing I noticed about the diagram in my hand was that this was not your usual corporate graphic design with square boxes and neatly arrayed chains of command. This one was drawn by hand using two different kinds of ball pens, each arrow and name underlined or dotted with different colours. The result was a sketchy, messy, multi-coloured drawing, looking like V had just sat down and produced it on the spot. Some names were crossed out, new ones added on top or squeezed in from the side. My assumption that afternoon was that this was an original handmade draft that V would soon give to a graphic designer who would then convert it into a real organizational diagram, the kind you would find on a corporation's official website or the kind that top managers use in their PowerPoint presentations when presenting their organization to the outside world. But this was no draft. As I am soon to realize, V is not that kind of manager.

V told me that she made this drawing when the European media giant had just bought up the entire media group that V works for, including all its subsidiaries and thereby also the *Paper*. The top executives flew in – suit and tie – to meet the Danish management team. V received the big boss in her office full of books and gave him this sketchy, colourful, handmade diagram as her best shot at communicating to him in one shot what kind of company the *Paper* was, and how it was different from the others they had visited. The broad smile she gave me while recounting this story told me my own was not inappropriate. 'Yes', she said, still smiling, 'I bet he will not forget that diagram anytime soon'. I couldn't help thinking that the impression she claims to have made on the executives that day was reflected in my own internal giggle that afternoon. The diagram itself, the story she tells about it and the way she handed it to me introduced me not just to the paper, or her understanding of it, but also to the way in which she presents herself as a particular kind of manager. One who does not think in square boxes and straight lines, one who is of another world than that of standardized corporate formats.

For example, V is not the kind of manager who would send out PowerPoint slides in preparation for a meeting. That is what other corporate managers do. I have never seen V use PowerPoints for written communication. V like prose text, not bullet points. V writes books, lectures, editorials, long, analytic newspaper articles and she has invented a whole genre of her own around food and cooking. She does not write PowerPoints. And emails with meeting invitations are not her style either. In fact, V does what she can to avoid meetings altogether. In a portrait interview series with Danish top managers broadcast on national television in 2007, V tells the interviewing journalist:

> Most managers are subjected to a huge bureaucracy that requires that you have meetings about it. And meetings take a horrible amount of time because they need to have a beginning, a middle and an end, much like a story you tell. And most of the things that happen in the beginning and the end, you can spare yourself from by simply going over to talk to people. . . . I conduct as few meetings as I possibly can because it's easier for me to talk to people. (Ahlefelt 2007)

If you are working at the *Paper*, you will know that V wants to see you when you see her knocking on the open door to your office with an easy 'hi', asking if you have time for a quick chat. If you agree, she will pay you a brief visit, converse with you and leave again shortly thereafter without writing anything down. If she does write to call you in for a meeting, you will receive an email demonstrating her full command of the Danish language. A PowerPoint presentation at the bottom of such an email would be like an uninvited guest who got the dress code wrong. 'Power Points are about the most forgettable thing in the world!', she says to me.

V cannot afford to be 'forgettable' when representing the *Paper* to the outside world. When reflecting on her story of this organizational diagram, V says her main concern was that the Danish media group that employs her made up only 4% of the international media giant that bought them. She tells me she made a conscious choice to use this hand drawn organizational diagram in order to make the *Paper* stand out.

V was recruited to do just this, stand out, do things differently. As the editor-in-chief she embodies a living brand for her organization. I'm not sure what came first, V's anthropologically informed prose and personality or the paper's reputation for in-depth, analytical and star quality journalism. With her background in anthropology and her past career as a university researcher, her editorials are always densely contextualized with historical facts and cultural analysis. This distinctly academic backdrop to her political and opinionated commentary is one signature feature of her as an editor-in-chief. Another is her award-winning use of the Danish language which makes room for an aesthetics of form quite unlike that of other Danish newspaper editorials. The *Paper*'s aesthetics and overall tone are themselves much in line with her own; the two seem to have become intertwined during her many years there, to the point where I cannot really tell them apart.

When it comes to design and layout, V and her main editor make sure that none of the graphic designers employed there get too creative and stray from the agreed design manual: a classic layout that will not distract the readers' experience with flashy colours or misplaced advertisement.

The *Paper*, as managed under V, has no standardized journalistic language as is the custom in Danish printed media. Writers keep their own unique style of prose and have their own group of faithful readers whose loyalty would be betrayed if the *Paper* suddenly decided to streamline their staff. In contrast to most printed media in Denmark, the *Paper* has never focused on breaking news but on 'well-written knowledge', as the slogan goes. This refers to the elite selection of thoroughly crafted and in-depth analytical articles covering developments in politics, science, humanities, art and cultural life. Lastly, the *Paper* has no digital platform under V's management.

The latter decision was not uncontroversial. V tells me that her strategy was questioned when she took the decision of not following suit when the rest of Danish printed media went digital. 'We simply couldn't see where the money was', was V's response to questions about this decision, as well as the one she made about not following the trend of giving out newspapers for free and counting on advertisement rather than journalistic content as the main source of income (Reseke 2017a, 2017b). She was also quick to point out that the strategy of not going with the digital flow is part of the reason why the *Paper* has been successful in creating a more profitable niche for itself. Much to the surprise of most media analysts, the strategy seems to be paying off (Reseke 2017a, 2017b). At the time of my fieldwork, the *Paper* was reaping the benefits of being the only newspaper in Denmark that insisted on sticking exclusively to print. When I came into the field, sales had been going up for a few years while most other Danish printed media were going down in flames (Reseke 2017a). There was clearly a growing niche market for old-school, slow-cooked, high-quality analytic journalism in print.

On that afternoon when V handed me the diagram, I felt the undeniable effect of her charisma but couldn't tell if it was deliberate or whether it had just become second nature to her. It was only the first week of our relationship and I was already starting to want a job there, something I would have sworn would never happen only a week before. I did not identify with the *Paper*'s liberal and slightly conservative profile and had no desire for a corporate career in the fast lane of Danish journalism. But on that afternoon, a need to become part of something different emerged in me: to be working there, alongside an elite group of intellectuals who refused to buy into the mainstream and yet make a serious impact on the public debate! I also now wanted to be old-school, unique and hand drawn. I wanted to lean back into all the classic academic virtues I wished I possessed. I wanted to write beautiful Danish prose infused by my own personal touch. I wanted to read, buy, wear and eat things that are hand crafted and take time to make – just like this newspaper. Most of all, I also wanted to be a successful academic whose relaxed, confident cashmere-presence silently says: 'Fuck the establishment'.

What is V doing when she distances herself from a mainstream corporate 'other'? If I asked V (who is a big fan of Frederick Barth), she would remind me that group identities are constructed not inside groups but in the encounters between groups. There is more, though. The identity constructed here is not just different, it is attractive in a very particular way. It awakens a desire to become part of it – in elite journalists, in a steadily increasing number of readers and in me. By pointing to what she is not, V carves out a space ripe with projections and dreams that is easy to connect to because it is easy to identify with.

Charismatic Leadership and Identification

We do not have to look far into the field of management and organization studies to find attempts to understand similar dynamics in the relationship between managers and their employees as they unfolded in and then moved away from bureaucratic organizations and towards enterprise and charismatic leadership (Du Gay 1994). The *Paper* is not the first organization in which the public image of the non-bureaucratic leader becomes indistinguishable from the brand of the organization as well as the conduct and self-image of the employee. My seduction by the self-presentation of V as embodying the antithesis to mainstream management does, at first glance, resemble the images by which management literature dispelled the dispassionate, bureaucratic organization and its associated style of management. Management scholar Paul Du Gay reviews key literature in the anti-bureaucratic critique and deduces the moral imperatives implicit in this era of management literature:

> In this reading, inefficiency, waste and inertia are directly related to the fact that bureaucracy does not function as an instrument of self-realization for its members. Instead, its very essence lies in a separation of work and life, reason and emotion, pleasure and duty which is disastrous for the productive health of the nation and the corporation and the moral and emotional character of the individual human subject. (Du Gay 1994: 661)

We could argue that the anti-bureaucratic ideas that flourished in management rhetoric in the early 1980s and went on well into the first decade of the new millennium are echoed in the *Paper*'s invitation to merge work and self-realization within a unique, creative literary expression. We could analyse the careers of superstar journalists that the *Paper* has given birth to through the years as an expression of the call to 'excellence', 'enterprise' and 'entrepreneurial spirit' that we find in the management literature that was published during V's years as an editor-in-chief (Peters and Waterman 1982, Osborne and Gaebler 1992). We could conceive of V as an example of charismatic leadership so characteristic for her generation of managers. As pointed out by Du Gay, the strict separation between public and private, rational and emotional that characterized the ethics of bureaucratic leadership is significantly blurred as the ethics of enterprise enters management literature and casts the role of the manager as a facilitator for the enterprising employee's self-actualization with a moral duty to merge what the bureaucracy separated (Du Gay 1994). The 'charismatic' and 'excellent' leadership figures that were born from the critique against bureaucracy are first and foremost charged with the reconstruction of the employees' conduct and self-image: 'In opposition to the "personally detached and strictly objective expert" characteristic of bureaucratic management the "excellent" manager was represented as a "charismatic" facilitator, encouraging others to take responsibility for themselves and fostering an "enterprising" sense of identification, commitment and involvement between employees and the organization for which they work' (Du Gay 1994: 664).

In the era of charismatic, excellent and transformational leadership, management literature assumes that leadership runs on the rails of identification processes similar to the one I experienced on my first day of fieldwork. V's self-representation does a good job at awakening a conscious – or unconscious – desire to be a little more like her, but not in the sense of mirroring or adopting her language, dress code, opinions or prose: mirroring a visibly detectable role model would be precisely unlike V. The dynamic of charismatic leadership rests on the premise that followers' self-concept, not necessarily their behaviour, mirrors that of the leader, the organization and the mission of that organization: 'For example, according to Shamir et al. (1993), the essence of the charismatic relationship is the presence of strong links between followers' self-concepts and the leader, the group and the mission of the group or organization' (Sinha and Jackson 2006: 235).

In this sense, V seems to embody precisely the kind of management role that is celebrated in the literature on charismatic, entrepreneurial and anti-bureaucratic leadership. She specifically did not give me a list of values that she stands for and wants her employees to commit to, neither did she discuss the content side of working for the *Paper*. She gave me a self-presentation that I could somehow identify with, despite our differences. And she did it in a light-hearted 'anti-establishment' tone that could imbue me with hopes and dreams, such as the dream that academics like me, whose job satisfaction rests on a need for free and creative expression, will be able to fulfil our needs while pursuing a corporate career. This image of the organization was also echoed in the way in which V's employees spoke about their workplace. As one of V's oldest employees told me, the strength of the *Paper* lies precisely in internal diversity and contradictions, not in everybody marching to the same drum. Although the *Paper* has an explicit liberal agenda, there are strong political disagreements between individual writers employed by V. Each of them is hired for their highly personal style of prose – and politics. What they have in common is being unique, different and special: just like V.

V sees management as a task of drawing this very diverse group of employees together to work for a common goal. She compares her job to that of coaching a football team. V sees it as her job to let her employees know what game they are playing, and how, by providing the greatest possible transparency around budgets and decisions as possible, so that employees can understand where the organization is going and why. In order to go where the *Paper* is going, V needs to give full rein to the unique journalistic expressions of each of her writers. So, rather than making her employees fit into a streamlined corporate mould, V seems to offer them an opportunity to make up their own. Her main job, she says, is to make the context of their creative self-expression clear. The identification process offered here is thus not about becoming more alike or aligning with a set of corporate values. It is rather about becoming different – but in similar ways, and thereby being able to identify with the organizational goal of creating a beautiful, well-written and top-quality newspaper.

When giving talks on Danish organizational culture, V is known to lash out against the tendency to disempower employees by managers taking on, what seems to her, a patronizing or overly caring attitude similar to that of some parents:

> Many organizations, especially today . . . are playing house, so to speak. You know. Let's pretend I'm the mother, right? And then you can chose if you want to be the child or the dog – because the dad is sort of over there as the chairman of the board and he is not even going to participate . . . – and then I will tell you that you now have to do this or that. For me! [gives the interviewer a pleading but invasive look while holding her head askew]. Right? And then as expected, I will not become angry but instead terribly hurt if you don't. And then you will in turn respond to me by becoming childish. . . . If you organize yourself as if you are playing house, then the employees cannot be anything other than children. (Ahlefelt 2007)

V is not the bureaucratic manager that tells you what to do. Neither is she the mother-manager who loves to solve your problems. The key, she says, is to address employees as responsible adults by being as transparent as possible about the *Paper*'s economic growth, budgets and problems 'because most people are fully capable of understanding these matters', she says. It is important to her that her employees know where decisions are coming from, and what context they arise in. She is highly critical of places she has been employed in previously where administrative functions seemed to her to grow out of proportion and organizational decisions 'fall in through the doors and walls', meaning that nobody knew where decisions were coming from and nobody would take responsibility for seeing them through.

We can thus detect a clear anti-bureaucratic tone in the way in which V presents herself as a manager, in that she is critical of heavy-handed administration, formalized meetings and decision processes that take place behind closed doors with no transparency and no opportunity for the individual employee to identify with management goals and objectives. This seems to align with the historical period of enterprise management and anti-bureaucracy discourse intrinsic to the context in which she worked. But as we are about to find out, V also presents herself as a manager who is in direct moral opposition to the boundary-blurring of the anti-bureaucratic doctrine. But really, this is neither paradoxical, nor surprising, because of course, V is not that kind of manager either.

Moral Boundaries: Anti-anti Bureaucracy

While we might expect well-read top managers like V to have a mainstream management bible or two lying around in their office, it is perhaps not surprising that V probably never did. When asked if, during her eighteen years in a leadership position, she ever took a course in management, V answers with a relaxed smile: 'I can't say that I did, no', and then, after a short pause, 'but I did teach in a few of them'. During my fieldwork with V, she repeatedly distances herself from mainstream management discourse either by making a virtue out of blatantly ignoring it or by explicitly positioning herself as a rational alternative to it. As much as she may sound like an echo of the anti-bureaucracy movement in management literature, she does not at all identify with that kind of management. Digging deeper into her views and her daily practice, I feel she appears at least as often like an anti-anti-bureaucrat. Having built her career in an era when the anti-bureaucracy movement went mainstream in Denmark, V seems to have ensured critical distance between herself and the management fads that were born from it.

As we will see in the following, V makes a moral point out of protecting the very divisions that the anti-bureaucratic movement set out to erode. She does not share the celebration of blurring boundaries between reason and emotion, public and private, manager and employee so intrinsic to anti-bureaucracy and its ethics of enterprise.

An example is her repeated dismissal of Danish mainstream management fads that advocated breaking down organizational hierarchies. V sees little or no enterprise-value in enhancing competition between employees. Her position is firmly critical when it comes to replacing traditional organizational hierarchies with a 'free market' approach where employees flexibly reorganize themselves in open office spaces depending on task and interest rather than on their formal job position or area of expertise. In the Danish mainstream management literature, this trend has been modelled on the concept of the 'spaghetti organization', a term coined by Danish top manager and author Lars Kolind who famously turned around a Danish hearing aid company in the late 1980s and quickly became an important player in spreading the anti-bureaucracy ethos in Denmark (Kolind 2006). The hype surrounding radical experiments in fluid organizations with little or no formal hierarchies left its physical mark in the architecture of many corporate offices in Denmark in the same period when V made her career as a manager. V was not impressed though. She tells me that she went upstairs to deliver an anthropologically informed protest speech in her manager's office, in response to the media group's decision to rearrange their employees in open offices with 'free seating'. V finds this idea to be a complete disaster as it undermines the employee's sense of safety, predictability and well-being and consequently slows down productivity. In addition, she says, free seating is a direct invitation to territorial harassment and turf wars between employees. According to V, any manager with even the slightest sense of how human groups work would prevent such 'heretic barbarianism' by sticking to the more traditional managerial style of leaving hierarchical separations intact and letting management assign desks to each employee. Her anthropological research has convinced her that when centralized state power retreats, violence ensues. This conviction is mirrored in her managerial insistence on maintaining formal boundaries that separates management and employees. V sees it as her moral responsibility to limit territorial conflicts between employees by staying 'in office' – so to speak. Her organizational diagram, although multicoloured and messy, is still pyramid shaped.

V thus sems to differentiate herself from the anti-bureaucracy trend in mainstream Danish management discourse by making an occasional and somewhat paradoxical return to old-school organizational hierarchy and traditional bureaucratic values. She is not the first Danish manager to make this move. Sørensen and Willadsen (2018) have shown how a highly controversial form of 'anti-establishment' management within the Danish creative industries tends to transgress professional, psychological and sexual boundaries to push creative breakthroughs while opportunistically drawing on occasional returns to 'old-school' managerial rights to hire and fire in a way that reinserts the organizational hierarchy and grants the manager the privileges of the sovereign.

By contrast, V seems to deploy her return to old-school bureaucratic values to reinforce those very same moral boundaries that the anti-establishment leadership makes a virtue out of transgressing. Her use of normative expressions like 'heretic barbarianism' when referring to trends such as free seating testifies to the moral aspect of her adherence to a more classical view on keeping hierarchies intact and protecting the boundaries between manager and employee. Quite contrary to the anti-establishment management described by Sørensen and Willadsen, V repeatedly points out the danger of transgressing the boundaries of the organizational hierarchy by becoming friends with her employees: 'Our relationship is professional. You cannot have an equal relationship to people you can fire. That's cheating. And its grossly inappropriate to force the employee to pretend that we are equal. . . . Because they will have to lie on an everyday basis. They will have to pretend that they don't know that I can fire them' (Ahlefelt 2007).

In contrast to the moral value that anti-bureaucracy management literature has for decades attributed to the intermingling of personal self-actualization and professional career development, V here seems to express quite the opposite view. She is not the kind of manager who uses words like 'passion', 'commitment' or 'love' when talking about management. In the soccer game that V is playing, that would simply be 'cheating'. V will point out how the public/private boundary can be detected in every modern society and tampering with it for strategic purposes seems to be not just inefficient, but also not fair play.

V's ability to simultaneously dismantle and resurrect the bureaucratic ethos in her management practice seems to allow for a self-presentation that sets her apart from other managers in several ways:

V is not the traditional bureaucratic manager, neither is she the anti-bureaucratic manager and she is definitely not the boundary blurring anti-establishment manager either. But what kind of manager is she then? As we are about to learn, V identifies more as an anthropologist than as any kind of manager.

The Anthropological Gaze

Already in my first interview with V, she told me that fieldwork and social analysis is an almost compulsive mode of functioning for her, a reading skill or view from above that is instilled in her by virtue of her training in anthropology. In my first interview with her she explains:

> Becoming an anthropologist is like learning to read. Once you have learned to read you can't help reading . . . you sit in the bathroom of complete strangers reading what it says on their shampoo bottles, despite the fact that you have the exact same ones at home. Because the letters simply jump into your head as meaning! And to become an anthropologist is a little bit like that. People's activities simply jump into your head as meaning, as patterns, as. . . you see? It's not a matter of 'now I'm going to do fieldwork'. I'm simply doing fieldwork all the time. (Interview 2016)

According to V, anthropology is what allows her to 'read' her employees with greater precision than other kinds of managers do, such as those who jump in with both feet when the latest business fad detects a new mode of reorganization. Anthropologists know about human groups and how they work, she says, and her particular training make her especially attentive to power dynamics. For example, V tells me she can tell if an employee is not thriving because they are seated with the wrong colleagues, and she sees it as her job as manager to do what she can to organize writers in ways that allow each of them to 'have a good time at work' and thereby be productive. Although it could be argued that the ability to read patterns and understand the motives and drives of her employees is a skill V shares with many other kinds of successful top managers, V very insistently attributes her ability to 'read' to her anthropological training. 'I don't get why there are not more managers out there that get a degree in anthropology on the side', she says (Ahlefelt 2007). V claims that a degree in anthropology also makes you acutely aware of perspectives on situations that are radically different from your own and hence helps to read and understand the employees in their own context rather than just seeing things from your own point of view (ibid.). Anthropology seems to be

at the root of her tendency to be curious about management and media trends as ethnographic phenomena rather than as prescriptions for
how to manage the *Paper*. In one of the few recent interviews with her,
she is asked to give her anthropological analysis of the media world.
She says:

> [In my close to twenty years as a manager] I have seen several cases of
> self-destructive mass psychosis . . . So I can conclude that going against the
> stream is not that common. There is a tendency for everyone to run over
> into one side of the boat, so that it rocks dangerously to one side – instead
> of having somebody that stays on the opposite railing so you can keep bal-
> ance. And remembers what it's all about. (V cited in Reseke 2017a)

V seem to attribute her own ability to 'remember what it's all about'
to her training in anthropology in a way that seem to involve a moral
obligation to 'rock the boat' in her superior's office if it takes the *Paper* back on a more responsible course. So, when V felt morally compelled to deliver her critique of free seating, this calling is not only
that of a manager concerned for productivity. To V, it is also the calling
of an anthropologist with a self-perceived overview which is slightly
detached from the logic of the media world. As an anthropologist, it
seems V feels she is functioning as a spokesperson for her employees
and the way in which they experience everyday organizational life.
Their well-being at work is what allows her to make a good newspaper, she says. V seems to see it as her job to protect her employees
and the *Paper* from morally questionable interventions coming from
management fads or abstract ideas crafted in management bibles or an
excel sheet somewhere, with no eye for the context and no sensitivity
to the social complexity of human everyday practice.

Consequently, V does not spend her time taking courses or reading
books about management. She rather discusses their content with the
observational interest of an ethnographer researching the documents
and concepts produced in a culture she is writing about. She will use
the lingo at times, but always with a critical or self-reflexive distance.

For example, V is observant of how charisma has become part of
her own conduct as a manager, and will let me know that she is actually quite wary of 'charismatic leadership'. She sees charismatic seduction as a dangerous drug and not necessarily a management tool one
should rely on. And the danger, V reminds me in an email correspondence, lies in getting high on the drug of charismatic seduction and
thereby becoming blind to the 'self-seduction' it inevitably entails for
the leader. V writes:

We are talking about strong emotions which can in effect overpower the one who exercises power, if that makes any sense. In a way where the process itself takes control. . . . It is my conviction that as a leader, you have to be very watchful towards this form of enthusiasm (*begejstring*), this means you need to keep cool – or at least cool off in between – by consulting reason. For example, by reminding oneself that this is only a game (*bare noget vi leger*). That can be done, if you are aware that the game has a limited purpose. (Email correspondence, June 2017)

So, although V recognizes that her management style is distinctly charismatic and involves an element of seduction, her sense of an underlying moral fault line in leadership prevents her from jumping on the anti-bureaucratic bandwagon of pure charismatic leadership. To her, the kind of leader-followership she needs to evoke if she is to be a responsible editor-in-chief and CEO depends on her being faithful to the boundaries and limits that are set by the goals of the organization. And, quite in line with the bureaucratic ethos, she makes a clear separation between reason and emotion. Contrary to enterprise management literature, where the separation between reason and emotion is essentially viewed as unethical in that it fails as a 'means for the realization of a moral personality' (Du Gay 1994: 661), V seems to present herself as a manager for whom this exact separation is part of her internal moral compass.

The same goes for the way in which she speaks about the public/private boundary. When asked what she has done over the years to 'keep cool' or 'consult reason', she will tell me she nurtures private relationships outside of work with people who are 'completely unimpressed' and have zero stakes in her role as a leader. She will also refer, time and again, to her firm resolve to keep a clear separation between her personal and her professional self: 'I AM not the editor in chief, it's just something I DO. A game we are playing. I have often repeated to myself and others that IN REALITY I am an anthropologist' (email correspondence, 2016). As an anthropologist, V seems to be watching things from somewhere outside the social order, from a place where things like full and passionate charismatic engagement seems more like a social script or a game, one that she attempts to assess the moral value and effectiveness of by way of her anthropologically informed analytical distance.

One of the writers let me know that V was criticized, especially in the beginning of her career, for not doing what most of her (male) colleagues in other newspapers have done: turn herself into a more visible public figure that merges her personality with that of the organization in order to represent the *Paper* more completely and give it more visibility in the public eye. V has been less willing to go as far into that endeavour as required by the ethics of charismatic leadership. When asked about why she has not been more visible in the media debate, she says that to her, it has always been more about the *Paper* and that she has no need to be a celebrity (Reseke 2017a). V says she does what she can to keep things separate, meaning she is wary of slipping into personally identifying with her leadership role and title.

Another example is V's policy around her own working hours. V is known to be one of the only top managers in Denmark who insists on coming in after ten almost every day and prefers to leave around four – except, of course, if it's an emergency. Some days she even leaves at three.[3] The rest of the corporate world, she claims, waste their time in long meetings. There seems be a moral aspect to V's insistence on maintaining a clear boundary between public and private self.

The classical work ethic of not wasting time is worth noticing here, but more so is that of maintaining a boundary between home and work. V has publicly stated that as a manager she is very much aware of how her own behaviour sets the standards for her employees and how especially 'the boys' have a tendency to get competitive around sitting in their office into the late hours. To her, it seems not just unethical but also inefficient when a manager stresses their employees and pressures them by mirroring their own over-performance (Ahlefelt 2007). So, V is often the first to leave the office rather than the last, and she will make a ritual out of her public goodbye as she walks through the secretariat carrying her bicycle helmet, coat and bag. On the few days I saw her working late, her exit included comments to one or two writers still sitting in their offices like 'What are you still doing here?' V is known for claiming that overworking is bad for productivity. Employees who continuously neglect their families get stressed or divorced, she says, and then they need to spend years in crisis mode where they are unable to do any real work which, from a managerial point of view, makes no sense (Ahlefelt 2007). V ascribes this ability to 'read' the long-term consequences of a competitive, boundaryless working environment to her anthropological sensitivity to the social and cultural scripts that guide human interactions. Consequently, she sees it as her duty to set an example by arriving late and leaving early.

I can tell, though, that she also works from home, even if she pretends not to and hardly ever talks about it, for example by her conversations with employees she talks to during the day: 'I'm so sorry I sent you that email in the middle of the night, it was because I just saw the news there but really, that was not cool (*ikke god stil*)'. The public display of her own sense of having crossed a moral boundary is worth noting.

If we analyse V's critique of 'mother-management' not for its content but for its function as a form of self-representation, it does almost the opposite of the anti-bureaucracy discourse: it portrays V as a manager who upholds the very boundaries that enterprise management and its charismatically driven leadership erode. It allows V to retain a sense of moral integrity when presenting herself as a responsible and morally accountable manager who plays fair by refraining from using guilt, shame and emotional blackmail to make her employees conform to the organization's goal. V's insistence on being transparent when it comes to finances and organizational changes distances her from the bureaucratic manager who works in closed loops that fail to involve employees. But at the same time, her disassociation with the kind of manager who is 'playing house' distances her from the opposite: unchecked, charisma-driven identification processes between manager and employee resulting in dodgy boundary blurring. Thus, it seems that the corporate, bureaucratically minded, mainstream other is not the only kind of manager that V is not. Clearly, she is also not the stereotypical echo of enterprise management either. Nor is she the head of a family business or a radically experimental anti-establishment manager. This cascade of negative definitions allows V to, almost in the same breath, denounce bureaucracy and insist on maintaining exactly what the anti-bureaucracy literature attempts to dismantle – the boundary between reason and emotion, public and private.

By not identifying as a manager, but as, 'really', an anthropologist, V has simply taken on the role of a manager for the time being and her moral obligation is to play that role responsibly as long as the game is on.

She thus willingly immerses herself in the charisma-driven leader-follower identification game, but at the same time she needs to keep cool by retaining a dispassionate observer status detached from that same game. Identification processes are thus at play in V's work, but it seems they are slightly different from those we see described in the literature on charismatic leadership. The moral problem here seems to be slipping into over-identifying with her employees or with her role as a manager and thereby risking conflict in response to the presence of the hierarchical difference that could easily get glossed over in this identification process. In V's understanding this could hinder employees in staying comfortable and productive while also rendering V less efficient as a manager.

Let's go back to our lunch at the oval table to have another look at how V handles the paradox of identification across the boundaries of hierarchical differences between herself and her employees, when needing writers to follow her lead.

Identification: Being 'Newspaper People'

This is the point where I decide to have another chocolate anyway. V is showing her colleagues a printed PowerPoint slide that was sent out by her managers upstairs, prior to this morning's meeting: six bullet points, black print, white background, the logo and name of the media company printed in a discrete blue tone at the bottom – classic corporate design.

V begins her summary of the meeting upstairs by stating that she is not the only person who looks like the living dead when dragged into the office for a meeting at the crack of dawn (*daggrysmøde*). One of the other editors-in-chief had looked at least as pale and grey as she did herself this morning, she says. V turns away from her colleagues and over to me to explain that 'in the newspaper world we work with cultural life, which means we do not necessarily go home when we leave the office'. Early morning meetings may be perfectly fine in other production companies, such as the ones that several members of the management upstairs came from, but not for 'newspaper people'. So, V was asked, or rather told to break her routine schedule and show up at 8 am. The silent exclamation mark between her eyebrows clearly indicates that this was not her cup of tea. As we already know, V is not that kind of manager: not the kind you find in the office at 8 in the morning or 7 in the evening, not the kind that always looks super busy. The only way you can tell that V is really busy, such as on the day where the *Paper* goes into print, is that she goes quieter, eats her lunch alone and stands writing in front of her computer most of the day. But there is no change of pace when she moves, no skipping lunch, no telling others how busy she is and absolutely no early mornings in the office.

As my fieldwork progresses it is made clear to me what it means to be 'newspaper people'. It seems related to an identity marker that was often used at the *Paper*: that of being 'editorial in the head' (*redaktionel oven i hovedet*). Most of V's employees are working as writers and, much like her, they see themselves as a whole different species from those who are 'commercial in the head' – often meaning those working in the group sales department or in the group administration or who are group executives. I learn from V and several of her editors that most media companies in Denmark will be characterized by strong divisions, if not opposition, between the 'editorial' and the 'commercial' part of the organization. 'Editorials' are interested in the content side of making newspapers, view themselves as 'creatives' and often feel they are in direct opposition to the commercials, who seem to them to be only interested in profit. The commercial part of the media world, in turn, simply 'don't get' the editorials. In my fieldwork, I was introduced by V to one of the top managers from the group administration who was on his way out from a short visit to her office. She explained to him that I was studying leadership at the *Paper*. He jokingly finished her sentence with 'Oh, you mean how to lead people who do not want to be led?' When I asked him to elaborate on this, he went on to explain that leadership in the media world does not work like in other places where he worked. He told me that in the media group, people will question your leadership much more than he was used to when he first arrived, and there seems to be no clear acceptance of the formal hierarchies and chains of command.[4] 'It's about earning respect by keeping your word and being consistent', he tells me. Apparently, newspaper people don't do as you tell them, just because you happen to be able to fire them.

Indeed, Danish journalism has a long tradition of conflict between journalists and their managers and in other Danish media companies the tone between them can be less than friendly and the work more characterized by high performance and precarity. When asking V about this divide, she will testify to its clear presence throughout the world of Danish media, but adds that 'in this house, we have more of a collaboration and less conflict'. She will point out, though, that history shows this was not always the case. In fact, the whole media group of which the *Paper* is a subsidiary was brought to its knees by striking journalists in 1980–1981.[5] According to V, it only rose again from bankruptcy because private capital from major Danish companies resurrected it.

The division would also crop up in the everyday negotiations between the *Paper* and the group concerning administrative decisions affecting their subsidiaries. The use and cost of phone sales, the choice of advertisement agent or the agreed ratio of advertisements to articles in any given publication, and of course the editorial budgets, became sites of minor turf wars during my fieldwork where the division between 'newspaper people' and 'commercials' became clearer.

And here, in our lunch meeting at the oval table, V is clearly showing her two colleagues (and me) on which side of this chasm she stands. V is not 'commercial in the head'. At work, she identifies as a newspaper person along with her employees. To begin with, I assumed that 'editorials' or 'newspaper people' would have to be either writers or editors. But V explains to me that this division is not just a matter of job function but a matter of interest and priority. V's CFO is in charge of finances and accounting but sounds as 'editorial in the head' as her editors do, when discussing business and strategy. V sums up the division to me like this: '*We* make money so that we can make newspapers, *they* make newspapers so that they can make money'(*Vi tjener penge for at lave avis, de laver avis for at tjene penge*).

V reiterates the above slogan several times during my fieldwork, such as in one of the editorial meetings on one Friday morning in the late autumn, midway through my fieldwork. V is sitting at the end of the oval table overlooking the crowded room, ready to say a few words on the current state of the *Paper* before the discussion of next week's writing projects begin. As in most weeks, only the first people to arrive can fit on the transparent chairs around her table, while the rest squeeze in on chairs brought from outside or stand leaning against the windowsill. Those who arrive late have to stay in the doorway, for lack of space. This week is a little different. The usual serving of coffee and croissants is accompanied by a few bottles of champagne. V is about to make a toast to celebrate the latest reader and sales statistics which came in the day before. This year has been one of the best in the recent history of the *Paper*, but due to a very successful sales strategy, last month's total topped all expectations. The paper is now only 2,000 readers short of one of the leading national newspapers, and as I understand it, that's a first.

'Congratulations, ladies and gentlemen, with the success!' V begins, while champagne bottles are passed around the office. 'Our number of readers have been going up and up this year, and when K [the CFO] comes back from a meeting with the management upstairs, I think we should all give him a big hand for devising an extremely efficient sales strategy. But', she continues, 'it's not just K's work but also the high quality of all of your work that makes such a big difference. Our subscribers are really pleased with their newspaper right now, thanks to your efforts'. She then goes on to explain that their total budget has grown with their success and that the numbers K is now juggling are now quite 'dizzying'. V makes a toast to her writers for a job well done and after the cheer settles, she ends with a little contextualization:

> As you know, we don't make newspapers to make money,[6] but the more money we make, the more freedom we have to make the kind of newspaper we want to make. So, it's good that we are in fact making money

and thereby also making the owners happy. Because the moment we don't, somebody will show up here and take control of how we do it. (Editorial meeting, autumn 2016)

Her last remark in particular tells us something about the points of identification where V and her employees can meet and merge as fellow editorials. In her toast, V not only identifies with being an editorial, she simultaneously disidentifies with those higher up in the organization whose main objective is to make money for the owners, and for whom the *Paper* is more like a means to an end than a goal in itself (cf. scales of objectification, Chapter 1). By pointing to the common goal ('making the newspaper we want to make'), she implicitly invites everyone in the room to identify with her as members of a particular species. In addition, the fact that V feels the need to explain why it is a good thing that the *Paper* is making money speaks volumes about the moral divisions that underpin her own sense of integrity when setting a common goal for herself and her employees. Apparently, V is not the kind of manager for whom the accumulation of profit alone will ever become a legitimate goal for the organization.

According to V, however, this is what it takes to get Danish journalists, who are famous for biting the hand that feeds them (as well as biting each other), to unite in their efforts in working towards a common goal. 'The main problem in this kind of leadership', she says to me, 'is how to lead people in a social order where the leader and the follower are so incredibly alike'. When I discuss leadership with V during fieldwork, she stresses that although she does have the formal mandate to hire and fire as she sees fit, her leadership depends more on voluntary followership by a group of people who are writers and academics much like herself and who have little or no respect for formal hierarchies. Most of her writers are so high up on the media career ladder, that many of them could pick pretty much any other newspaper to write for. They could also choose to digress from her game of 'making money so we can make newspapers' and serve their own interests such as going away for months to write award-winning books, hosting their own TV show or beginning a career in politics. And the fact that some of the writers at the *Paper* are receiving the highest salaries in the world of Danish journalism is no guarantee that they stay in V's 'soccer team', let alone accept her role as their 'coach'. When asked about this, V will invoke Barth's ethnography of political leadership among the Swat Pathans to explain to me how her leadership depends more on the power of persuasion than on the formal power of the sovereign king. 'People have to be enticed, not forced' (*Folk skal lokkes ikke tvinges*), she is known to say, when asked for her opinion on leadership (Ahlefelt 2007).

But how? Leader-follower identification is relatively easy to establish while celebrating a joint victory in champagne. But the almost 'perfect transaction' (Sinha and Jackson 2006) that seems to be taking place here is challenged by the underlying conflicts of interest that are intrinsic to organizational hierarchies and therefore part of the leader-follower relationship. In the precarious, high performance world of Danish media the fact that you had champagne for breakfast does not mean the rest of the day will turn out well.

Disidentification: Not Being Commercial

On the very same morning as V and her writers are celebrating the new statistics, her CFO, K, is upstairs in a meeting with V's management; they were hardly in the mood to celebrate. When he comes back downstairs, he stays in the doorway and even though he smiles at the big applause that meets him from the crowd inside V's office, he does not come in but leaves quietly after a few minutes without saying very much. At lunch he is back at the oval table with V and I learn that he has received a rather authoritarian reprimand upstairs concerning the *Paper*'s budget for the previous month and the consequence it may have for the remaining year. According to the upstairs management, the editorial costs had grown to inappropriate proportions over the past few months, and due to last month's excess, the *Paper* is in danger of failing to meet their set annual goal of bringing in a profit matching 20% of their total revenue.

This is probably the only time I have seen V visibly upset. She seems to take it to heart that the meeting upstairs turned out to be a rather dramatic event and keeps repeating that she is impressed with K's smile and composure, because she for one is quite concerned. The prospect that she may be ordered to fire writers in order to get the budget back in line seems very disturbing to her. And the timing is terrible too. It was only a few days ago that one of V's writers left her editorial post and V now has to find money in the budget to pay another writer to do her job. Meanwhile, two younger women are away on paid maternity leave, which accounts for a substantial part of the increased costs. Lastly, none of the writers has taken a self-paid leave over the summer months where they normally go off and work on their own projects and this had actually been part of the budget calculations. The cost of having so many people on the payroll is significantly higher than expected, not just in salaries but also in the production costs, travel expenses and the like. Normally, things balance out at the end of the year, but the management upstairs were very particular about last month's overspending and wanted it fixed 'asap'. V will need to find this money fast if she is to keep all her current staff. At the table, V, K and her main editor discuss different scenarios, and one solution appears later in the form of an email sent out by V, addressed to all employees at the *Paper*. V writes:

> Dear all
> If there is anyone among you who are planning a leave, the last two months of this year would be a very welcome suggestion.
> We always budget with one or two people being away, but nobody went either in the summer and or through the autumn, and now we are getting reprimanded because we are overspending on the editorial budget.
> Even tiny snippets of leave would be helpful. . .
> Have a nice weekend.
> V

We can read the 'we' in this email as ambiguously referring both to 'we the management team' or to 'we the editorials' or simply as 'we the *Paper*'. The last two options are what makes it possible for V to send out this request, which in most media companies would be completely untenable. The sentence 'we are being reprimanded' refers implicitly to the management upstairs and encourages the 'we' addressed in the email to collectively disidentify with the top management.

It seems that V presents herself as being one with the organization when she self-identifies as a 'newspaper person'. At the same time, she dissociates from the organization by showing that it is not her but the 'commercials' upstairs who are behind the proposed change in the contractual relationship between V and her employees.

Surely, in the age of the flexible organization, management is expected to willingly fire people when things get rough and rehire when times are better. By now, however, it will come as no surprise that V is not that kind of manager.

The distance V puts between herself and the managers upstairs tells us something about the moral work that underpins V's self-presentation as a manager. Here, it seems we could pursue the line of inquiry followed in symbolic interactionist perspectives on the leader-follower identification (Sinha and Jackson 2006; Sørensen and Willadsen 2018). In this perspective, the identification process will always carry 'the underlying contradiction that the leader and follower are joined, yet separate, from one another' (Sinha and Jackson 2006). Whereas leader-follower identification allows for a form of 'heroic management' in which management see themselves engaged in non-exploitative transactions (ibid.), the separation inherent to the division of labour between leader and follower is bound to create 'worker alienation' and hence conflict with the story of heroic – and therefore morally justified – leadership (Sørensen and Willadsen 2018). As pointed out by V herself, no matter how alike she and her employees seem to be, no matter how mutually committed they are to make the kind of newspaper they believe in, she still has the formal power to fire them. In a symbolic interactionist perspective, the paradox of leadership lies in the fact that 'one must navigate distance and identification at the same time, achieve identification between leader and follower yet maintain the distance that serves to uphold the superiority intrinsic to being a leader' (Sørensen and Willadsen 2018: 1062–63).

Keeping the balance between identification and distance in order to maintain the relationship and not create conflict seems to be the issue here. Let's see how V resolves this dilemma.

The Power of Double Disidentification

After the weekend, V is back in her office and once again, the managerial trinity meets for lunch at her table. When asked how the weekend went after Friday afternoon's budget cliffhanger, V conveys that she had been terribly worried at first, but then she made a decision that cleared it all up for her. V simply came to the conclusion that if the management upstairs are actually serious about Friday's dramatic response to last month's budget, this might actually be a perfect opportunity for V to 'get rid of the job'. She says she made up her mind that there was no way she was going to go along with firing people on account of one bad budget month taken out of their best year ever. And that given the fact that none of the other newspapers in the media group are expected to come anywhere near the 20% mark required of the *Paper*, she felt no obligation to fulfil this demand if it required her to fire anyone. 'They can fire me instead', V says with a big smile, and claims to have slept fantastically after this decision was made. V will now do her best to balance the budget without firing anyone, and if that's not enough, she will pack her things and depart, effective immediately, leaving it to her management upstairs to produce next week's paper on their own.

V has already sent out another email before lunch, announcing that all travel plans that are not agreed directly with her in person are cancelled for now, that editors are to limit their purchase of single articles from freelancers and that they will have to make do with whatever the in-house people on contract can produce. And that 'since all tenured staff is in the house right now that should be possible'. The email continues: 'I am asking you to be as careful as possible and to save where you can. Unfortunately, this is really a serious situation'. At the end of the email followed a small P.S. where V mentions the names of three employees who have already volunteered to go on self-paid leave and lets everyone know how much this is appreciated, but also that 'actually, we still need more'.

V sighs and looks directly at me across the table with a pale smile. 'Yes', she says, 'It's like peeing one's pants to keep warm, but that at least it will make the budget look better'. The next morning, I run into V, looking sharper than usual in a grey, knitted dress and a minimalist silver necklace. As it is the custom among women at the *Paper* to compliment or ask each other about clothes, I remark that I like her outfit and also ask her if she has been upstairs yet. V confirms that she just came down from a meeting with the entire management group this morning where her colleagues from the other papers were also participating along with the top management. At lunch she gives K, her main editor and me a full report: 'It does look like the *Paper* at least is out of the woods', she says, hinting that some of the other newspapers were still in trouble. 'Concerning our budget, I think we really need to make an effort for the remaining year. People are spending their own money on this now, so really, we owe it to them'.

Apparently, V's solution this morning was to report back to her manager and everyone else at the table that within the last forty-eight hours she had managed to find five people who were willing to go on unpaid leave and that the budget was now back on track, according to this year's estimations. She continues to explain how the other managers responded to this news: 'I mean, they couldn't even *look* at me!' she says, to us and hides her face in her palm while looking down into the shiny white surface of the table. The three of them break out in spontaneous laughter at this little performance. I don't get the joke, so V and her main editor explain to me that it's annoying for the other managers in the group that V can do things that 'nobody else here is capable of'. As one of V's editors – who has spent an entire career in media – tells me: 'In other newspapers, this is unthinkable, to get people to go on a self-paid leave at such short notice, in order to save the company budget, because they basically treat people like dirt in this business'. V says that being successful in requesting writers to invest their own payment really requires that you 'treat people well'. I take it that this involves being able to 'read them' or 'get them' and that being an anthropologist on permanent fieldwork is of help to V in this respect. V may not like to play house, and you will never hear her refer to the *Paper* as a family where her employees owe it to her as the parent to sacrifice their salaries for her. But, she says, there has to be some kind of community around the newspaper, a sense that 'we are here for something' or that 'this is something we produce together'.

The identification processes necessary to establish such common goals are, as we saw above, always in danger of getting too close (playing house) or too distant (dispassionate bureaucratic management). In both extremes, conflict can arise. According to the analysis of anti-establishment management as described by Sørensen and Willadsen, we would now have to look for ways in which V as a leader identifies a scapegoat whose sacrifice redeems the inherent guilt arising from such a conflict; we could ask what real or symbolic sacrifice needs to be made, in order for V to re-instantiate the order of leadership.

First, V resolves her moral conflict over the weekend by substituting the upstairs management's proposed sacrifice (firing writers) with a more morally defensible sacrifice: V's own job position ('they can fire me instead'). V gets a good night's sleep as soon as she has identified herself as the symbolic sacrifice, which we could interpret as her way of re-establishing her own sense of moral integrity and thereby her sense of exercising power in responsible ways: what has also been termed 'heroic management' (Sinha and Jackson 2006).

However, in the end V does not become the sacrificial victim in this episode of the organizational drama. She keeps her leadership going by resolving the conflict at a lower level in the organization: between herself and the employees. It is rather the five employees who, mirroring the rationale given by V, decide to sacrifice a part of their own salary for the sake of all the other editorials keeping their job – including V. This parallel displacement of the necessary sacrifice that re-establishes the moral order of V's leadership rests on the strong sense of identification between leader and follower. As both V and her employees identify as editorials, the sacrifice that V tells me that she was originally willing to make can be substituted with that of the one her employees are ready to make in their commitment to a common goal.

This completes the process, a symbolic sacrifice made by leader and follower through collective disidentification, with the management upstairs as the scapegoat or common enemy. Now, even though V would not herself conceive of things in the vocabulary we are using here, she is in fact very conscious and aware of the strategic advantage that she gains by disidentifying with a common enemy. Late in the evening after my last day of fieldwork, V and I continue a conversation on email that we had during the day, a conversation about what kind of manager she really is, that continues well into the writing process that followed the fieldwork. V writes: 'There is always a possible aggression, or at least danger, in everything we do together, the employees and I. It is a condition, no figment of anybody's imagination. Drama! And I spend a considerable amount of energy directing this aggression to other places, remoulding it into loyalty for the common project. With common enemies, necessarily'.

V knows her Marx and Freud. She also knows that Danish journalists cannot be counted upon to do her bidding solely on account of her formal title as their manager. Without a series of continuous not-that-kind-of-manager moves V would be standing right in the line of fire of her writers' messy and multicoloured aggression. What her changing disidentifications do here is channel the conflict – and thereby also the sacrifices – away from herself and away from the goal of making newspapers. The 'common enemy' changes frequently during my fieldwork with V, depending on where the danger lies, and hence the direction that aggression could take.

One day she may stress to her employees the division between 'our' writing and 'their' commercial interests, meaning the enemy is upstairs, inhabiting the commercial part of the organization or in an executive office somewhere in western Europe. Another day the enemy 'other' may be a competing newspaper, Facebook, fake news or someone who filed a lawsuit against the *Paper*. Similarly, V will define the common goal of the paper slightly differently depending on context, according to whatever will allow her to live up to her own idea of integrity when inviting employees to identify with the *Paper*'s mission. It seems that her deepest self-identification as being 'really' an anthropologist charges V with being, at least in her own eyes, a truthful spokesperson for her employees' perspective, so that her charismatic leadership does not transgress the moral boundaries she has committed to. This in turn allows V to present herself as a manager who invites writers to work towards a common goal by way of what she senses to be an almost non-exploitative transaction between leader and employee.

It is not my task to evaluate the moral integrity of V's management. Neither is it my task to deliver a critique of the self-representations by which anthropologists negotiate their own sense of moral justification. My objective here has merely been to describe the moral work that V does as an anthropologist to secure her own continued sense of integrity in a professional field fraught with mutually exclusive moral imperatives. In this, her continuous ability to move to a new position and become 'not that kind of manager' seems to be closely tied not just to her own sense of moral justification but also to the kind of power she is able to exercise and to her undisputable success as a manager: a form of power that allows her to manage her employees with little or no resistance.

Birgitte Gorm Hansen is an independent consultant and researcher. She is trained as a psychologist from the University of Copenhagen and received her PhD in science studies and management from Copenhagen Business School in 2011. Her postdoctoral research on anthropologists working in leadership positions formed one of the four sub-studies conducted in the Department of Anthropology at the University of Copenhagen.

NOTES

I would like to thank the anthropologist-informants who engaged with me as an interviewer prior to the fieldwork presented here. I am grateful for their reflections which form the backdrop to the material presented here and helped me to focus my inquiry around moral work among anthropologists. I would also like to thank several employees at the *Paper* who tolerated my constant presence in their office and shared with me perspectives on their workplace and its position in the world of Danish media. I am greatly indebted to Bent Meier Sørensen for helping me to contextualize this material within corporate Denmark's ongoing conversation with changing theories of management and their accompanying business trends. A special thanks, of course, goes to my main informant V, for her hospitality, her academic engagement with my work and her trust in the fieldwork process.

1. The material presented in this chapter forms the bulk of my postdoctoral work conducted at the department of Anthropology at the University of Copenhagen as part of the project 'The Practice of Anthropology – People and Ideas in Action'. The first step of the study was to conduct twelve interviews with anthropologists working in management or leadership positions. The interviews enquired into informants' academic training, career trajectories and whether/how their background in anthropology played a role in their everyday working life. One interview was conducted online with a UK-based anthropologist and business owner and one with an anthropologist living and working in Greenland. All other interviews took place in Denmark and with one exception were conducted live in the informant's workplace. Most informants were Danish, apart from two who were born and trained in the UK and one born in Greenland but trained in Denmark. All were trained in anthropology to MA level and apart from the two mentioned above they received most of their academic training in one of the two Danish departments

of anthropology. The informants occupied very different types of leadership positions: about half of the informants were business owners or founders, the other half were employees mostly in the private sector. One was the leader of a political party. From this sample, two anthropologists agreed to become part of the ethnographic fieldwork. The first fieldwork lasted for one and half months and took place in Copenhagen with an anthropologist who founded a public/private partnership where he managed both employees and a loosely connected group of volunteer workers. The second fieldwork with V also took place in Copenhagen and lasted close to three months.

2. It would require much more extensive fieldwork to map precisely why anthropologists in my fieldwork presented with such diversity while other fields, such as the medical anthropologists we met in Chapter 1, presented as a more homogenous group. One good guess is that whereas the anthropologists I sampled from this study were trained in very different academic settings, were separated by a large age gap and were in conversation with a field worker coming from outside their own discipline, the anthropologists we met in Chapter 1 were all trained in the same department and programme and were studied by a fellow medical anthropologist.

3. One should add here that even though V's late mornings are quite unusual, it is not exceptional to see a Danish knowledge worker leave the office between three and four. Danish culture is very much centred around family life and, since the 1980s, the role of parent has become increasingly important, meaning that employees with families often go home early but continue working from home in the evening, once their children are in bed. However, this pattern rarely extends to the top of the organizational hierarchy where V is positioned.

4. Again, the regional context speaks to this tendency towards low employee compliance and a more trust-driven type of leader-follower relationship. When studying research managers in a Danish university in 2007–2009, I learned from managers hired from other European countries that they were almost in shock over how little power their formal titles as managers really held, and puzzled about what it would take to make their employees follow their lead. The commercial manager who I was talking to at the *Paper*, however, was employed in Denmark before the came to the media world. This testifies to the *Paper* as a rather extreme example of an organization where leader-follower relationships are based more on identification than on formal hierarchy and contractual relationships (Gorm Hansen 2011).

5. At the time of my fieldwork, this incident of a one-and-a-half-year strike that drained the media company of funds and forced it to close was described on the website of the Danish media group. Today, this detail has been removed from the company timeline.

6. 'Vi laver jo ikke avis for at tjene penge'. The little insertion of the Danish word 'jo' in this particular iteration of V's slogan, signifies an implicit agreement with the receiver of the statement, making the statement almost rhetorical. By using 'jo', V is implying an identification between her and the employees. The sentence can be translated along the lines of: 'I know you already know this' or 'as we all know' . . . 'we don't make newspapers to make money'.

REFERENCES

Ahlefeldt, C. 2007. 'Chefens sjæl: Anne Knudsen'. Television series originally broadcasted by the national Danish Tv channel DR. Retrieved 14 January 2021 from https://www.youtube.com/watch?v=p8v56ZlXQKE.

Du Gay, P. 1994. 'Making up Managers: Bureaucracy, Enterprise and the Liberal Art of Separation', *British Journal of Sociology* 45(4): 655–74.

Freud, S. 1939/1973. *Civilization and Its Discontents*. London: Hogarth Press and the Institute of Psychoanalysis.

Goffman, E. 1959. *The Presentation of Self in Everyday Life*. London: Penguin Books.

Gorm Hansen, B. 2011. *Adapting in the Knowledge Economy – Lateral Strategies for Scientists and Those Who Study Them*. Copenhagen: Samfundslitteratur.

Kolind, L. 2006. *The Second Cycle: Winning the War Against Bureaucracy*. Philadelphia: Wharton School Publishing.

Osborne, D. and T. Gaebler. 1992. *Reinventing Government: How the Entrepreneurial Spirit Is Transforming the Public Sector*. New York: Penguin Books.

Peters, T, and R. Waterman. 1982. *In Search of Excellence*. New York: Harper & Row.

Reseke, L. 2017a. 'Jeg har ofte forventet at blive fyret'. Retrieved 20 October 2020 from https://mediawatch.dk/Arkiv/?query=anne+knudsen&sortBy=date&pageNumber=2.

———. 2017b. 'Krasnik skal Finde Weekendavisens Digitale Gangart'. Retrieved 20-10-2019 from https://mediawatch.dk/secure/Medienyt/Aviser/article 263392.ece.

———. 2017c. 'Weekendavisen holder formkurven'. Retrieved 20 October 2020 from https://mediawatch.dk/secure/Medienyt/Aviser/article9603416.ece.

Sinha, Paresha N. and Brad Jackson. 2006. 'A Burkean Inquiry into Leader–Follower Identification Motives', *Culture and Organization* 12(3): 233–47, DOI: 10.1080/14759550600865966.

Sørensen, B.M. and K. Willadsen. 2018. 'Penis Whirling and Pie Throwing: Norm Defying and Norm Setting in the Creative Industries', *Human Relations* 7(8) 1049–2071.

CHAPTER 4

Going Native in Data Science
An (Auto) Ethnography of
Interdisciplinary Collaboration

Morten Axel Pedersen

'Interdisciplinarity' and 'collaboration' have become buzzwords in research policy and discourse, and the field of anthropology is often highlighted as central to this vision, not least by the anthropologists themselves (Estalella and Sánchez Criado 2018; Rabinow and Stavrianakis 2015; see also Lassiter 2005; Holmes and Marcus 2008). Indeed, over the last decade or so, Danish, EU and private funding bodies have funded several large-scale interdisciplinary collaborations between anthropologists and natural scientists in Denmark and elsewhere in Europe (the US seems to 'lag behind' in terms of this development, but that is another story). Yet, as Callard, Fitzgerald and Woods observe, while 'interdisciplinarity is often framed as a unquestioned good within and beyond the academy, one to be encouraged by funders and research institutions alike . . . there is little research on how interdisciplinary projects actually work – and do not work – in practice' (2015: 1). Accordingly,

> there has been strikingly little attention to what large-scale and complex interdisciplinary projects actually look like in the making. We still know remarkably little of the mundane detail of what it looks and feels like to labour in an interdisciplinary setting. Nor, more importantly, do we have much sense of the consequences of this unfolding, uncertain, hybrid and multiple science-and-humanities-and-arts-in-the-making for what is, in fact, increasingly coming to be understood as the basic (indeed, correct and proper) praxis of interdisciplinarity today. (2015: 6)

This knowledge lacuna is particularly deep for fields and disciplines that remain peripheral to the technical, natural and life sciences. In fact, as Callard et al. also note, 'there has not yet been any significant emergence of research on practices of interdisciplinarity within the social sciences and humanities' (2015: 1). Anthropology is a case in point. Barring a few exceptions, many of which, perhaps not incidentally, are Danish[1] (Hastrup 2018; Flora and Andersen 2017; Madsen et al. 2018), little has been published on what anthropologists think and do (or think that they do) when engaged in research projects and other collaborations with scholars from other disciplines. Certainly, 'there remains no sub-field of ethnographic collaboration studies, and no sustained attention to the micro-practices of interdisciplinary working, despite the prominence of this norm within the contemporary academy' (Callard et al. 2015: 4).

The present chapter seeks to push towards the development of such a 'field of ethnographic collaboration studies'. My ethnographic material stems partly from my own experiences with and role in the development and the institutionalization of the interdisciplinary field of 'social data science' in Denmark, and partly from interviews with other scholars who have partaken in research collaborations between anthropologists and researchers from other disciplines.[2] Combining auto-ethnography with ethnographic data from these other interdisciplinary contexts, I make two overarching points, which challenge both established wisdom concerning anthropology's relationship to other disciplines in general and data/natural science in particular. In the chapter's first part I show how a focus on the 'complexity' and 'uniqueness' of individual fieldwork experiences leads anthropologists to feel methodologically, epistemologically and morally compromised when sharing their data and findings. As a result, anthropologists are sometimes perceived as 'flow-stoppers' by collaborators from other disciplines. This in contrast to many anthropologists' view of themselves as superior collaborators due to an alleged ability to understand, reflect upon and navigate different social-cultural positionings and epistemological, political and moral worlds. I also discuss how this 'moral economy of anthropological collaboration' is inseparable from the marginal status that anthropology and anthropologists often occupy vis-à-vis other disciplines.

Whereas the first part of the chapter draws on ethnographic interviews with anthropologists from Denmark and elsewhere in Europe, the US and Japan, the central protagonist of its second part is me, who, in my treble capacity as science ethnographer, novice data scientist and an anthropologist studying anthropologists, has entertained multiple and at times contradictory roles within Copenhagen's social data science community. I thus chronicle the tale of a classically trained anthropologist, who first thought that he was going to study data scientists from the cosy vantage of critical data studies (boyd and Crawford 2012); but who ended up 'going native' in data science and in this process came to attain a more distanced and sceptical view of his native discipline's more or less tacit norms, assumptions and conventions, including its moral economy of collaboration and the identity work associated with it. So, if at first blush the chapter's two parts may seem little connected, what unites the ethnographic account with the auto-ethnographic one is a critical engagement with the moral economy of anthropology as discussed in this book's Introduction.

Anthropological Identity Politics

Ruth: I was incredibly resistant to plans as a novice PhD student. So much so that I fought my supervisor over whether to write a project proposal before going to the field. I thought, 'this is completely un-anthropological, to say beforehand what I am going to do!'. I felt it was a betrayal of the people in the field whom I had not even met, yet whose interest I was going to follow.

Me: So, it was an ethical thing, more than just an epistemological question?

Ruth: Yes. I told my supervisor: 'This managerial format that you are putting me through is in complete disagreement with the commitments that I have to knowledge'. I felt that it was completely serving the institution, the paper work, the bureaucracy; it was not serving me.

Me: But does not most if not all science barring that strange beast we call anthropology, actually operate in this way, by making plans. There is nothing inherently 'neoliberal' or 'managerial' about that, that's simply how science works?

Ruth: Yes, I can completely see that. But the way this was being filtered through the anthropology department, was like 'oh, this is not really us, we just have to do it [to get funding/because we are told to] and therefore you just have to do it too'. But the struggle in my case was particularly strong because I love planning [as a person]; I am a person who tends to think very synthetically.

Me: Aha, so [the resistance to planning] was also a struggle against yourself?

Ruth. Yes. The non-determinacy of anthropology is very much something I learned [as a student of anthropology] and then have gotten very attached to. But I can totally flip between them. So if you tell me that anthropologists cannot follow plans and that others think this about them, then I am in total disagreement. I think it depends on which version of the anthropologist I am.

Me: So, where does the intensity of this insistence among you and other anthropologists to not want to plan come from? It seems almost to be like an affect?

Ruth: Yes, definitely. I actually used to have a great deal of [issues] with proposals because I felt they were promises that I could not keep, i.e. lies. I think I have a different relationship to it now. I see my students come to me with such desperate vagueness that all I can give them is a semblance of a plan. So I see the research proposal as a different kind of lie now. It is not necessarily a bad lie. It is an explicit lie, which opens up the question of whom you are lying *for*. If you are lying to yourself, that's when the affect erupts. If you are 'just' lying to other people [laughing] then you are in a state of a different kind of ethical freedom!

Thus went one of the several conservations about the anthropological aversion to research planning that Ruth and I had in the course of the several hours of interviewing and dialogue. A mid-career anthropologist with extensive experience with interdisciplinary collaboration as both a junior and senior team member, Ruth emerged as a central informant in my early investigations (in fact, I was so impressed by her ethnographic sensibility that I asked her to swap roles and interview me in in my own capacity as a co-PI (Principal Investigator) in the interdisciplinary project, now centre, which I am going to be discussing in the second part of this chapter).

Numerous themes and questions are at play in the above interview snippet. For present purposes, let me hone in on what has clearly presented an important dilemma for Ruth in her professional life, namely the design and planning of research. Indeed, Ruth is by no means the only anthropologist to have expressed similar aversions to research planning (or planning writ large!) to me, whether in their role as interlocutors in the research project on which this book is based, or as colleagues and students in more informal contexts. Both among senior anthropologists (myself included, at least until I started subjecting these gut feelings to critical scrutiny) and among junior researchers, there is widespread scepticism towards the planning of ethnographic research. In both Denmark and especially in the UK, I have often heard professional academic anthropologists going as far as saying that it is downright 'un-anthropological' to make research proposals – especially if one believes in what one writes in them, God forbid! (this is almost akin to a form of madness). Even more widespread is the notion that any attempt to formalize the collection, processing, the analysis of ethnographic data is not just uncool (or 'uncouth', in Ruth's words), but also morally and epistemologically tainted, because doing so directly contradicts the 'non-determinacy of anthropology'. As Ruth put it, 'there was a sense among [us] anthropologists that by collaborating, you were betraying. "To collaborate" meant that we were at risk, and others were also at risk by working with us, by bringing in outsiders into a conversation about something that was supposed to be local'[3] (see also Metcalf, Moss and boyd 2019).

Due to this association (and projection) of 'research planning', 'determinacy' and indeed 'collaboration' itself with researchers from other disciplines, it follows that 'they' are imagined to be fundamentally different from 'us'. Elsewhere in this volume, it is described how, within various communities of anthropological practice (e.g. health [Chapter 1], business [Chapter 2]), a moral economy is constructed around images of specific Others (capitalists, bureaucrats, etc.) who are seen to be located outside its perimeter, and who for the same reason are seen as polluting to the deeds, thoughts and effects of the practicing anthropologists in question. So, who might these anthropological Others be in the case of interdisciplinary collaboration? Well, judging from what we have learned in this section, they comprise all scholars whose data are not collected via long-term ethnographic fieldwork, and who may have less epistemological and ethical reservations about pooling their data with team members from their own and perhaps (especially) other disciplines.[4] Naturally, this will often amount to a large share of the researchers within these interdisciplinary teams. In fact, in some cases I studied, there was only a single scholar, who was not part of this bloated Other, namely the anthropologist him- or himself!

Such is the logic behind the identity work undergirding what I, in keeping with the general definition outlined in this book's Introduction, will here call the moral economy of anthropological collaboration. While the degree to which this moral economy is directly played out in my interlocutors' work practices and reflections and evaluations of these varies between the handful of cases of anthropological collaboration I have examined, the underlying logic is clear. Since We are not doing the (methodologically, epistemologically and ethically) dubious things that scholars from other disciplines do, it follows that We are not just fundamentally different from Them, but also that We are inherently Better than them (for other and more explicit examples of this logic, see also Chapter 1). This begs the question: what does this purist and essentialized image of anthropological practice look like from the vantage of collaborators from other disciplines? To explore this, I now introduce another interlocutor, Bodil, an experienced female research leader, who has been the PI of interdisciplinary projects involving a number of anthropologists:

> Bodil: That is just how it is with case studies: anthropologists are best at doing them. Or that's what I believed. I thought, if in-depth knowledge about a certain place is needed – and this was a very place-specific project – there needs to be someone who feels like going there. Someone who wishes to do it, who has the time for it, and who is trained to do it. For everyone thinks they know how to do ethnography and that's a huge problem. A lot of people don't know what it takes, you know also physically. Taking notes . . . and be bored like hell. Plus having the drive to book plane tickets and then later go, etc. But having said that, I also need to say that there is a different side of the coin.
>
> I can now see how all that later became a problem. For it is super hard to elevate oneself from [*komme op fra*] that place. Those [junior anthropologists], they are very ethnographic. And they believe it is the field that must speak to them. And it does not, well then . . . That's a real problem with being so good at obtaining empirical data. The problem shows in two ways: You can never get enough data. And if the data does not, well speak out [*anråber*] to you in such a way that it makes you feel something [*så du føler noget*] and senses that 'this is right', then it is not good data. And you cannot use it.
>
> Me: So, what you are saying is that it is not so much in spite of but actually because of the special things that the anthropologists are able to do, that certain challenges have arisen? Could you try to come a bit closer to what these challenges are: is it that you are waiting at the other end of the pipeline for something, which then does not come? Or is it rather that they do not see any equivalence between other peoples' data and their own?
>
> Bodil. No, it is not so much about equivalence. It's more this thing that I perhaps consider rather old-fashioned – but I guess I am not supposed to say that? [laughter] – 'the it is "my field" idea'. That it is only this one person who is supposed to sit on [*sidde på*] this data until that 'fantastic moment where everything makes sense' [mock-enthusiastic]. For just when does one . . . one can supervise, but . . . Well, I guess we do have some examples in our project where we share data. But it is difficult, it really is.

Let us recall our definition of the moral economy of anthropology from this book's Introduction. We suggested there that anthropologists divide the world into two spheres, representing, supposedly, amoral abstractions into dead numbers and moral concrete everyday life, respectively. Bodil's anthropological collaborators' unwillingness to generalize from their data or share these with the rest of the team can be seen as an example of this moral economy of anthropology in action. If what it means to be a 'good anthropologist' (in the dual sense of being both good at anthropology and a good person) is perceived to be the opposite to 'being abstract', then small wonder that Bodil is facing an uphill battle as PI. Due to the central role played by a cluster of interlinked concepts like 'the concrete', 'the everyday' and 'the intersubjective' in the narrative of uniqueness that undergirds the anthropological politics of identity, anthropologists partaking in interdisciplinary collaborations are faced with a personal and professional dilemma (the two are closely interlinked, and especially so in the case of anthropology). Both in the case of Bodil's junior collaborators and in the case of more senior scholars such as Ruth, the anthropologist is faced with an ethical and epistemological double-bind that is directly tied to anthropology's moral economy: any attempt to collaborate with other scholars – especially people from other disciplines but also in some cases fellow anthropologists (Bunkenborg, Nielsen and Pedersen in press) – about the collecting, processing and analysis of one's data is often deemed not just epistemologically but also morally and politically inferior. Or to adopt one of Ruth's points: all collaboration that is not taking place with members of the community studied is collaboration in the negative, 'traitor' sense of the term!

Against this background, there may be reason to question the widespread understanding among anthropologists that professional members of this discipline are not just good at collaborating with others, but better than others at it, presumably, or so the logic seems to go, because 'we are good at seeing things from different perspectives', and 'we are trained to reflect about our own and other's positioning', etc. Actually, according to my own experiences from the different interdisciplinary projects in which I have been involved (see below), and from my conversations with non-anthropological PI's as part of the research project on which the chapters in this book are based, the truth seems to be that anthropologists involved in interdisciplinary research within or outside the academy, as a whole, are quite bad at collaborating. The problem is not just that they are perceived to be overprotective of their data and reluctant to share them with others, and are as a whole wary and cagey about any general inferences and conclusions that might potentially be deduced from these data in its own right or by pooling them with other people's data, whether qualitative or quantitative. The problem is also that, in addition to an unwillingness 'elevate oneself from one's fieldsite' (c.f. the interview passage above), anthropologists also expect their collaborators to abide to this injunction of 'sitting on the data' (ibid.). Indeed, some anthropologists do not just expect but demand this of their fellow team members.

A similar dynamic is discussed by Rosalynn Vega (2019). 'Sociocultural anthropology', she writes, 'was originally conceived of as a science conducted by one person'. Yet, one of the consequences of this 'reified notion of anthropological research as a fundamentally individual enterprise', she suggests, is that it 'render[s] mixed-methods research among a team of distinctly trained professionals impossible' (2019). What is more, through

> the solo practice of ethnography, anthropologists have inadvertently contributed to a long-standing split between . . . anthropology as a qualitative science, and the quantitative . . . sciences . . . The underlying assumption undergirding this interdisciplinary split is that qualitative and quantitative sciences are in many ways incongruous . . . A related assumption is that in order for . . . anthropologists to collaborate with professionals trained in positivist science, they must sacrifice some theoretical acuity. (Vega 2019)

What is happening here, I suggest, is the extension of the moral economy of anthropology to encompass not just the anthropologists themselves but also their partners from other disciplines and fields. Naturally, not all collaborators are able, willing or positioned to abide with this injunction, which then defines them as not just epistemologically unreflexive and theoretically primitive but also ethically tainted and morally flawed from the vantage of the anthropologists, who in turn find ways of conveying this dissatisfaction with and negative judgement of their peers in more or less tacit ways. The result is what seems to be a rather unfavourable reputation of anthropologists among other scholars with whom they collaborate. Rightly or wrongly, I have heard anthropologists being described as 'self-indulging', 'conservative', 'difficult' and, above all, 'arrogant'. Indeed, my interviews have left me with the sense that some collaborators from other disciplines have been victims of forms of objectification, essentialization and dehumanization that are reminiscent of what modern anthropology has criticized as a sorry feature of its own colonial pasts (Said 1978; Clifford and Marcus 1986) as well as in the treatment of citizens by state professionals in contemporary neoliberal contexts (Biehl 2005; Povinelli 2008). Certainly, several of my interlocutors have relayed tragic-comical (and in some cases almost traumatic) experiences, where anthropologists have talked to them – and about them – in patronizing ways (see also Chapter 5 this book).

Admittedly, I have been making the above case in very strong and highly provocative terms. Of course, a good number of my informants (including not least Ruth) were perfectly capable of looking at and describing themselves in self-reflexive and self-critical ways. To be fair, many anthropologists – including, as we saw, Ruth herself – are quite aware of the practical dilemmas and logical paradoxes that arise from this purist stance towards interdisciplinary collaboration. And to be sure, it is not hard to find examples of interdisciplinary projects in which anthropologists (and their local collaborators) have been marginalized and treated in ways that can only be described as insensitive if not unethical. Indeed, even when anthropologists have played leading roles in interdisciplinary research projects – as several of my interlocutors in the present study have – they have been engaged in an ongoing and by no means always successful struggle for recognition and respect from their collaborators from other disciplines. Take, for example, the cases of Ole and Maria, who have both served as co-PIs in huge interdisciplinary projects with partners from numerous faculties, including medical professors with many years of experience, and egos to match. Or Catherine, who has been the PI of several projects where the development of new formats for the collaboration between anthropologists and natural scientists have been a key ambition and output criterion. In spite of many differences (in terms of funding structure, institutional affiliation, geographical scope, etc.), a number of common dynamics between the three examples of Ole, Maria and Catherine can be identified from my interviews. Two of the most significant such shared features are as follows.

The 'Anthropologist as Impresario' Trap

Each of the three anthropologists discussed above had a very ambitious (some would say romantic and idealized) notion of what it means to work with other scholars. Catherine recalled how she often became filled with a strong sense of disappointment and resignation after having partaken in collective activities with the other project members. The problem was not social: the 'non-anthropologists' (as Catherine liked to call them) in question were friendly enough to be around during meetings and other joint events. Rather, her mounting dissatisfaction inhered in what she and the other anthropologists perceived as a lack of interest in their professional work and ideas. 'It was always us who had to take the initiative', Catherine lamented (and I here paraphrase from a long interview I conducted with her towards the end of the project): 'We asked a lot of questions about their research, and really tried to understand how and why they asked the questions and used the methods they did. Yet, they never seemed particularly interested in what we were doing; and eventually we gave up trying – and always insisting on trying – to explain how anthropologists do fieldwork and why'.

Ole voiced similar concerns. However, his main source of disappointment – and eventually irritation and then resignation – had to do with a different perception of asymmetry between himself and his co-PIs from other disciplines. As Ole explained, it was always him who had to come up with the new ideas for joint activities, and to a large extent he also ends up being responsible for their organization as well as their execution. Not that Ole was expected to do all this work by himself; there was plenty of money in the grant to hire assistance to help with all sort of things, but someone still had to allocate the resources and later account for how they had been spent by logging into various bureaucratic procedures and platforms. This was the case both for activities whose purpose was explicitly social (get-togethers, outings, etc.) and for internal project workshops, as well as conferences with invited speakers, where the so-called scholarly and the so-called social dimensions were more or less seamlessly combined and integrated (I stress 'so-called', since the very distinction between something 'scholarly' and something 'social' is of course itself the product of a specific socio-cultural and political-economic configuration). The problem with all this, Ole went on to explain, was not lack of gratitude from his fellow research leaders for this work. In fact, the other co-PIs were full of praise for what they saw as a vital contribution to the well-being of the team and the success of the project. The problem was that, precisely because Ole ended up investing so much time and energy on organizing these collaborative activities, he neither had the time nor was he expected to contribute as much to 'the actual research' (as he and, presumably, the other PIs referred to it) as he wanted to do. In short, due to a combination of a factors including Ole's personality and other contingencies arising from the unfolding of the project, he ended up playing the role of an impresario within the division of labour between himself and the co-PI running the project with him. Having originally entered the group of principal investigators and the project team as a scholar representing a certain set of social scientific skills, he increasingly found himself relegated to and defined as an expert on the orchestration of good social events and vibes.

The same dynamic – that the anthropologists end up up taking charge of the organization of collective events – can be detected in other interdisciplinary contexts, including the Copenhagen social data science community (see below). And while there is no doubt that the other project members in many cases are more than happy about this division of labour (he/she 'is so good at it, much better than I am'), the anthropologists are not without blame either. For one thing, many anthropologists seem all too happy to buy into the unwarranted notion that just because they are experts in the empirical and theoretical study of social relations, they are somehow also imbued with superior social skills themselves (a fallacy calling to mind the notion that children of pastors are better Christians, or that psychologists are more mentally sane than others). Secondly, and partly following from this, all of my informants (and I am sure, me too) seemed to harbour unrealistic expectations about interdisciplinary work. On more than a few occasions in my conversations with Ole, Catherine and the others, I could not help wondering if they – and I – had not unwittingly adopted and extended the idea(l) of romantic love to our colleagues from other disciplines. I am referring to the characteristic (and, coming to think of it, really quite peculiar) underlying hope of an almost transcendental melting together of two hitherto separate entities – anthropology and NN non-anthropology – into a single shared essence; all, or course, in accordance with terms dictated by anthropology. Small wonder that the actual flesh-and-bones researchers with whom we work have trouble living up to (and interacting with) this specific variant of tragic unrecruited love.

'Add Anthropologists and Stir'

Another concern that was voiced to me in my interviews with the three senior anthropologists was a more or less pervasive sense of marginalization. Indeed, this seems to be a very widespread experience among anthropologists and other qualitative social science/humanities scholars involved in interdisciplinary research. Even when employed as full professors, and even when occupying a position (as, for example, steering group members) on par with their co-PI's, the senior anthropologists suffer from a creeping sensation that they are not being taken seriously. This sense of being barely tolerated, as opposed to respected or celebrated on equal terms with people from other disciplines, appeared to be particularly pervasive in biomedical research, where there seems to be a widespread expectation and assumption that anthropologists by their very presence represent a humanist touch, whose 'people skills' can be used to benchmark the project ethically (with respect to national and international guidelines for research practice) and legally (GDPR and other data protection laws).

To borrow a mock-slogan from the first generation of feminist anthropologists (Moore 1988), we could call this the 'Add Anthropologists and Stir' problem. In coining this term, I refer to the fact that, within biomedical and tech research, it has become common to advertise positions with associated work packages and earmarked budgets, whose job is to serve as experts in and deal with privacy, culturally sensitive and other ethical issues. And it seems to be just such positions that anthropologists (along with philosophers and other 'ethicists') typically apply for and are employed in, which only reinforces the notion amongst themselves and their employers that there is a particular dimension of research that anthropologists excel at and belong in, namely morality. But then again, the anthropologists can surely be said to bear some of the blame for this themselves, considering how easily and happily they have bought into the idealized image of the 'wise sage', who is simultaneously ethically superior, culturally civilized, socially sophisticated and of course politically progressive.

So to sum up, there is little doubt that in many interdisciplinary collaborations, the anthropologist(s) ends up playing second fiddle. More or less consciously, and more or less willingly, anthropologists tend to become stuck within the increasingly narrow and lonely role of 'ethical experts' and/or 'social impresarios', whose chief responsibility and competency is associated with tasks which scholars from other disciplines either consider themselves less competent at or simply are not interested or willing to do themselves, perhaps because less prestige is associated with them in comparison with other tasks, such as being the lead author of a publication in a high-end journal, or representing the research project in collaborations and negotiations with private companies, policy makers, journalists and other external partners.

Against this background, it is now much more understandable why so many anthropologists entertain a purist image and an exceptional narrative concerning the nature and role of anthropological practice within interdisciplinary contexts, for it is inseparable from the sense of marginalization if not stigmatization that so many anthropologists experience when working with scholars from other disciplines generally, and natural/biomedical disciplines in particular. The result is what might be called 'anthropological identity politics'. As in all other such processes of othering, the anthropological identity is the product of constant boundary work with respect various kinds of Others (Barth 1969; Fabian 2014). And as with all such other processes of othering, this symbolic work entails an element of reification, stereotyping and sometimes even demonization and dehumanizing. Indeed, there are anthropological Others, who, within interdisciplinary contexts, are perceived as more Other than all other Others, as it were. I am referring to people from the natural/technical and the life/medical sciences, as well as – and perhaps above all – people with a social science (and more seldom, humanities) background, whose research relies on quantitative data and methods.

Consider a conversation that I recently had with a prominent professor from a very prestigious US anthropology department. Having mentioned my involvement in the Copenhagen Centre for Social Data Science (see below), I asked her whether there happened to be any collaboration between her department and a newly established interdisciplinary data science initiative at the university. 'No, not at all!', was her curt reply. 'Why do you think that might be?', I then proceeded to ask, to which her no less definitive answer was, 'well, they are all doing boring quantitative work, aren't they, the place is full of economists and so on'. This particular professor is not alone in making such very categorical judgements. As the reader may recognize, quantitative methods – and quantitative social scientists from various fields in particular – have been in pretty bad standing amongst anthropologists since at least the early 1970s. And among all these quantitative social science Others, one certain figure stands out as perhaps the most demonized and the most inhuman of all, namely that of 'the economist'.[5] In fact, as I sometimes like to put it when attending an anthropological meeting,[6] or just overhearing a chat between two colleagues inside or outside academia, one is sometimes left with the sense that professional anthropologists are quite happy to talk about economists in the same way that Donald Trump talks about Muslims, or Mexicans!

So, the figure of the 'quantitative scientist' generally and the 'economist' in particular can be said to play very much the same role among anthropologists involved in interdisciplinary research as the figure of the 'businessman', the 'bureaucrat' or the 'corporate manager' is shown to play within other anthropological communities of practice elsewhere in this book. But this begs the question of what might happen when an anthropologist or a group of anthropologists embarks upon a collaboration with quantitative social scientists around a shared research agenda. It is to this question that I shall turn my attention in the second part of this chapter.

Going Native in Data Science

Over recent decades, researchers in anthropology, sociology and science and technology studies (STS) have engaged in many collaborative and cross-disciplinary endeavours, to experiment on new forms of complex data generation, analysis and visualization (Housley et al. 2014; see also Ford 2014; boyd and Crawford 2012; Nafus and Sherman 2014; Wilf et al. 2013; Knox and Nafus 2018; Mills 2019; Jemielniak 2020). Partly overlapping with wider development, a predominantly critically-minded anthropological literature has emerged that discusses the often strained relationships between 'small' and 'thick' qualitative ethnographic versus 'big' data approaches (Stoller 2013; Erwin and Pollari 2013; Boellstorff 2013; Ford 2014; Boellstorff and Maurer 2015; Abramson 2016; Blok and Pedersen 2014; Madsen, Blok and Pedersen 2018; Pedersen forthcoming).

It is to this discussion that I seek to contribute here.[7] I do so both as co-leader of a handful of anthropologists, sociologists and STS scholars (known as the 'AntSoc Group' or the Critical Algorithms Lab), who from 2012 to 2016 collaborated with quantitative social scientists and data scientists on a large computational social science research project, and in my capacity as Deputy Director of the Copenhagen Centre for Social Data Science (SODAS), which since 2016 has served as an interdisciplinary research centre and teaching hub at the Faculty of Social Science UCPH. In these two roles, I have been involved in a wide range of collaborative activities with partners from all faculties at this and other Danish universities, different public/state institutions, and private companies. However, my most sustained interaction and closest professional relations have been with four fellow researchers (a sociologist, an economist, a psychologist and a political scientist) from the Social Sciences Faculty as well as a data scientist/physicist from the Computer Science department at the Danish Technical University, a group who have colloquially become known as the 'core group' (*kernegruppen*).

While I have certainly adopted an ethnographic stance (including, as we shall see, participant observation, note taking and semi-structured interviews) during especially the first years of this collaboration, I have over the years become a still more central and active figure within the incipient field of data science in Denmark and beyond. In that sense, as I have argued together with Madsen and Blok (2018; c.f. Marcus 1993), this involvement has taken the form of an ongoing oscillation between doing ethnography 'in' and doing ethnography 'of' social data science. At the same time, I have been experiencing a growing estrangement from anthropology, which has been aided by the critical distance towards and objectification of my original discipline which I have adopted in order to carry out the ethnographic research upon which the first part of this chapter is based. That is, I have gone native in data science. This, then, is a third way in which anthropologists might engage collaboratively with data science and data scientists, namely by doing anthropology not 'of', nor 'in', but as data science.

What remains of this chapter is organized around this tripartite distinction. Accordingly, in what follows I describe three different phases of my involvement in the social data science initiative at UCPH as it developed from its inception almost a decade ago to the institutionalization of SODAS as a permanent research and teaching centre. In so doing, I want to accomplish three things. I wish to chronicle the story of what seems to a be unique case of anthropology as a key social data science component and stakeholder.[8] Interspersed across this account, I will present a number of 'collaborative moments' (Korsby and Stavrianakis 2018; Hastrup 2018) from my time in the Copenhagen social data science community. And finally, I shall tie the account of social data science at UCPH and my own role in it to anthropology's moral economy and to anthropological identity politics more generally.

Phase I: Anthropology 'of' Social Data Science

In retrospect, the reason why what is now a fairly large research and teaching centre came into being was an optimal mixture of timing, ambition, ability, connections, boldness and a good deal of co-incidence/luck. Social Data Science at Copenhagen University started in 2011, when Troels Østergaard Andersen, then dean of Social Science, created a 'Forum for Young Research Leaders' at the faculty. The idea was to create an interdisciplinary forum where aspiring research leaders from the five departments at the faculty could meet to share experiences, discuss ideas and simply get to know each other. A second but less overt purpose was to give the dean (and the then prodean Birgitte Sloth, who sometimes substituted for him) an opportunity to 'test the waters' in relation to a number of potential new cross-faculty initiatives in the making. Meetings took place on a monthly basis, and were usually kicked off by a short presentation from one of the participants about their current research in their research projects or groups, even though on a couple occasions external guests (for instance two members of the Parliamentary Research Committee) were invited to give presentations instead. While the heads of departments were instructed to actively promote the initiative among those members of the staff they found most fitting for it, the forum was in principle open to all 'younger' (that is, anyone up to forty years old) scholars, who already were or were planning to be leading or co-leading a team of researchers around a common project.

Predictably, most of the ten or so scholars who became regular attendants in the first year of the forum's existence were male.[9] I was one of these men, and so were two others of the total of four scholars, who after some months met to discuss the possibility of a collaboration. For in the meantime, the dean had launched another idea: a seed money initiative for which scholars from the faculty could apply under the condition that their group and theme of research were explicitly inter-disciplinary. It was Søren Kyllingsbæk, an experimental psychologist (and later professor and head of the psychology department), who first brought the original 'core group' together. In addition to representa-tives from four of the faculty's five departments (for reasons I cannot remember or don't know, no one was at this point invited from the political science department, although this gap was eventually filled some years later with the inclusion of the award-winning and noted professor Rebecca Adler Nissen [henceforth Rebecca]), the group in-cluded Sune Lehmann Jørgensen (henceforth Sune), then assistant professor at the department of computer science at DTU. With a PhD from the Niels Bohr Institute and several co-publications with famous social physicists from the US (e.g. Pentland 2015), Sune had already made a name for himself within the new field of computational social science, and Søren (who had met Sune at a workshop some years back) knew that Sune was looking for 'new playmates' (*nye legekammerater*) in Denmark. As for myself, I was asked to identify 'someone from the sociology department' to join our incipient research group. Although the two departments are located in the same buildings, I knew very lit-tle about my sociology colleagues back then, but I knew I was looking for someone interested in transcending the methodological and epis-temological divide between qualitative and quantitative approaches, so I picked Anders Blok (henceforth Anders), a sociologist that I had got to know from my role in the (then) bourgeoning interface between anthropology and STS in Denmark and abroad. And so we found our-selves with just enough funds (7,500 Euro) to launch the grandly (and cumbersomely) named CCCSS: Copenhagen Centre for Computa-tional Social Science.

We ended up spending all the money on a one-day workshop in the spring of 2012. In addition to various internal UCPH presenters and participants, it featured four invited speakers from other univer-sities, including the Cambridge-based anthropologist Matei Candea. And that was more or less it, at least as far as I was concerned. While I liked the company of my new-found collaborators intellectually as well as socially, there seemed to be no clear path forward for our still very loose and vaguely defined 'computational social science' vision. Clearly, forging such a path would entail a significant amount of time and resources, and this was not an investment that I was able or will-ing to make at the time, also in light of my commitments to a number of anthropology-centric projects in Denmark and abroad. But once again, a new opportunity came about out of the blue, which drastically improved our prospects. I am referring to the so-called '2016 Initiative', a large internally funded Centre of Excellence Program at UCPH, which was explicitly targeting the establishment of radically interdisciplinary collaborations between so-called 'dry' (social science, humanities, law and theology) and 'wet' (natural and life science) faculties. (The story of the 2016 Initiative is too long to recount here, but it undoubtedly is one the biggest and most truly interdisciplinary research programmes launched in Denmark.) The decision to apply was quickly made between the five of us, along with two senior scholars invited from the Department of Public Health and the Niels Bohr Institute. As the only professor in the original core group, David Dreyer-Lassen (a noted economist and recipient of several elite grants) took charge of piecing together the bits and pieces provided by the rest of us into a coherent whole. To everyone's surprise, the application received very favourable reviews by the external reviewers and the internal award committee at UCPH, and so we found ourselves in charge of a $4 million research project spanning eight departments, three faculties and two universities.

The Social Fabric project (aka Sensible DTU and Copenhagen Networks Study) was a large computational social science experiment funded by 16 million DKK from the UCPH '2016' Centres of Excellence Program (PI David Dreyer Lassen) in combination with a 7 million DKK Young Investigator Grant (PI Sune Lehmann Jørgensen) from the Villum Foundation. Framed as a bold ambition to develop technical, methodological and analytical tools to transform the 'big data' revolution into a new 'deep data' vision, social data and meta-data was logged from call and SMS logs, Bluetooth, GPS geo-location, and other digital channels in 800 free smartphones distributed to an entire freshman cohort at the Danish Technical University north of Copenhagen. In addition, the project used many other social scientific quantitative or qualitative methods and data, ranging from questionnaires and other surveys (including personality tests), text data and meta-data mined from social media ('likes', etc.), register data, as well as ethnographic data obtained via participant observation, interviews and focus groups (for two overviews, see Stopczynski et al. 2014 and Blok and Pedersen 2014).

The project had three overarching research questions (I cite here from the original application): (1) how information and influence is transmitted and transformed in the DTU students' 'social fabric'; (2) how friendships, networks and behaviours form, offline and online, and; (3) how the researchers involved in the project themselves study 'big data' and handle issues of ethics and privacy. Within this framework, the AntSoc Group, which in addition to Anders and myself comprised an anthropology/STS postdoc (Antonia Walford), two PhD students (Tobias Bornakke Jørgensen from sociology and Mette My Madsen [henceforth My] from anthropology) and several aspiring computational social science students, explored a number of questions: (i) Fieldwork – how can ethnographic studies of friendship and other social network relations amongst students enrich or challenge computational approaches, and vice versa?; (ii) Quali-Quantitative Methods – does the rise of computational social science lead to a reconfiguration of traditional splits between quantitative and qualitative research methods?; (iii) Big Data Experiments – what kinds of anthropological and sociological experiments does the Social Fabric experiment enable, and how might these enrich existing social-scientific designs?; (iv) The Social life of Big Data – what new ethical, political and organizational challenges and opportunities do the rise of large-scale social databases pose to the social sciences and indeed to science and society at large?; and (v) Research Collaboration – taken as an object of science and technology studies (STS), what may be learned about cross-disciplinary collaboration from the research programme itself?

Departing from what could broadly be called a STS approach, various constellations of people associated with the AntSoc Group have explored the combination between ethnographic and other qualitative data on the one hand and 'big data'/quantitative methods on the other (e.g. Blok et al. 2017; Madsen 2017; Madsen et al. 2018; Birkbak and Carlsen 2016; Due and Bornakke 2016). Some of these studies have explicitly touched upon the theme of collaboration, including the awkward and sometimes marginal role that My found herself in as a junior female ethnographer in 'sea' of quantitative data scientists who were mostly male and her senior. Indeed, hers and other accounts by the AntSoc team call to mind other anthropologists involved in interdisciplinary collaborations, including the sensation of playing second fiddle and never being taken quite as seriously as team members from fields such as physics and economics. Indeed, especially during the roll-out phase of the Copenhagen Networks Study, I sometimes suspected that my role was to be the icing on the cake, whose status as 'house anthropologist' could be used internally and externally to 'tick the ethics box' and as living proof of the project's privacy-sensitive and humanistic credentials.

However, this suspicion was proven totally wrong. For one thing, as I was also at pains to stress to the other co-PIs from Day 1, my experience with and knowledge of research ethics and privacy based on an Oxbridge PhD and decades of fieldwork in Mongolia was not sufficiently professional to be of much use to my team members. But fortunately, this did not represent too big a problem. Several of my co-PIs turned out to be highly ethical, reflexive and privacy-conscious, and as far removed from the stereotype of the nutty professor who will break all the rules in the quest for truth and fame as one could imagine. Thus, Sune had already developed a privacy-sensitive and ethically sustainable software and hardware platform for the collection and storage of digital social data in conjunction with a pilot version of the project. Paired with David's and other quantitative social scientist's extensive experience with survey and register data and analysis, the Copenhagen Networks Study came to rest on a solid and extremely well thought through data legal/ethical framework.

But if my role was not (and had never been envisioned to be) that of the 'house ethicist', then what was it? There is no doubt that, in the early stages of the Copenhagen Networks Study, it was hard for anyone beyond the confines of the AntSoc group to envision what purpose anthropology played in the project. To illustrate this early sense of confusion, let me now zoom in on a couple of revealing snapshots from the very first (and, coming to think if it, in fact also the only) occasion on which the entire Social Fabric/Sensible DTU research group was gathered.[10] The meeting, which took place shortly after the official beginning of the project, was held at DTU: in many ways a fitting venue given that it was both home to one of the central project partners (Computer Science) and the physical, institutional and sociological site of its object of study, viz. first year engineer students. In what follows below, I quote more or less directly from the 'raw' field notes, which I (in my new role as science ethnographer) diligently took on my laptop during the three hour-long event:

> David: My starting point is that economics is a method: it is a science about how people behave when resources are scarce and they try to maximize a certain objective. Now, the thing is that it is very hard to identify network effects (causalities) in observational social networks, unless one formalizes the study. So, what I am looking for as an economist cannot just be an observational network; randomization is key. And this is precisely what our experimental context 'naturally' provides [due to the standard DTU practice of dividing of freshmen students into random social 'matrix groups' across different degree programs].[11] What is more, the Social Fabric experiment also allows for randomized interventions by slicing up the sample, as a complement to the external randomization. For example, we could remind [via the mobile phones distributed to them] a sample of stu-

dents about the next municipal election in the days prior to it. By doing this [imagined example of a randomized intervention], it would be possible to see whether and how the act of casting a vote spreads in the network.

Sune/Morten:[12] Speaking of scarce resources, how about making an experiment involving free beers? Somewhere on campus we start handing out 500 beers and then trace what happens as the rumour starts to spread among students. It is a bit like injecting contrast liquid in a vein prior to a scanning: we will be able to trace the spread of information across the network and the movement of people in it!

NN1 (Associate professor in Public Health): As a medical doctor I am all too aware of the negative effects of alcohol on the human body. I have previously been involved in research on drinking patterns among Danish youth and I would not be comfortable about the signals this kind of experiment would send. So perhaps we could come up with something more ethical than beers?

Me [with a playful/sarcastic tone]: Green salad, for example?

NN1 [irritated]: No, since obviously it has to be something the students want!

NN2 (Prospective PhD student in psychology): We might also consider inviting some companies to help in financing the experiments.

Me: Well, the most important thing is that it should be a scarce resource and an experimental set-up. It clearly does not need to be beers, but on the other hand I would find it much more unethical to collaborate with a company, for example.

Sune: Actually, there has been some discussion [among the software engineers in his DTU group] of us developing an attractive game [for the project app installed on the phones], where students could then participate in an act out of various experimental formats. Perhaps My [the aforementioned PhD student doing fieldwork among the student cohort] can become involved in this somehow.

NN1: Fine, but we will still need to find a way for the rest of us in the project group to be informed about these things, so that we will be made aware of the contamination of the experiment caused by an anthropologist doing fieldwork.

A range of observations could be made based on the above, but let me here make three. First, it is hard not to take notice of the notion that anthropologists represent a source of 'contamination'. Indeed, as My has discussed elsewhere (Madsen 2019; Madsen et al. 2018), this was not the only occasion when her role as ethnographer was referred to in such terms by team members from public health or psychology. Needless to say, being seen as impure is not exactly conducive for collaboration, even when this perception is the result of methodological and epistemological, as opposed, say, to racialized or gendered concerns. Nonetheless, gender was another dimension that undergirded not just the above conversation but many other discourses and situations that unfolded in the course of the five-year-long Copenhagen Networks Study. In fact, as My convincingly shows in her PhD dissertation (2018), gender plays a central if largely tacit role in the socialization of new engineer students at DTU, including what she calls 'playful masculinity' (2018: 126). 'Playful masculinity', she explains with reference to Hasse (2008), is a particular attitude (or to be more precise, the capacity to perform this attitude) characterized by 'being average or above average in narrow professional terms (*faglig dygtighed*), but superior when it comes to the ability to play with physics [by] for example relating it to science fiction, tell jokes and make fun in a curious way about assignments and research infrastructure' (Madsen 2018: 85; my translation). The reason why this attitude (which can also be found among female students, while not all male students subscribe to it) is associated with high status at the DTU has to do with a general notion and consensus among physicists that 'it is the desire and the capacity to play and being curious which gives rise to new scientific discoveries' (2018: 85; my translation).

In many ways, I suggest, being 'playful' in this 'physicist' (and gendered) way was what Sune and I were competing about in the above example. In coming up with the half-serious idea of distributing free beers in order to track the spread of information in the social network,[13] and in the 'salad joke', we were (without fully being aware of it) tapping into a discursive space, which celebrates the ability to make sharp and witty comments in a way that takes neither oneself nor the issue at hand too seriously (see also Gell 1998). Now, clearly, both the rules of this game and the *illusio* displayed by us in mastering it are highly privileged with respect to several parameters, including not only gender and race, but also ethnicity, generation and possibly class. However, what I wish to focus on here – and this is my third and final observation – is a more personal and thus also idiosyncratic dimension of the interaction and collaboration between Sune and myself. I am referring to the coincidental (but I think very important) fact that whereas Sune originally studied philosophy at UCPH before enrolling at the Niels Bohr institute, I started out as a physics and mathematics students at the University of Aarhus before moving to and doing my masters at the anthropology department at the same place.

In addition to being in possession of elementary knowledge about and basic practical experience with each other's disciplines, this symmetrical reversal in our respective educational paths and scientific careers also had some wider, and, it now seems to me, decisive ramifications. As the above conservation snippet offers a glimpse of, on numerous occasions during those first years both the interests and the attitudes of the anthropologists (myself and My) and the physicists (Sune and his DTU group) turned out to overlap significantly. What is more, these unexpected similarities between the concerns of ethnography/anthropology and of data science/physics typically became manifest in situations where otherwise invisible divergences were exposed between different groups of quantitative scholars, such as psychologists versus data scientists, or quantitative sociologists versus econometric economists. While it is hard to put one's finger on where these resonances originate from, there seemed to be a greater degree of openness and flexibility among physicists and anthropologists towards the possibility that a given experiment may not generate the expected type and form of data; and more generally, an acceptance and awareness of the fact that not all questions and hypotheses can be deduced beforehand and thus need to be continuously adjusted or even rejected. Although this is likely to surprise both parties, the classic ethnographic ideal of 'grasping the native's point of view' (Malinowski 1961) thus reappeared among computational social scientists collecting data 'in the wild' (Dyson 2019). Certainly, in the case of both the DTU physicists and the AntSoc group, a 'blue sky' approach to the study of social reality was being pursued, whose ambition was to detect unknown or unexpected patterns that came closer to the concerns of classical anthropology as well as certain kinds of physics than the hypothesis-driven approaches that dominate the social sciences (DiMaggio 2015).

This, then, might be a viable path for ethnographic dinosaurs like myself in interdisciplinary teams, where people neither want nor need anthropologists to 'help educate' them into being 'better' collaborators. Instead of pretending (to ourselves and others) that our professional training has endowed us with unique and superior social and/or ethical expertise, we might instead think of ourselves as a sort of qualitative physicists, who have geeky interests and ask unexpected but therefore often productive questions. Surely, as scholars conducting our work 'in the wild', we have built up a certain degree of robustness and resilience when it comes to handling unexpected situations, events and crises, and we are thus able to adjust our research designs and eventually our conclusions and our theories accordingly. In practical terms, this semi-conscious but highly embodied capacity might take different forms, one of which could be some version or another of the 'playfulness' discussed above in a general atmosphere of curiosity, humour and permitted failure. Certainly, this ability and willingness to be a fellow geek-in-crime and not a besserwisser/flow-stopper, worked well for several members of the AntSoc group, including My and me.

Still, the concrete interactions between myself and the other anthropologists and the quantitative oriented scholars remained minimal at this stage. While the social and professional relationships between us was characterized by a great deal of sympathy, tolerance and curiosity, little actual mutual collaboration took place between us, and it was hard to imagine how things might be different in the future. Nowhere was this polite distance or 'inter-patience' (Candea 2010) better illustrated than in the 'Complementary Social Science' paper that Anders and I wrote during the early stages of the Copenhagen Networks Study (Blok and Pedersen 2014). Drawing loosely on Niels Bohr's concept of complementarity, we argued for a division of labour between ethnographic and other qualitative researchers on the one hand, and data scientists and other quantitative researchers on the other – which, for all its nice words about mutual respect and amiable relationships, at the end of the day reaffirmed and reproduced the perception of a 'great divide' between the two sides.

Phase 2: Anthropology 'in' Social Data Science

As the Social Fabric project entered its final phase, the dean of the Social Science Faculty once again made a decision that was to have a lasting and positive impact on the Copenhagen social data science community. Following some initial probing with David (who in turn informed the 'core group'), it was decided to capitalize on what both the dean and others[14] deemed as Social Fabric's success and to launch a new strategic initiative at the faculty. Accordingly, in 2016 the Copenhagen Centre for Social Data Science (SODAS) was established at the Faculty, involving faculty and students from anthropology, economics, political science, psychology and sociology, as well as data scientists from DTU. SODAS' vision was (and still is) to create a social data science research and teaching community focused on – and I paraphrase here from our website (www.sodas.ku.dk, assessed in June 2020) – (i) leveraging advances in data science and in the collection of digital and/ or big data and new data forms for the benefit of social scientists; (ii) enriching and combining qualitative and quantitative methods; and (iii) studying how such data, and not least their ethical and privacy-related challenges, transform the ways of doing social science. At the heart of SODAS' work, then, lies the ability to do data collection, visualization and analysis based on new digital data forms – that is, data from dedicated and non-dedicated digital data collectors, social media, web scraping, etc. – to explore key social science themes and questions, including the mathematical structure of networks; privacy, law and ethics; quali-quantitative data integrations; peer effects measurements from high frequency data; political language and mass political discourse such as 'fake news'; the combination of social, historical and register data; machine learning in the social sciences; text mining; visualization; mobility data, etc.

With the establishment of SODAS and my increasingly central role in its leadership and management along with David and Sune,[15] it became clear to me and people around me that a fundamental shift had taken place in terms of my positioning vis-à-vis not just the UCPH social data science community and initiative, but also vis-à-vis my department and the discipline of anthropology. As discussed in the previous section, this gradual professional (as well as existential) change from being an anthropologist conducting an ethnography *of* big data to being an anthropologist working *with* big data had already begun during the early phases of the Copenhagen Networks Study, as it became clear that my role as a co-PI was different and involved other competences than my collaborators and I had envisioned. Two developments, however, made the situation now different from those earlier years. For one thing, the combination of skills within the AntSoc group had by now reached a point where constellations of quantitative and qualitatively oriented scholars started working on data from the Copenhagen Networks Study (e.g. Blok et al. 2017). Compared to the earlier think piece written by Blok and me (2014) that stressed the purportedly radically different nature of qualitative and quantitative approaches, our work in the AntSoc group during this phase can in broad terms be described as 'quali-quantitative' (Venturini and Latour 2010): that is, combinations of different kinds of data from ethnographic field notes to digital traces from mobile phones and other digital devises and platforms (see also Moats and Borra 2018; Arora et al. 2018; Curran 2013; Ford 2014; Hsu; 2014; Pretnar and Podjed 2018; Madsen and Munk 2019;; Breslin et al. 2020; Isfelt et al. forthcoming).[16]

Concurrently with the AntSoc group's deconstruction of the 'quali-quantitative' divide, other developments within SODAS generally and the steering committee in particular further fostered the shift from a mainstream science-ethnography 'of' approach to a more explorative mode of anthropology 'with' data and data scientists. As a result of a combination – so characteristic of the story of the UCPH social data science community – of pragmatic, personal and professional reasons, I gradually found myself working together with David not just on all sort of things pertaining to the daily management of SODAS, but also in relation to various funding possibilities and partnerships with external stakeholders. While a comprehensive outline of all this is beyond the remit of this chapter, our bilateral (and sometimes trilateral, with Sune or Rebecca appearances and activities included: co-organizing a session on 'Big Data and Human Relations' at the science festival Bloom and two panels about 'Sustainable Big Data' and 'Human Digital Traces' at the politics and policy festival Folkemødet; applying for research grants from the Danish Innovation Fund (in 2017 and 2018, unsuccessfully) and from the European Research Council (Advanced Grant 2019, successfully); joint presentations at numerous events at UCPH and other universities about interdisciplinary collaboration between social science/humanities and STEM (Science Technology Engineering and Medicine) scholars and institutions; and numerous meetings with the dean and the rest of the faculty leadership about the role and place of SODAS within the future development of research, teaching and impact activities at the Social Science Faculty.

In addition to these numerous collaborations centred on practical, managerial and organizational issues, a growing (albeit by no means full) epistemological alignment began to happen between David and me with the realization that certain questions posed in empirical anthropological and empirical economic research were quite similar. I am referring to the sense in which so-called behavioural economics (Kahneman 2011) – an influential recent alternative to traditional neoclassical economics – resembles what anthropologists and sociologists call practice theory (Bourdieu 1977). Notwithstanding their many epistemological differences, both behavioural economists and practice anthropologists thus share a basic scepticism towards relying on people's (over)rationalized accounts of their own and other's motives and actions, favouring instead methods (e.g. participant observation and digital meta-data) which provide better access to peoples' so-called actual behaviour.

Coupled with a growing sense of respect and trust between us, as well as (not to be forgotten) matching interests in terms of our vision for the future of SODAS and the social science faculty, I found myself agreeing about more and more crucial research and educational questions with a hard-core quantitative economist specialized in economet-rics and predictive modelling.[16]

Small wonder that on the rare occasions that I had the time (and energy) to discuss my work at SODAS with fellow anthropologists, I found myself torn between two contrasting roles. On the one hand, there was the 'moral anthropologist' (c.f. Kapferer and Gold 2018) dis-cussed in the Introduction to this volume. Here, my role in SODAS would be to serve as an epistemological-cum-ethical police officer, whose responsibility in collaboration with 'non-anthropologists' is to patrol and uphold a vital but fragile boundary between a 'moral' inside and an 'immoral' outside. Seen from the insular and (I really do think) fundamentalist logic of this moral economy of anthropological collab-oration, my close professional collaboration with David represented danger if not betrayal of not just my professional and personal ethics, but of the discipline of anthropology (and qualitative social science) writ large. But on the other hand, there was also a very different role available for me in the Copenhagen social data science community in general and vis-à-vis 'economists' like David in particular. According to this version, the potential 'moral' upshot from partaking and (as in my case) playing a leading role in interdisciplinary collaborations is not the product of a superior (again in the dual sense of being more professional and morally better) ethical compass let alone a more de-veloped epistemological reflexivity or more progressive politics. In-stead, thinking and acting in an ethically informed and morally decent way is here a question of being less of 'an anthropologist', if by this we understand the identity that has been constructed around the politics depicting economists and other quantitative scientists as its Big Other. Or, put differently, the role that I have chosen and gradually learned to perfect involves thinking and behaving anthropologically to do away with, or exorcise, 'the moral anthropologist' within me!

Let me conclude this section with a comment on a PowerPoint slide from one of many joint presentations made by David and me. As has often been the case, the presentation was made at a seminar where 'in-terdisciplinary collaboration' was an explicit theme; indeed, this was the very reason we had been invited in the first place. The venue was a one-day-workshop organized by the Vice-Chancellor of the Copen-hagen Business School (CBS), who had gathered all heads of depart-ments and the deans from his own school as well as numerous heads of departments and other managers from the Natural Science Faculty at UCPH. The slide contained 'Five Do's' and 'Five Don'ts' of interdis-ciplinary collaboration:

Table 4.1 'Five Dos' and 'Five Don'ts' of interdisciplinary collaboration

Do	Don't
Design a shared 'machine'/experiment in the middle	Submit to a Jane Austen fantasy of romantic love
Foster a culture of permitted failure and psychological safety	Impose a single methodology/theory/data standard
Facilitate intense collaborative moments e.g. data sprints	Only go for top journals and reproduce hierarchies
Secure a physical space for the core team and events	Accept 'innocent' jokes about minor sciences/juniors
Support outreach (key platform for interdisciplinarity)	Assume that you can remain faithful to your discipline

If I have accomplished nothing else in eight years of studying and do-ing interdisciplinary collaboration in practice as well as in theory, I would like to believe that this particular slide serves as a testimony to the 'success' (however one want to measure this) of the UCPH social data initiative as this was envisioned and set in motion by our (then) dean Troels Østergaard in 2011. But that is not all. I also think that that the slide counts as 'evidence' of a more specifically anthropolog-ical 'impact' on the manner in which interdisciplinary collaboration is being conceptualized and (so I would like to think, or hope) prac-tised within (and perhaps also beyond) the now well-established and fast-growing social data science community in Copenhagen. I am, of course, referring to the specific and very explicit way in which both the original questions and the actual findings of the research project on which this book is based have found their way into the 'Five Do's' and (no less crucially) the 'Five Don'ts' of interdisciplinary collaboration, which I formulated for the aforementioned event and have been tour-ing with and promiscuously sharing with whomever wanted them ever since.

Conclusion: Anthropology as Data Science

By way of closing, let me begin by making a few observations and re-flections about the most recent (and possibly last) stop in my interdis-ciplinary journey: the anthropology 'as' data science phase. I should note here that due to reasons that are both pragmatic and principled, what follows will be much shorter in length than the above account of the two other phases. In pragmatic terms, I simply do not have sufficient space available here that would permit me to describe, even in the abridged form used above, the developments that has taken place in the UCPH social data science community over recent years, including: (1) the relocation of SODAS to much bigger, centrally located and very attractive premises; (2) the rapid growth of researchers fully or partly employed by and based at SODAS (presently around fifty people); (3) the application and approval for a new MSc in Social Data Science that commenced in 2020, largely managed and taught by SODAS people; (4) the expansion and formalization of a SODAS leadership with David as Director and myself as deputy director with responsibility for the academic quality of the new degree (following David's appointment as pro-rector at UCPH in Jan 2021, I took over the directorship of SODAS with Rebecca as the deputy director); (5) a permanent establishment and embedding of SODAS within the faculty's organizational, financial and administrative framework, with the future possibility that SODAS may be transformed into a fully-fledged department at the social science faculty at some point; and (6) numerous new research grants from public and private funding bodies in Denmark and Europe, including a SODAS-based ERC Advanced Grant with me as PI and David, Sune and Anders as co-PIs, which commenced in January 2020.

But there is also a more principled reason why it would not be feasible to provide an account of the present anthropology 'as' data science phase. I am referring to the fact that this phase is, precisely, ongoing and still in the making. While the second half of this chapter was based on past experiences and events, which could be made subject to the distanced gaze and the necessary objectification that is required to produce a genuinely (auto) ethnographic account, the situation is quite different with respect to the present moment. After all, as alluded to above, it is not just SODAS's role and status with respect to the other departments at the faculty that is currently subject to big changes; the same also goes for my own position and role, including the question of my future professional affiliation and place of employment. There is no doubt that the story and the argument that I have presented here have comprised its own share of epistemological blind spots as well moral(izing) biases. To be sure, the fact that my professional identity is presently undergoing a 'transitioning' from one disciplinary community of practice to another is bound to have influenced my analyses. For the same reason, the present account should not be understood as a new version of the classic anthropology-as-hero narrative associated with Malinowski and the countless students of anthropology who have undertaken the professional *rite de passage* still to this day associated with long-term individual fieldwork (Stocking 1983). Rather, what I have presented is a deeply situated personal-cum-professional micro-history/autobiography, which remains part of the overarching moral economy of anthropology discussed in this volume.

Zooming out, it also remains an open question whether an integration can be made between anthropology and data science, and if so what (and how) such an anthropology 'as' big data would be. What can be said and anticipated at this point, however, is that such a methodological and analytical transmutation of anthropology into a form of data science (and vice versa) will entail a fundamental rethinking of some of the most cherished norms and ideas regarding the place of anthropology vis-à-vis the natural sciences in particular and the contemporary world writ large. Indeed, for such an anthropology as data science to be realized, it would involve questioning some of the most deeply held qualitative social scientific methodological, epistemological and ethical/political conventions. First, it would entail bracketing and thus 'provincializing' fieldwork as the only, or primary, method of anthropological inquiry (see also Ingold 2014). Secondly, it would require deploying and integrating into the heart of anthropological inquiry social data science methods like text mining, machine learning and natural language processing (see Pedersen forthcoming). Only through such a double disruption of mainstream anthropological dogmas might it become possible to experiment with the creation of distinctly computational, or could we say 'machinic', anthropology. But of course, it is an open question whether such a new breed of 'computational anthropologists' would be welcomed, not just by other and more established data scientists from quantitative/computational social science, but also by the national and international community of anthropologists. That, it seems, is the big 'if' – and it is, as I hope to have shown, a question which is inseparable from the wider epistemological and indeed moral question of what the role of anthropology vis-à-vis other disciplines is, and could be.

Morten Axel Pedersen is a Professor at the Department of Anthropology and Director of SODAS. After having spent two decades doing anthropological research in and on Inner Asia, he has for the last eight years been working on political forms and digital economies in Denmark.

NOTES

This research was made possible by generous economic and institutional support from The Danish Research Council for the Humanities as well as from the University of Copenhagen '2016' Centre of Excellence Grant. I thank many researchers from the Copenhagen Networks Study research program and the Copenhagen Centre for Social Data Science, as well as my interlocutors from a handful of other interdisciplinary projects based in Denmark, UK, the US and Japan, for finding time to talk to me and being interviewed about the nature of interdisciplinary collaboration. I would also like to thank the other members of the Practice of Anthropology team, Hanne Overgaaard Mogensen, Birgitte Gorm Hansen and Jasmin Cullen, as well as Lise Røjskjær Pedersen, Mette My Madsen and Steffen Jöhncke, for stimulating intellectual discussions and good company.

1. I am not suggesting here that Danish anthropologists are imbued with superior wisdom or a more encompassing perspective on these matters. But I do think that Danish anthropology may represent an extreme case in terms of the degree to which academic anthropologists have been engaged in interdisciplinary research projects over the last two decades. While the reasons behind this are many, there is little doubt that the fundamental changes in research funding structures – including a transfer of funds from individual and mono-disciplinary to collective and multi-disciplinary research projects – that followed the neoliberal reforms of the universities in 2001 played a key role (Gorm Hansen 2011; Wright and Ørberg 2015; Pedersen 2018).

2. A total of eight semi-structured interviews lasting one hour or more were conducted between January and October 2016. Care was taken to select interviewees representing different positions (junior/senior; project leader/ project member), genders and disciplinary backgrounds (e.g. anthropology, sociology, STS, economy, political science). In addition, a substantial number of more informal interviews and conversations pertaining explicitly to the topic were carried out with members of especially the Danish but also international (e.g. British, American and Japanese) anthropological community in the course of the project period.

3. As pointed out by one of the peer reviewers of this volume, this perceived risk of epistemological betrayal is at one and the same time in continuity and in tension with the more general idea(s) that the practice of anthropology involves a moral obligation to 'do good', which is discussed in more detail in several of this book's other chapters. After all, as the reviewer aptly asks, how can Ruth do good for others if she does not (yet) know what is good for them?

4. This may possibly be a feature of – or at least be especially outspoken in – the handful of research projects that form the empirical basis of the present chapters. After all, as another peer reviewer put it, 'I know of several other Danish led interdisciplinary projects where the anthropologists share their data *without any of the[se] considerations*' (my emphasis). This may be true, but then again, this very categorical refusal ('without any') seems to indicate that this reviewer is deeply positioned and has explicit stakes in this moral economy.

5. According to one of the peer reviewers of this article, my observation that anthropologists 'distance themselves from economists, scientists and en-

gineers . . . seems somewhat constructed for the occasion'. I fundamentally disagree with this suggestion. Indeed, once again, the reviewers themselves could be suspected to themselves be part of the empirical field under investigation rather than simply observing it from a safe distance. After all, in claiming that he/she/they 'cannot recognize this at all', is it not strongly indicated and laid bare that there is indeed something vital going on here, which is quite general to our discipline's understanding of its own mission and practice?

6. I first made this point as a discussant at the 'Towards an Anthropology of Anthropological Practice' panel organized by Hanne O. Mogensen at the Annual Anthropological Association meeting in 2017. While the comparison between anthropologists and Trump was well received, the expressions on peoples' faces were considerably more negative when Birgitte Gorm Hansen later the same day quoted me during a comment made by her at the (much bigger and more well-attended) 'What is Analysis?' round table.

7. As will also become clear below, my position within the Copenhagen social data science community – as well as within Danish anthropology – is hardly neutral or innocent. Surely, my status as a white, middle-aged, middle-class, Cis-male professor with economic and cultural privileges carries with it a significant baggage of implicit biases and politics, as well as all sorts of epistemological and bodily normativities along with social, cultural, economic, heteronormative and racialized blind spots.

8. Over the last couple of years, an increasing number of computational science or social data science research hubs and degree programmes have been set up in Europe (e.g. LSE, UCL, Helsinki, Oxford, Goldsmiths) and USA (e.g. Berkeley, Harvard, Chicago). However, to the best of my knowledge, anthropologists and anthropology do not seem to play any significant role in these initiatives.

9. This over-representation of male scholars may be explained not just by the fact that most PI's at the faculty were men back then, but also because it was easier for these male scholars to classify themselves and be classified as 'research leaders' than their female peers and because they found the form of the forum easier to partake in.

10. Additional meetings concerning the running of the project as a whole took place over the next years. But barring annual year's receptions, these were restricted to steering group members. Instead, the community of scholars involved in the project eventually congealed into several layers. The inner layer was comprised by the steering group, who (during the most intense early years) met around once a month. The outer layer was a loosely defined group of twenty-five, plus computer scientists, physicists, economists, psychologists, philosophers, sociologists and anthropologists, who collaborated within different constellations, and in more or less direct, intensive and amicable ways. Additionally, the original 'core group' also meet occasionally, sometimes in conjunction with professional or social activities at the social science faculty (e.g. inaugural lectures, Christmas parties, etc.), but also with the explicit purpose of discussing faculty-specific questions and developments pertaining to our common agenda. And finally, there were numerous more discipline-specific groups of researchers, who would meet, at various intervals and with

various meeting lengths, to discuss their own or another's data, results and writings.

11. For details, see Madsen 2019 and Sekara et al. 2016.

12. It is not clear in my notes whether this was said by Sune or me. Very possibly, we both talked by constantly interrupting and commenting/joking about each other, in the incessantly playful and purposefully meandering way that has so often characterized our interactions (see below).

13. Incidentally, a scaled-down version of this experiment was later carried out during an outreach event in Copenhagen following a conversation between Sune and the Danish science writer Tor Nørretanders.

14. The research project received significant coverage in national media and more specialized publications about research and university life, just as David was invited to talk about it to audiences comprised of leading figures from both government and private research institutions and funds. The project also received a very favorable assessment by the external peer reviewers appointed to review this and other 2016 Initiative projects.

15. For various reasons (including maternity leave and fieldwork abroad), the three other members of the steering committee from sociology, psychology and political science were less involved than the rest of us in the daily running and management of SODAS during the first years of its existence.

16. It is beyond the scope of this chapter to present any elaborate description and discussion of concrete instances of this realization on behalf of myself and the economists and other quantitative social scientists with whom I collaborate. But for some examples of the sort of research that has been made possible in this interface between computationally augmented anthropology and explorative empirical economics, see the numerous Covid-19 related blogposts and articles (e.g. https://coronakrisen.github.io/; Breslin et al. 2020), which have been produced and published by SODAS researchers during the spring and summer of 2020.

REFERENCES

Abramson, A. 2016. 'What in/Is the World is/of Big Data? Fieldsights – Cultural Anthropology'. Retrieved 16 March 2017 from https://culanth.org/fieldsights/833-what-in-is- the-world-is-of-big-data.

Andersen, A.O., J. Flora and K. Lampert. 2017. 'From Data to Findings: Validating Interdisciplinary Data in Piniariarneq', in K. Hastrup, B. Grønnow and A. Mosbech (eds), *The NOW Project: Living Resources and Human Societies Around the North Water in the Thule Area, NW Greenland: Annual Report 2016*, pp. 33–38.

Arora, Millie P., M. Krenchel, J. McAuliffe and P. Ramaswamy. 2018. 'Contextual Analysis: Towards a Practical Integration of Human and Data Science Approaches in the Development of Algorithms', *2018 EPIC Proceedings*: 224–44.

Barth, Frederic (ed.). 1969. *Ethnic Groups and Boundaries: The Social Organization of Culture Difference*. Oslo: Universitetsforlaget.

Beaulieu, Anne. 2017. 'Vectors for Fieldwork: Computational Thinking and New Modes of Ethnography', in L. Hjorth, H. Horst, A. Galloway and G. Bell (eds), *The Routledge Companion to Digital Ethnography*. London: Routledge, pp. 29–39.

Biehl, Joâo. 2005. *Vita: Life in a Zone of Social Abandonment*. Berkeley, CA: Berkeley University Press.

Birkbak, Anders and Hjalmar B. Carlsen. 2016. 'The Public and Its Algorithms: Comparing and Experimenting with Calculated Publics', in Louise Amoore and Volha Piotukh (eds), *Algorithmic Life: Calculative Devices in the Age of Big Data*. London: Routledge, pp. 21–34.

Blok, A., T. Bornakke, H. Bang Carlsen, M.M. Madsen, S. Ralund and M.A. Pedersen. 2017. 'Stitching Together the Heterogeneous Party: A Complementary Social Data Science Experiment', *Big Data & Society* 4(2). DOI: https://doi.org/10.1177/2053951717736337

Blok, Anders and Morten Axel Pedersen. 2014. 'Complementary Social Science? Quali-Quantitative Experiments in a Big Data World', *Big Data & Society* 1(2): 1–6.

Boellstorff, T. 2013. 'Making Big Data, in Theory', *First Monday* 18(10). Retrieved 14 January 2021 from http://firstmonday.org/article/view/4869/3750.

Boellstorff, T. and B. Maurer. 2015. *Data, Now Bigger and Better!* Chicago: Prickly Paradigm Press.

Bourdieu, P. 1977. *Outline of a Theory of Practice*. Cambridge: Cambridge University Press.

boyd, d. and K. Crawford. 2012. 'Critical Questions for Big Data: Provocations for a Cultural, Technological, and Scholarly Phenomenon', *Information, Communication & Society* 15(5): 662–79.

Breslin, S.D, T.R. Enggaard, A. Blok, T. Gårdhus and M.A. Pedersen. 2020. 'How We Tweet About Coronavirus, and Why: A Computational Anthropological Mapping of Political Attention on Danish Twitter during the COVID-19 Pandemic'. Retrieved 14 January 2021 from http://somatosphere.net/forumpost/covid19-danish-twitter-computational-map/.

Bunkenborg, Mikkel, Morten Nielsen and Morten Axel Pedersen. In press. *Collaborative Damage: An Experimental Ethnography of Chinese Globalization*. Ithaca: Cornell University Press.

Callard, F., D. Fitzgerald and A. Woods. 2015. 'Interdisciplinary Collaboration in Action: Tracking the Signal, Tracing the Noise', *Palgrave Communications* 1: 15019.

Candea, Matei. 2010. '"I Fell in Love with Carlos the Meerkat": Engagement and Detachment in Human-Animal Relations', *American Ethnologist* 37(2): 241–58.

Clifford, James and George E. Marcus (eds). 1986. *Writing Culture: The Poetics and Politics of Ethnography*. Berkeley, CA: University of California Press.

Curran J. 2013. 'Big Data or "Big Ethnographic Data"? Positioning Big Data Within the Ethnographic Space', in *Ethnographic Praxis in Industry Conference Proceedings*, University College London, 15–18 September 2013. Wiley Online Library. Arlington, VA: American Anthropological Association, pp. 62–73.

DiMaggio, Paul. 2015. 'Adapting Computational Text Analysis to Social Science (and Vice Versa)', *Big Data & Society* 2: 1–5.

Due, Brian L. and Tobias Bornakke Jørgensen. 2016. 'Big Thick Blending: Quali-fying Service Design Thinking through Behavioural Methods and Network Granularity & Extension', *Working Papers on Interaction and Communication* 2.

Dyson, G. 2019. 'AI That Evolves in the Wild', Friday 25 October 2019. Re-trieved 14 January 2021 from https://www.edge.org/conversation/george_dyson-ai-that-evolves-in-the-wild.

Erwin, K. and Pollari, T. 2013. 'Small Packages for Big (Qualitative) Data'. EPIC 2013, 1. Retrieved 21 February 2018 from www.epicpeople.org/small-pack ages-for-big-qualitative- data/.

Estalella, Adolfo and Tomás Sánchez Criado (eds). 2018. *Experimental Collabora-tions: Ethnography through Fieldwork Devices*. Oxford: Berghahn Books.

Fabian, Johannes. 2014. *Time and the Other: How Anthropology Makes Its Object*. With a New Postscript by the Author. New York: Columbia University Press.

Flora, J. and A.O. Andersen. 2017. 'Whose Track Is It Anyway? An Anthropological Perspective on Collaboration with Biologists and Hunters in Thule, North-west Greenland', *Collaborative Anthropologies* 9(1–2): 79–116.

Ford, H. 2014. 'Big Data and Small: Collaborations between Ethnographers and Data Scientists', *Big Data & Society* 1(2). DOI: https://doi.org/10.1177/205 3951714544337.

Gell, A. 1998. 'Introduction: Notes on Seminar Culture and some other Influences'. In E. Hirsch (ed.), *The Art of Anthropology: Essays and Diagrams*. London: Ath-lone, pp. 1–28

Gorm Hansen, Birgitte. 2011. 'Beyond the Boundary: Science, Industry, and Man-aging Symbiosis', *Bulletin of Science, Technology & Society* 31(6): 493–505.

Hasse, Catherine. 2008. 'Learning and Transition in a Culture of Playful Physi-cists', *European Journal of Psychology of Education* XXIII(2): 149–64.

Hastrup, Kirsten. 2018. 'Collaborative Moments: Expanding the Anthropological Field through Cross-Disciplinary Practice', *Ethnos* 83(2): 316–34.

Holmes, Douglas R. and George E. Marcus. 2008. 'Para-Ethnography', in L.M. Given (ed.), *The SAGE Encyclopaedia of Qualitative Research Methods*. London: Sage, pp. 595–97.

Housley, W., R. Procter, A. Edwards et al. 2014. 'Big and Broad Social Data and the Sociological Imagination: A Collaborative Response'. *Big Data & Society* 1(2): 1–15.

Hsu, W.F. 2014. 'Digital Ethnography toward Augmented Empiricism: A New Methodological Framework', *Journal of Digital Humanities* 3(1). Retrieved 14 January 2021 from http://journalofdigitalhumanities.org/3-1/digital-ethn ography-toward-augmented-empiricism-by-wendy-hsu/.

Ingold, Tim. 2014. 'That's Enough About Ethnography!', *HAU: Journal of Ethno-graphic Theory* 4(1): 383–95.

Isfelt, A, T. Enggard, A. Blok and M.A. Pedersen. Forthcoming.

Jemielniak, Dariusz. 2020. *Thick Big Data: Doing Digital Social Sciences*. Oxford: Ox-ford University Press.

Kahneman, Daniel. 2011. *Thinking, Fast and Slow*. London: Penguin Books.

Kapferer, B. and M. Gold. 2018. 'Introduction: Reconceptualizing the Discipline', in B. Kapferer and M. Gold (eds), *Moral Anthropology: A Critique*. Oxford: Ber-ghahn Books, pp. 1–24.

Knox, Hanna and Dawn Nafus (eds). 2018. *Ethnography for a Data Saturated World*. Manchester: Manchester University Press.

Korsby, Trine M. and Anthony Stavrianakis. 2018. 'Moments in Collaboration: Experiments in Concept Work', *Ethnos* 83(1): 39–57.

Lassiter, Luke E. 2005. 'Collaborative Ethnography and Public Anthropology', *Current Anthropology* 46(1): 83–106.

Levi-Strauss, Claude. 1963. *Structural Anthropology*. Translated by Claire Jacobson and Brooke Grundfest Schoepf. New York: Doubleday Anchor Books.

Madsen, Anders Koed and Anders Kristian Munk. 2019. 'Experiments with a Data-Public: Moving Digital Methods into Critical Proximity with Political Practice', *Big Data & Society*: 1–19.

Madsen, Mette My. 2017. 'Data as Monads: How Digital Data Can Be Understood as the Sum of the Components in the Process of Locating It', *Intersections: East European Journal of Society and Politics* 3(1): 15–30.

———. 2018. *Fællesskabets Ingeniører: En antropologisk analyse af sociale studiestartsaktiviteter for ingeniørstuderende*. PhD Dissertation, Department of Anthropology, University of Copenhagen.

Madsen, M.M., A. Blok and M.A. Pedersen. 2018. 'An Ethnography in/of Computational Social Science', in H. Knox and D. Nafus (eds), *Ethnography for a Data Saturated World*. Manchester: Manchester University Press. DOI: https://doi.org/10.7765/9781526127600.00017.

Malinowski, Bronislaw. 1961. *Argonauts of the Western Pacific*. New York: E.P. Dutton.

Marcus, George. 1993. 'Ethnography in/of the World System: The Emergence of Multi-sited Ethnography', *Annual Review of Anthropology* 24: 95–117.

Metcalf, J., E. Moss and d. boyd. 2019. 'Owning Ethics: Corporate Logics, Silicon Valley, and the Institutionalization of Ethics', *Social Research: An International Quarterly* 82(2): 449–76.

Mills, Kathy A. 2019. *Big Data for Qualitative Research*. London: Routledge.

Moats, D. and E. Borra. 2018. 'Quali-Quantitative Methods beyond Networks: Studying Information Diffusion on Twitter with the Modulation Sequencer', *Big Data & Society* 5(1). DOI: https://doi.org/10.1177/2053951718772137.

Moore, Henrietta. 1988. *Feminism and Anthropology*. Minneapolis: Minnesota University Press.

Nafus, D. and J. Sherman. 2014. 'Big Data, Big Questions: This One Does Not Go up to 11: The Quantified Self Movement as an Alternative Big Data Practice', *International Journal of Communication* 8: 1784–94.

Nielsen, G.B. and N. Jordt Jørgensen. 2018. 'Engagement beyond Critique? Anthropological Perspectives on Participation and Community', *Conjunctions: Transdisciplinary Journal of Cultural Participation* 5(1): 1–13.

Pedersen, L.R. 2018. *Fact Finders: Knowledge Aesthetics and The Business of Human Science in a Danish Consultancy*. PhD Dissertation, Department of Anthropology, University of Copenhagen.

Pedersen, M.A. (ed.). Forthcoming. 'Machine Anthropology'. Special theme issue of *Big Data & Society*.

Pentland, Alex. 2015. *Social Physics: How Social Networks Can Make Us Smarter*. London: Penguin.

Povinelli, Elisabeth A. 2008. 'The Child and the Broom Closet: States of Killing and Letting Die', *South Atlantic Quarterly* 107(3): 509–30.

Pretnar, Adja and Dan Podjed. 2018. *Data Mining Workspace Sensors: A New Approach to Anthropology*. Retrieved 14 January 2021 from https://e-knjige.ff.uni-lj.si/znanstvenazalozba/catalog/download/120/214/3104- 1?inline=1.

Rabinow, Paul and Anthony Stavrianakis. 2015. *Demands of the Day: On the Logic of Anthropological Inquiry*. Chicago: Chicago University Press.

Ruppert, E., J. Law and M. Savage. 2013. 'Reassembling Social Science Methods: The Challenge of Digital Devices', *Theory, Culture and Society* 30(4): 22–46.

Said, Edward W. 1978. *Orientalism*. New York: Pantheon.

Sekara, V., A. Stopczynski and S. Lehmann. 2016. 'Fundamental Structures of Dynamic Social Networks', *Proceedings of the National Academy of Sciences* 113(36): 9977–82.

Stocking, G.W. (ed.). 1983. *Observers Observed: Essays on Ethnographic Fieldwork*. Madison, WI: University of Wisconsin Press.

Stopczynski, A., V. Sekara, P. Sapiezynski, A. Cuttone, M.M. Madsen et al. 2014. 'Measuring Large-Scale Social Networks with High Resolution', *PLoS ONE* 9(4): e95978.

Stoller, Paul. 2013. 'Big Data, Thick Description and Political Expediency', *Huffington Post*, 16 June. Retrieved 14 January 2021 from www.huffingtonpost.com/paul-stoller/big-dat a-thick-description_b_3450623.html.

Vega, Rosalynn. 2019. 'Syndemics: Considerations for Interdisciplinary Research. Somatosphere'. Retrieved 14 October 2019 from http://somatosphere.net/2019/syndemics-considerations-for-interdisciplinary-research.html.

Venturini T. and B. Latour. 2010. 'The Social Fabric: Digital Traces and Quali-Quantitative Methods', in *Proceedings of Future En Seine*, 2009. Paris: Editions Future en Seine, pp. 87–101.

Wilf, E., J. Cheney-Lippold, A. Duranti et al. 2013. 'Toward an Anthropology of Computer-Mediated, Algorithmic Forms of Sociality', *Current Anthropology* 54(6): 716–39.

Wright, Susan and Jacob W. Ørberg. 2015. 'Autonomy and Control: Danish University Reform in the Context of Modern Governance', in S.B. Hyatt, B.W. Shear and S. Wright (eds), *Learning under Neoliberalism: Ethnographies of Governance in Higher Education*. Oxford: Berghahn Books, pp. 178–200.

CHAPTER 5

You Win. Forever

Moral Positioning in a Field with No Going Home

Birgitte Gorm Hansen and Lise Røjskjær Pedersen

While located in the slightly claustrophobic situation of studying the moral work of anthropologists ethnographically, we have encountered the challenge of finding a moral compass of our own. How do we position ourselves productively in relation to our interlocutors in a field where the distinctions between good and bad anthropology are already defined and given moral value by interlocutors? As our interlocutors were often older, more experienced and more powerful anthropologists with voices of their own, they were both willing and able to beat us at our own game when it came to coming up with normative criteria for distinguishing between good and bad ethnography, good and bad fieldwork, or good and bad analysis. As we seemed to operate by way of the same moral divisions, we found ourselves engulfed by, rather than reflecting on, what we later decided to call the moral economy of anthropology. As a result, we found ourselves enrolled into a competitive logic where we and our interlocutors competed for the same moral high ground by taking turns in doing the final analysis. This dynamic took shape as a series of 'counter ethnographic' moments (Holmes and Marcus 2008). Whereas the 'counter' aspect of counter ethnography is often downplayed in the existing literature, we will propose that the productive relationship to interlocutors is not, as often assumed, dependent on a playful, collaborative process where researcher and interlocutor co-create descriptions based on mutual interest or common ground. It was the more intimidating push-backs, the competitiveness and the challenges we received from our powerful and analytically capable interlocutors that compelled us to think about our own moral position and invent new attempts to define what it means to operate responsibly as researchers and analysts of our own societies. As a side effect, going through this process of finding our own feet when studying other anthropologists has helped us to rethink our rather rose-tinted ideas of 'collaboration' as the future of anthropological fieldwork.

Through a series of counter-ethnographic fieldwork experiences we will show how our fieldwork amongst anthropologists involved playful but also unstable and precarious relationships. We describe how we and our interlocutors took turns in altering each other's position as data. Luckily, we are not the first to encounter the problem of being entangled in fieldwork relations that feel not only too close for comfort but also slightly competitive.

Anthropological researchers increasingly study not only 'their own societies' but also people within these societies who hold similar academic titles, occupy positions of power and have stakes in what is being written about them as well as the power, connections and qualifications to do their own writing (Riles 2000; Maurer 2005; Miyazaki 2013). Our 'own societies' are parts of knowledge economies, meaning that science, policy, technology and business are entangled – and stakes and interests are both competing and overlapping. The study of these societies involves getting close to people who may feel disturbingly unfamiliar to some academic anthropologists: white men and women in suits and heels, armed with degrees of their own, excel sheets, budgets, bullet points and friends in high places. Doing fieldwork 'back home' increasingly involves getting familiar with territories where fieldworker and interlocutor already inhabit the same entangled jungle and the university researcher is in no way guaranteed a place in the top of the analytical food chain. Given this context, anthropologist Annelise Riles asks how ethnography is to be conducted when the central problem is not so much the researcher's own position in the field as 'the way the field is both within and without' the researcher (2000: 20).

This problem is arguably not only relevant to anthropologists studying anthropologists. Academic researchers are increasingly in competition with other knowledge producers in ways that call the illusion of our analytical distance and independence into question (Irwin and Wynne 1996). As research policy changes and public funding dwindles, academic researchers are increasingly challenged to navigate dual relationships with multiple stakeholders, collaborate across disciplinary and institutional boundaries, and struggle for scientific authority within a public territory pervaded by competing modes of reasoning (Horst

2003; Sismondo 2011; Gorm Hansen 2017). Whereas our academic colleagues in medicine, biotechnology and climate science have been grappling, for some time now, with the dilemmas of commercial and political interest as well as competing representations coming from journalists, social media and fake news, we in the social sciences and humanities still seem somewhat surprised that the people we study are now competent to represent themselves in ways that successfully compete with, and in some cases trump, the stories written by academic researchers.

In this chapter we ask the following questions: what is the future of anthropological fieldwork and analysis under these circumstances, where informants may no longer be satisfied with playing the role of 'raw material' for our analytical work and are fully capable of expressing themselves academically? How do we think of 'good' anthropology when our own 'go-to' position for normative evaluation is already occupied by our interlocutors? When both sides of the relationship claim the moral position of being authentic spokespersons for human reality, what becomes the normative distinction by which to assess the integrity and productiveness of our own work?

The chapter builds on material from two research projects focusing, each in their way, on the work of anthropologists outside academia. Lise's project is about the consultancy ReD Associates, a strategy and innovation consultancy that bases its consultancy method in the human science disciplines and especially in ethnography and anthropology. Birgitte's project is a study of anthropologists working in leadership positions in Denmark.

Let us begin one month into Lise's fieldwork.[1]

The Balinese Cockfight Moment

Lise is participating in a discussion on the LEGO Minecraft team, consisting of Jay, the project manager, Hannah, an experienced business anthropologist, and two other consultants.

The discussion in the team has been going on for a couple of hours and the consultants are writing up notes on their laptops from yellow and green post-it notes on the wall. Lise sits next to them. The office manager comes in to tell the team that they need to leave the room as soon as possible as a group of visitors from China is coming in, and she needs to clean and prepare the room. She is clearly stressed. Jay, the project manager, an ethnologist by background, assures her that they will be out of the room in time. He asks if somebody can please take a picture of the post-its on the wall so that they are captured for later use. Lise volunteers. Jay looks up and smiles; he seems surprised.

A couple of minutes later he asks Lise if she would mind cleaning the table of coffee cups, glasses and papers. She does what he asks. When she returns from the kitchen, Jay says, now with a larger smile on his face: 'Lise, I think you just had your Balinese cockfight moment! You know, the moment when Clifford Geertz and his wife escaped the police together with the natives in Bali . . . that was the moment when he was truly accepted by his informants and he felt accepted for the first time'.

A couple of hours later, Jay sends out an email to the team, including Lise. It says:

> Thanks Lise.
> Like I said, I think this was truly the Balinese cockfight moment of your research:
> The first Manifesto session the researcher attended with the LEGO Minecraft team was broken up by Majken [the office secretary], and the experience of clearing the table, aligning the chairs and photographing the post-its allowed Lise Røjskjær Pedersen to break the tension between herself and the 'consultants'. . . .

Lise is somewhat surprised by Jay's meta-analysis and replies immediately – using the same jargon:

> I love your meta-analysis on my project Jay – keep them coming, they are wonderful data:)
> By the way . . . great session today . . . looking forward to more and to go through it later on.

Now, one of the other consultants – Hannah – replies to this. She says:

> Ha-ha, yeah that was a really big turning point in your research Lise

Then Jay writes:

> Yeah, forgot to respond to this. Love how you get the last word no matter what – as no matter what I/we do – we will end up as data.
> You win. Forever.

This was one of those moments that you know will be important – an 'ethnographic moment', if you like – and if this reply wasn't dense enough, Hannah's last comment made up yet another meta layer. She closed the dialogue with the comment:

It's interesting that you should say this, Jay. I look forward to reading about what this means in Lise's Ph.D.!

Both of our fieldwork experiences were full of these types of episodes. We were constantly drawn into loops where who was researcher and who was informant was up for grabs. The positions were not fixed. Especially in Lise's fieldwork, every dialogue felt like a negotiation, sometimes even a combat over who was 'on top' and who had the right to define the premises of the situation.

In this case above, Jay is clearly not comfortable with the role of 'informant'. His quick analysis of the situation as a 'Balinese cockfight moment' is an act of resistance towards being analysed and objectified as data. By using the Geertz reference, he reconfigures the situation and becomes the analyst himself, and he renders Lise and her project as data in turn. Lise, however, manages to wrest back the analytical upper hand by encompassing his comment as a new piece of data, but Hannah, the other consultant, gets the final word by combining researcher and informant as an instance of 'meta data' that she looks forward to seeing analysed in Lise's dissertation.

Jay's comments echo a general attitude amongst especially the seniors of the consultants of ReD Associates. They often expressed that it was painful, risky and somewhat annoying to have an anthropologist observing their work. As such, partners and managers were somewhat ambivalent towards the project and Lise's arrival in the company. One partner said: 'I think it is great that you have chosen us, and we will learn a lot from it. It is going to be a painful process for us', and a senior manager commented: 'I hear that you are doing a study about ReD, that is scary and I don't understand how you can get anything structural out of something that is as weird as what we are doing. It's exciting [to consider] what will come out of it, good luck'.

Lise had formal access to study the consultancy's work processes, including project activities with clients and internal meetings. Still, she was introduced to the staff with the following comment by one of the partners: 'You might have gotten access formally, but as we all know, that access is something that you negotiate from day to day'. First, the partner makes sure to inform the staff that while Lise had officially got permission to study them, it was now entirely up to each employee how (and whether) they consented to be studied. Second, note how the partner prefaces his reassurance with 'as we all know'. We read this statement as a reminder to everyone present that the consultants in the room have the same status as Lise. They too know all about access negotiation when doing fieldwork. This attempt to even out or potentially reverse the hierarchies between the researcher and those researched was a common thread through both our fieldworks.

Lateral and Para Ethnography

We bring up this example to illustrate the kind of conditions we are grappling with while doing fieldwork in our research about anthropologists and other social scientists, and how these comprise both constraints and possibilities. The kinds of 'counter ethnographic moves' we see here are not new to anthropologists. Douglas Holmes and George Marcus describe 'para sites' as those ethnographic sites in which some sort of 'research expertise' is integral to a particular community and where the anthropologist finds, in one way or the other, 'reflexive subjects whose intellectual practices assume real or figurative interlocutors'. As such, these are field sites where the researcher encounters a 'preexisting ethnographic consciousness or curiosity' (Holmes and Marcus 2008: 82) and what tends to happen in these para ethnographic field sites, according to Holmes and Marcus, is that the anthropological researcher becomes inscribed into interlocutor roles already anticipated and routinized by the people studied (ibid.: 95).

Holmes and Marcus use their relation to a particular informant, a law professor who ended up writing a book about 'ethnography' using the two anthropology professors as informants, to describe the creative potential of the genre of 'para ethnography'. They argue that 'para sites' call for new ethnographic methods and analytical approaches: in conversations with what they call 'epistemic partners', such as a law professor, different perspectives are set in motion that alter the anthropological inquiry. Based on these experiences they define the aim of contemporary ethnography as the endeavour to 'integrate fully our subjects' analytical acumen and insights to define the issues at stake in our projects as well as the means by which we explore them' (ibid.: 86).

This includes, they argue, making certain instances of 'counter ethnography' the objects of research: that is to say, instances such as the conceptual work of informants in which the roles of researcher and subject are reversed (ibid.: 90) – such as the 'Balinese cockfight episode' just described. Using these instances, not only as data but also as a means to explore interlocutor relations and the nature of anthropological fieldwork, can feel risky as it questions the authority of the researcher as the sole analyst. However, as Holmes and Marcus suggest, it is exactly the blurring of these positions that makes up a creative space for exploring relations of collaboration and contestation of parallel modes of inquiry.

Another line of reasoning that we build on here is 'lateral ethnography'. The lateral perspective does not necessarily take its point of departure in 'para sites', but in an attempt to reinvigorate anthropological conceptualization by radically reversing the order of researcher concepts vis-à-vis informants or native concepts. Bill Maurer launched the term 'lateral reasoning' in 2005 as a particular experimental analytical approach in his work on Islamic banking and alternative currencies. For Maurer, the lateral approach is a particular way of 'connecting' across and beyond such divides as informant-researcher-reader. What is achieved is a form that is parallel to that of 'the study object', but which grows from intense enmeshments and mutual influence. As Maurer has it, the lateral 'does not try to "describe cultures" so much as to place the effort to so do in the same frame as that which takes for granted cultural difference and the knowledge apparatuses that it warrants' (2005: 17). More recently, scholars within the field of Science, Technology and Society (STS) Christopher Gad and Casper Bruun Jensen defined 'the lateral' as processes of concept development that 'work on the basis of a mutual modification' of academic concepts and informants' concepts (Gad and Bruun Jensen 2016: 5), whereby a collaborative dynamic of rethinking what it means to do analysis is set in motion (ibid. :10). Other instances of this line of reasoning are found in the work of Martin Holbraad, who suggests 'recursivity' as an anthropological method (Holbraad 2012), in Viveiros de Castro's notion of 'controlled equivocation' (2004), in the proposal of 'infra critique' (Verran 2014; Gad and Winthereik 2016) and indeed in the recent much-debated 'ontological turn' in anthropology (Holbraad and Pedersen 2017).

The overarching aim of these different approaches is to reconfigure the hierarchical relation between the concepts and practices of the researcher and those of the informants, using the reconfiguration as a heuristic tool to consider anthropological analysis in new ways (cf. Riles 1998). Riles asks the question of how to conduct ethnography when the phenomenon studied is in a sense too known (Riles 2000: 20). When there is no 'outside' to the field, the challenge seems to be to find a possible analytical space from within.

Thus, studying parallel communities and practices and using them as productive resistance to rethink anthropological concepts is not new. But what has perhaps not been given sufficient attention in the above literature is the counter aspect of 'counter ethnography'. In the literature on para sites and lateral moves, the relationship between researcher and informant may look awkward and slightly strained but seems to take place in an atmosphere of playfulness, experimentation and partnership. It is often framed as collaboration between two different species of thinkers that may challenge the researcher's position, without jeopardizing it completely. But what happens when we are already enmeshed in similar and competing logics and modes of reasoning even before making the first ethnographic move into the field? When informants not only 'do what we do' (Riles 2000) but occupy almost identical professional identities, academic titles and skill sets?

In order to unpack what 'the counter' aspect does in researcher-interlocutor encounters, we turn to Birgitte's fieldwork. As part of her postdoctoral research in a department of anthropology, Birgitte did close to three months of fieldwork in a Danish newspaper (hereafter referred to as the *Paper*), following the day-to-day work of an anthropologist who was at the time employed as the CEO and Editor-in-Chief. Birgitte thus did fieldwork with a senior anthropologist who not only knew the rules of the ethnographic game, but was also more competent than her in playing by those rules.

The 'Counter' of Counter Ethnography

'Anthropologists all over the place', said the headline of an email that Birgitte's informant, V, had sent out to all her employees the day before she began her fieldwork. V is an anthropologist and was, at the time, the CEO and editor-in-chief of a Danish newspaper; Birgitte is a psychologist whose extensive experience with ethnographic fieldwork within STS and management studies landed her in the very same department of anthropology that V used to work for in her past career as a university researcher. Moreover, the *Paper* had printed the writings of several Danish anthropologists on a regular basis over the years, one of the journalists employed by V was an anthropologist by training, another one was married to an anthropologist. Anthropology and ethnography were indeed 'all over the place'.

A few weeks later, Birgitte walked right into one of those ethnographic moments that tend to occur when 'they do what we do'. As always, it was preceded by a playful joke. V had offered to gift Birgitte a copy of one of her books that she needed for her background research, and Birgitte made a joke about V signing the book for her like some celebrity author and made a remark about gift-giving. To this joke V replies, still smiling: 'Yes, but you have to take care never to become indebted to your informants'. Birgitte responds: 'Of course, but are we not always in debt to each other somehow?' 'Yes, that goes without saying!' says V, and continues: 'But I do mean you have to be careful here. And that that is why I rejected your kind offer to take both of our plates to the dishwasher today after lunch, and that is why you are not doing [any] work for us while you are here'.

V's humorous, yet unsolicited, advice to Birgitte on how to manage her relationships with informants was one of the first, but certainly not the last, instances of V taking on what felt, to Birgitte, like the role of a manager or a supervisor of some sorts, a role that to Birgitte seemed genuinely motivated by V's desire to share her experience with, and love for, anthropology. We bring up this example because it reflects a situation we frequently found ourselves in: being more or less politely corrected by the anthropologists we met in the field. We have encountered interlocutors who scrutinized our research design and questioned its contribution before even accepting to meet with us. We have interviewed anthropologists who displayed impatience, if not overt irritation, with the way we chose to conduct the interview. One interviewee even paused the interview several times, questioning the relevance of the questions, to then finally, after a deep sigh and a long silence, say: 'Okay, last chance!' We have been in casual conversation with interlocutors in the field who suddenly turned the tables on us and said something like: 'You just broke the first rule of fieldwork right there'. As unsettling as these exchanges may seem, and as much as we resisted them, these episodes and our own slightly defensive or even competitive responses to them are instances of valuable analytical material. They teach us something about the normative distinctions that are being made between 'good' and 'bad' fieldwork in a field where there are indeed 'anthropologists all over the place' and therefore no outsider position to refer to when making judgements about the integrity of our own position.

In the above example with V, we do see the order of the 'para site' played out in the way in which she inscribes Birgitte into the pre-existing interlocutor positions already present in the field. Prior to this job, V was employed at a university for many years where she functioned as a researcher, a supervisor for students of anthropology, and an editor and reviewer of academic research. She now also occupies a managerial role along with the editorial one. In addition to this, her interest in Birgitte's independence and accountability closely resembles aspects of the work V does as an editor-in-chief. V's primary task, she says, is to protect the credibility of the *Paper*. In order to do so, she must make sure the integrity of her writers and the independence of their writings is not compromised. The kind of warning she extends to

Birgitte here, not to become indebted, mirrors the one she frequently extended to journalists about not getting entangled in political or commercial interests that could question the accountability of their writing. It is quite easy to interpret the above exchange as V's more or less automatic recruitment of Birgitte into a similar role. In addition, Birgitte's employment at an academic university makes her a representative for free academic research, something V is naturally invested in, given her background in academic anthropology. So far, we can follow the shared experience of the para site described by Holmes and Marcus.

But there is more. First, V's remark can be seen in the context of establishing and forming her relationship to Birgitte as a fieldworker. Like Lise's informants, V is expressing the genuine playfulness of a fellow academic confident enough in the relationship to also turn the table on Birgitte once in a while. In fact, when recalling this episode, V says her intention with the dishwasher remark was to communicate precisely that Birgitte was not her employee to manage or order around, hence there was no need to please her or do her any favours. V's stated intention in making the above remarks was to signal that her relationship to Birgitte as a fieldworker was of another kind than the one V has with employees. As a side effect, one could argue, the conversation about debt and dishwashers thereby also sends a message to Birgitte that she and V have a special relationship outside the existing interlocutor roles of this field site. V momentarily positions herself outside the field alongside the fieldworker. This manoeuvre also precludes future situations in which V would be reduced to mere data by Birgitte.

Second, and this is where the counter aspect of counter ethnography kicks in, there is a subtle and mutual competitiveness to both the Balinese cockfight moment described above and this little exchange with V. Unlike the para site of Holmes and Marcus, two professors in anthropology forming epistemic partnerships with a professor in law, our fieldwork experiences involved engaging in a more precarious power dynamic. The reflexive playfulness of our interlocutors invites us into a territory in which researcher and interlocutor take turns positioning each other in what looks like a subtle pecking order. In addition, the perception Birgitte had of a slightly prescriptive tone from V shaped her relationship to V in a way that made her not just any fellow academic, but one who was understood to be somewhat superior to her, working above her pay grade in several ways.

Birgitte was no stranger to studying fellow academics who feel entitled to be met as thinkers in their own right and take an active part in the research process. But contrary to her previous fieldwork with research managers within nanoscience and synthetic biology, researching anthropologists seemed to add competitiveness to the epistemic partnership in a way that further challenged her academic authority. Birgitte received her draft papers back from her previous interlocutors with track changes rather than comments and was given unsolicited advice by physicists and biologists on how to manage her academic career (Gorm Hansen 2011). But her former interlocutors would never pose as more competent ethnographers, they would not question the quality of her data material or her understanding of the field of research she was contributing to, and they would not come up with an alternative analysis which fully competed with her own. In short, studying physicists and biologists as fellow academics posed less of a threat in that their suggestions could easily be rendered as data rather than as a sobering critique from a more competent academic reviewer. Studying anthropologists was much 'closer to home', hence it involved more risk.

Birgitte's status as a 'non-anthropologist' (the expression alone speaks volumes)[2] studying trained anthropologists ethnographically in their own half of the playing field formed a much less symmetrical relationship where Birgitte had to earn the right to use the methods and theories that were the anthropologist's native language. The subtle pecking order within which this fieldwork took place is quite a far cry from Holmes and Marcus' counter ethnographical writing experiments.

In the case of ReD Associates, the predator-prey game rested upon certain important stakes. One was that the company is a successful business with a solid base of returning clients and with books of their own, describing and branding the consultancy method. Lise's work and publications were thus a potential threat to the consultancy brand and business. This was one of the reasons why Thomas and his colleagues made sure to read and comment on both unfinished and final dissertation chapters. However, it was as important for ReD consultants to keep good relations with and be respected as practising applied anthropologists by the academic anthropological community, not least the Department of Anthropology in Copenhagen (see Pedersen 2018).

Ethnographic moments like these allow us to get a sense of the risk involved in doing academic research in a knowledge economy jungle where the academic scholar is no longer the privileged explorer but simply just another sub-species. Rather than lamenting the loss of our academic privilege to speak authoritatively about a silent empirical world, we prefer to inquire further into what kind of pecking order we are dealing with here, and what analytical resources it may hold.

Predator/Prey Relationships

How do we think of these instances of counter ethnography where it is not just our fieldwork options and analysis that are on the line but also our academic authority? How do we work productively with that sense of being beaten in our own game?

A logical response would be to 'do what they do'; to pull the material back into our own half of the playing field; to make sure we really do win forever by getting the final word. We can both testify to having felt this slightly defensive knee-jerk reaction. Reasserting our right to analyse as we see fit seems to be both a legitimate and sensible response for two university researchers, one we both feel completely entitled to move forward with in the interest of independent academic research.

This 'game' of getting the final word is intrinsic to science itself. Philosopher of science Isabelle Stengers has characterized this as the tendency for scientific practices to engage in what she calls a predator/prey relationship: 'Practices that maintain a stronger definition of objectivity will freely define others as potential prey; and all sciences will define as prey whatever is not scientific' (Stengers 2011: 60).

According to Stengers, predator/prey relations are unilateral: one species captures and consumes the other and the story ends there, with no further entanglements. The analytical predator works by imposing categories on the object of study which 'do not concern it' and thus gets to address the object of research as a 'silent empirical world' (2011: 57). The prey does not need to agree to, understand or even relate to the terms by which it is made into an empirical example of a more general phenomenon. Playing this game is tempting here. Our interlocutors may be academic scholars like us, but we are the ones representing the university and the right to publish using this material is solely ours. The academic predator/prey game is a hierarchical game in which there is only one winner and that winner is always an academic predator. One relationship in Lise's fieldwork aptly illustrates this dynamic.

Thomas is an anthropologist by background, educated at the Department of Anthropology at the University of Copenhagen. His master's thesis about 'innovation' was based on studies of the consultancy, ReD Associates, when he was employed in the company as a student assistant. Some six to seven years later, he became a partner in the consultancy, which has grown considerably, both in size and reputation, since its founding in 2005. Today it is one of the most influential consultancies using anthropological methods and approaches as part of their services.

Thomas was also one of Lise's key informants during fieldwork in the consultancy in 2013, and the relationship was peculiar. Lise and Thomas had worked together several times prior to the fieldwork, when she worked in the consultancy. Back then, they had many discussions about anthropology, and the greater purpose of anthropological knowledge in society. During the fieldwork, these discussions were taken up again, only now the relationship had changed: Lise was there to study the consultants and their work practices, and it quickly became clear that Thomas, with his background in anthropology and his position as partner, was going to become a key figure in her research: he was influential both inside the consultancy and a public figure outside as well as an 'epistemic partner' in different business and research communities, including academic anthropology departments.

Over time, Lise and Thomas developed a routine of meeting every Monday right after the joint Monday morning meeting, to update each other. Thomas would tell her about his plans for the week and ideas for future projects and provide the status of current projects and Lise would deliver ethnographic observations about the consultants and their work. Interestingly, no matter what point the conversations took off from, they almost always ended up as a discussion about 'academic anthropology' versus the consultants' version of anthropology.

For one of these conversations, Lise had prepared a list of topics that she wanted to present to Thomas. She began by saying that the topics were emerging insights stemming from a bunch of interviews and some general observations. Thomas quickly responded: 'I'm so bad at just listening to long stories without knowing what it is about. Could you please provide some sort of table of contents [*indholdsfortegnelse*], like five points or ten things'. Lise answered that she had 'four points', in the form of what looked like schisms between seemingly opposed modes of reasoning amongst the consultants whom she had identified in her data. One such split was between the consultants' striving for building what they call a 'storyline' on the one hand and their fondness of dramatic and affective storytelling in client presentations on the other. Another theme was around the tight structure of the consultancy method, neatly divided into project phases, versus the consultants' frequent use of the office kitchen for what was often referred to as 'jamming sessions': to Lise these sessions looked like fun and slightly forbidden conversational spaces outside the formally defined rules of how ideas are supposed to develop in this company.

Conveying the insights to Thomas in the pristine meeting room, situated in one of Copenhagen's most expensive neighbourhoods, made what Lise had at home found to be fairly confined points seem unclear and vague. In the company of Thomas, her insights appeared foggy and her style of explanation felt slow and hesitant, if not clumsy. A sense of defeat arose in her as she was presenting, and it was deepened when Thomas started disproving her points one by one. He explained to her how these different approaches in the consultancy made complete sense and should by no means be analysed as contrasts. However, Thomas did find the schism between 'storyline' and 'storytelling' useful and asked Lise to elaborate on this so that the consultants could gain clarity about what he saw as a difference between the 'analytical' part of the consultancy method and the 'communications' part. Understanding this difference, he said, 'could be very helpful for us'.

What happened here? It seems that Thomas assumes the role of the academic predator by moving the ideas and points proposed by Lise over onto his own half of the playing field where he restates them in 'consulting terms' rather than academic terms. Thomas was generally frustrated with what he saw as inaction and lack of participation in public debate among academic anthropologists. He found anthropology to be a 'navel-gazing' occupation that was obsessed with 'long stories' but made little impact in the world and he often found ways to remind Lise that the consulting approach was a 'useful' and 'helpful' discipline with 'real impact' in the world, unlike academic anthropology. As one can perhaps imagine, these discussions with Thomas could go on for a while. Lise found them both interesting and provocative and she often, to her regret, ended up representing academic anthropology as a refined whole. The conversations reproduced again and again a clear-cut division between anthropology and consultancy as different and competing approaches.

During fieldwork in the consultancy, Thomas continuously tried to identify points of action from what he took to be Lise's rather fuzzy ideas. How could her research become a tool that the consultants could use to 'get things right', just like the consultants work to get people right (Madsbjerg and Rasmussen 2014)[3] and 'close gaps' between companies and customers, as they often put it? Not surprisingly perhaps, Lise's stay at the consultancy as well as her writing did not produce explanations of this kind. Rather, her ethnographic approach became part of an unstable relational dynamic. She was inscribed into a different relational form already rehearsed and routinized in ReD

Associates, namely the consultant-client relation: a relationship that is simultaneously competitive and seductive. For in consultant-client relationships, the client is both challenged as a counterpart and seduced as a collaborator. This was exactly what happened in her conversations with Thomas: contesting the ideas and insights that Lise presented was usually followed by a seductive redefining of the premises and terms of those insights as a way of impelling the researcher onto the interlocutor's part of the playing field, as a way of consuming the other as prey.

Our fieldwork experiences speak to pecking orders and competitive dynamics that neither we nor our informants are prepared for or desire. When counter ethnography gets more competitive, things feel a lot less playful and the creative potential of 'studying those who study us' can easily be flatlined in a defensive freeze response.

Our informants had their own voice, one that could not just reframe our ideas but potentially also question our academic accountability. They were the kind of professionals who would get book contracts of their own faster than we can find our next job. Thomas sat on the advisory board of the very department where Lise was employed while she was doing fieldwork with him. V has more readers than any of us will ever dream of and she is extremely well connected, not just in the world of the Danish press and national television: her professional and personal network extends far into publishing houses and back into academic departments. Our interlocutors simply own the part of the jungle where we do fieldwork as well as parts of the territory within which we attempt to pursue our careers. Their veto power towards us extended much further than other interlocutors we have worked with whose worst-case scenario would be to withdraw from their roles of study-objects or refuse to work as our gate-keepers. Perhaps this is part of the reason why our informants played with open cards, challenged our approach and findings and gave us access in the first place to observe them in their work. They could afford the risk.

V made a point about engaging with Birgitte as a colleague and maintained a respectful mode of engagement during the fieldwork itself. And later in the process, when she responded to Birgitte's writing, V engaged playfully in long email exchanges with Birgitte where she offered even more perspectives, reflections, reinterpretations and suggestions for how she could further make sense of the material. When other field participants asked V about Birgitte's close presence in meetings and hallways and lunch breaks, she would jokingly give the same response: 'Never underestimate the power of human vanity!' This joke effectively moved the focus of attention away from Birgitte as a possible threat (to the participants in the meeting or to V herself). To Birgitte, this remark seemed to send a clear signal that V had nothing to hide and, more importantly, nothing to lose in this encounter. Thomas, for his part, showed up with two other partners and a senior manager from the consultancy at Lise's PhD defence, in suits and sunglasses, carrying the largest present in the room: a gigantic bottle of champagne. Their extremely well-dressed presence in the reception was topped up with an eloquent speech, declaring that the academic department and the consultancy 'look in the same direction' and share the same vision of being at the forefront of the discipline of anthropology. As a response to some of the discussions during the defence concerning the question of critique, Thomas thanked Lise for the very interesting collaboration and underscored that Lise had in no way been uncritical of the consultants, but that she had given them lots of material to think about. The ease with which these statements were delivered by our interlocutors speaks to our sense of the ease with which they claimed their space significantly higher in the pecking order at every stage of our research. In other words, they were not only worthy opponents, but also academic predators to be reckoned with.

It seems these common fieldwork experiences of ours have an interesting double bind to them: on the one hand, our interlocutors were genuinely interested in the research process and wanted to play along with this role with the stated intention that they might learn something from us. On the other hand, their 'counter moves' show how, once the fieldwork got going and quite far into our writing process, they insisted on us learning from them, not just when it came to what happened in their work but also when it came to anthropological theory and the art of doing good fieldwork. And we did exactly the same. The elegance and conviction with which we each inscribed each other into existing relational repertoires, the subtle competitiveness that arose on both sides (not least our own!), tells us that we are not alone in feeling entitled to be met as thinkers with analytical repertoires of our own. If there is a pecking order here, it revolves around who gets to do the final analysis.

We could have played this game with our interlocutors: continued to take turns in framing each other as data. We could keep writing 'You win. Forever', forever. We could enter into an analytical staring contest. This would have involved insisting on our right to be social science predators who debunk the underlying mechanisms that we claim are behind the actions and decisions of our powerful interlocutors. All we would need to do is stop talking to them and go home. We could reserve the right to gain some critical distance by moving the game from field site to desk site. We could reframe our informants' practices with big concepts like 'late capitalism', 'neoliberalism', 'managerialism' or other terms by which we are trained to deconstruct the logics we would claim that our informants subscribe to. We could subsume the protests of our informants under some conceptual order that we as university scholars feel entitled to instantiate. We could carry off our material to our own corner of the woods where we would consume it alone, protected by the thick walls of whatever is left of the academic university. In the company of like-minded colleagues who would back up our privilege to speak authoritatively about our field participants, we would peacefully lick our wounds, digest our material and finish off our papers. We wanted to. We tried. Instead, something like this happened.

The Barth Situation

As it is probably clear by now, V was not the kind of interlocutor who readily accepted being preyed upon. She did not play the role of mute, passive data material very well. As one of her employees put it, V was a 'typical anthropologist' in that she never entered fully into the dramas played out on the scene in the organization, and instead took a position akin to a 'Greek god' gazing down from up high, occasionally descending to deliver a nuanced, dispassionate and multi-faceted analysis, from every angle of the situation. As productive as this seemed to be for V's managerial practice, it posed a challenge to Birgitte as a fieldworker. Whatever concepts or frameworks Birgitte attempted to wheel out as 'deus ex machina' when writing about her, V would playfully up the game and suggest more or better ways of reframing the material.

As a field site, the *Paper* was itself a place where desk site and field site quickly merged into an impenetrable swamp. During fieldwork, as well as into the writing process, the conceptual and the empirical seemed to be in continuous variation in this field site. The right to gain distance and think conceptually from a place above it all had to be earned in free competition, not just with the anthropologists working there but also with journalists who did their own academic writing, and even with the receptionist, who knew her French philosophers and management theory. In the phase of writing up this research, the right to define what constitutes a good analysis was not based on solid academic criteria available only to the researcher and her future reviewers, but rather had to be conquered in the face of an ever widening pack of academics who had no problem defining the fieldworker as their 'less scientific' prey.

Around a month into her fieldwork, Birgitte arrived in the office carrying a brand new copy of *Big Men & Great Men*. She was preparing a talk for a seminar back at her university department. The invitation was to share news from the field and present some rudimentary material. Her working title was 'From the Anthropology of Leadership to the Leadership of Anthropologists'. As Birgitte was conducting a single person ethnography with someone virtually impossible to anonymize in a Danish context, she felt it would be ethically appropriate to openly discuss the material with V before presenting it to her old colleagues back at the department. Allowing V to have a say in how she was represented – giving voice to her native perspective, so to speak – seemed like the right thing to do, given the trust V had displayed in giving Birgitte complete access to observe almost every part of her working day.

Upon discovering that Birgitte was reading a classic in the anthropology of leadership, V's whole face lit up. Comparing a corporate media company in Denmark to *Big Men & Great Men* was clearly a source of amusement to her. 'Maybe the exotic isn't that exotic after all', she said. Over the next two weeks, Birgitte and V engaged in several conversations about Birgitte's upcoming presentation. It seemed V just could not help suggesting more anthropological references. Birgitte gladly took this opportunity to get to know her informant's 'native concepts' so she decided to have a look at the books that V felt most passionate about. Her idea was to take her seriously as a fellow compulsive thinker.

'It may be an idea for you to look at Bourdieu, especially *L'Algérie* or maybe Barth's book on political leadership among the Swat Pathans', was V's first response. As Birgitte read up on the Swat Pathans, she would debate with V whether she was more similar to Barth's chiefs or whether she was in fact more a saint. V voted jokingly for saint at first, but in the end agreed to being represented as a chief sitting at one end of her oval editorial meeting table like it was a Pathan 'men's house'. It clearly amused her to hear the description of how giving champagne toasts at office celebrations, serving coffee and croissants at editorial meetings and creating a prestigious and high quality journalistic working environment was a necessary strategy for her to keep her 'men' from leaving the *Paper* to pursue their careers in competing media companies. V had several other takes on the material and the discussions were both lively and cheerful.

V's amusement and willingness to engage in making sense of the material was, however, not at all shared by Birgitte's anthropologist-colleagues back at the university. Birgitte had, perhaps naively, expected her colleagues in anthropology to approve of her somewhat participatory design and her commitment to learning about her interlocutor's native concepts. She had taken great care to represent V's everyday practice in native, that is anthropological, terms rather than coding them with concepts imported from STS or critical management studies, her own disciplinary corner of the woods. But when presented with the material at the annual seminar, her anthropologist-colleagues had different appetites. Instead of taking apart and co-digesting her rather raw data material, they sank their teeth into Birgitte's relationship with V in a way that directly questioned her academic accountability.

'I'm not sure whether this is her analysis or yours', a colleague remarked. Birgitte's first response was defensive, assuring her colleague that this was indeed her own analysis. But inside, she was not so sure. Was this even an analysis at all? The status of her so-called 'paper' was not clear. 'I get the feeling that you have just written her story – about how terribly hard it is for your informant to have all the power and privileges she enjoys in her very secure top management job', Birgitte's colleague continued. This invoked something that can best be described as a cheer in the room, faces turning to the colleague and heads nodding in agreement. 'There is a real problem with her taking over your analysis like that', the colleague continued, 'but maybe that's just the deal when you work like this with your informants or your . . . friends or whatever you call them'.

At the time, Birgitte took this comment as an indication that the 'real' anthropologists in her department somehow felt that she and V had become too close or friendly with one another. Quite a few responses implied that she was not critical enough towards V. The real problem was, of course, that Birgitte's paper had only shown how V saw herself but had yet to show how Birgitte as the ethnographic researcher saw V. This separation was, however, almost impossible to tease out, given the conceptual/empirical continuum inherent to this particular field.

This meant that in the eyes of the academic anthropologists who were her colleagues, Birgitte had completely failed to show that she was willing to make the cut and drag her material out of V's half of the playing field and into her own. In other words, she failed to successfully pose as an academic predator who brought some meat to the table. A strangely familiar sense of defeat spread through Birgitte's body as the seminar continued. It took quite a while to work out that her colleagues had essentially given her the same kind of response that she had by now got used to dealing with from her anthropologist-interlocutors; that even though the seminar took place at the university and she was officially not doing fieldwork, this was not a desk site. It was yet another field site. She had not left the field to go back home and digest her prey, she had taken yet another step into the conceptual/empirical swamp where new packs of anthropological predators awaited at every turn!

Coming back to V on Monday morning after the seminar, Birgitte shared with V her surprise over this request for more critical bite in her analysis. Birgitte's impression was that ethnographic fieldwork was a method used to ensure that she really understood her informants on their own terms, gave them a voice of their own in her analysis and took care to do justice to their native language and concepts. V nodded thoughtfully on hearing the reflections about giving voice to informants. 'Yes', she said, 'in your particular case it seems you are damned if you do, and you are damned if you don't'.

V here spells out the general moral dilemma we encounter when we find ourselves in a field where distinctions such as 'your analysis' and 'my analysis' merge but where we nevertheless move on to produce anthropological accounts. Let us look at the different options we tried out.

We are dammed if we do: as just described in the 'Barth situation', one challenge and critique we encountered in producing our ethnographic narratives that we often met was our lack of critical distance and the danger of us 'going native'. This is, of course, a well-known critique and pitfall, but it seems that for our anthropologist-colleagues back at the university, the risk of going native while 'studying up' was a lot more controversial. This resulted in our academic authority being put on the line in a fundamental way when we attempted to give voice to our powerful, privileged interlocutors in the same way we would, had they been, say, victims of structural oppression, poverty, war or ruination. It seems that in order to counter this critique and regain our academic privileges, we would need to reduce people like Thomas and V to mute ethnographic material that remains dead while we and our academic colleagues chew them through.

We are equally dammed if we don't: in trying to meet precisely the above critique, we have also received the opposite response, however: that our representations were unnecessarily critical, veering towards being ethnocentric and judgmental, that we did not take our interlocutors' version of anthropology seriously. Thus, if we present an analysis of our interlocutor's moral work solely in our own terms while completely ignoring their right to be met as thinkers just like us, our analysis will be found wanting on the exact same value scale, the scale in which we can claim to have spoken for the concrete, lived life experience of real human beings we met in the field. Describing the people we study without including their say on the matter would be to portray them with utter disregard for who they are and how they understand themselves. This would not have gone down well with either those anthropologists who are our interlocutors or those who are our colleagues (and we are frankly a little more afraid of the former group than the latter).

It seems the kind of para ethnography we have been involved in collapses distinctions such as studying up or down and reconfigures them as lateral, sideways trajectories where normative distinctions between good and bad anthropology are used as collateral rather than as founding principles and guidelines. We are left with a strange feeling of self-reference. It is no surprise then that the third and final mode of response to our accounts has been that they were overly self-reflexive and that the original study object seemed disturbingly out of focus. Lise once received the comment on one of her draft papers that her analysis was an incidence of a particular style of ethnography titled 'Hocus pocus, me in focus'! (We plead guilty as charged.)

Where do we go from here? The challenge seems to be to persuade two mutually exclusive audiences. Our field includes anthropologists both inside and outside the university who happen to position each other very differently in the moral economy of anthropology. How to find moral ground in a field that claims and engulfs all outside positions and normative distinctions as its own?

Normativity from Within: Ecological Relationships

One probably doesn't have to be a climate scientist to have realized by now that the future of academic research is likely to offer us further entanglements of this kind where the academic privilege of doing the final analysis can easily be revoked or eaten up by competing knowledge producers. The future of fieldwork is likely to require training in how to manage unstable epistemic partnerships and think through para sites. As fieldworkers we might as well get used to including competitive attempts at counter ethnography as part of our material.

The question we want to ask now is: how to use these uncomfortable and risky dynamics productively in our research? What constitutes a good researcher position in this type of fieldwork where the researcher is not the strongest predator? It seems that the challenge posed to us here is to learn the art of simultaneously thinking with and against the ideas of our informants. If the para site really is to become a collaborative space for creative writing processes, we first have to drop the idea that collaboration necessarily depends on equality, mutual interest or common ground. In fact, as we have shown, para sites and their counter ethnographic moments are also expressions of diverging interests rather than convergent agendas, of antagonism rather than harmony, of pushback, instability, power asymmetry and risk. Perhaps the time where we could retreat to an isolated desk site protected from stakeholder interests has passed and we now need to take up the challenge posed by Riles and find the analytical space 'from within' in relation to epistemic partners who have strong agendas and the power to push them through. As our field sites extend into a larger whole that includes not just our interlocutors but also our colleagues (and soon, we suspect, our reviewers too), there is clearly no separate position we can take as researchers, no identity by which we can claim to be saying something that is more scientific or academically valid than the multiple actors who make up our immanent field. But perhaps we can work with this dynamic in a way that makes us capable of producing accounts that are different from the ones both we and our interlocutors could have written before we met?

Perhaps it makes sense then that Stengers' alternative to the rather unproductive predator/prey relationship is to think of modern science as an 'ecology of practices' (Stengers 2005). If we were to zoom out and see our researcher position as part of, rather than separate from, a larger ecology, we might be able to abandon 'all temptation to conceive of nature as submissive, manipulable, assimilable to some "raw material" on which we would be free to impose whatever organization we choose' (Stengers 2010: 34). In Stengers' normative philosophy, this would hold true for the relationship between physicists and neutrinos as well as between ethnographers and their interlocutors.

If we are to come up with a normative criterion for distinguishing between good and bad ethnographer positions or good and bad para site anthropology, we would suggest that we become more willing to run the risk of analysing our interlocutors in their habitat as the living, competing academic predators they are. As there is obviously no going home from this type of field, we find inspiration in Stengers' ecological approach to thinking normatively about science, and specifically about the roles we occupy as researchers versus research objects. Ecosystems are good concepts for thinking about a field which has no outside. If we zoom out to see the relationship with our interlocutors as part of a complex ecology from which there is no external, normative position to refer to when defining 'good ethnography', we discover that the roles of each species in this ecology is not defined in isolation. In ecologies there are no single, unilateral relationships: all relations are external to their terms. Stengers writes about the concept of ecology: 'The populations whose modes of entangled coexistence it describes are not fully defined by the respective roles they play in that entanglement, in such a way that we could deduce the identity of each on the basis of its role. This role is by definition "metastable"' (Stengers 2010: 34).

If we resist the knee-jerk predatory reaction to 'make the cut' with our interlocutors when being corrected in our craft, when being challenged in our mode of analysis and when being preyed upon by several competing sub-species of anthropologists, we might, according to Stengers, enter into a more transformative relationship with all of them as part of the same ecology. But it would require that we refrain from pretending that we can take away their power to contest our academic authority by reducing them to data that passively awaits our analytical inscription. Of course, anthropologists are normally quite comfortable with this kind of relationship to interlocutors. In many ways, the essence of anthropology as a craft is to learn by way of participation and become able to think in terms other than one's own. As Bruce Kapferer asserts, anthropology is a discipline that has the potential to:

> challenge accepted knowledge (scientific or otherwise) by virtue of going outside, becoming external to, the domains of knowledge from which they travelled. This stress in anthropology of becoming external is a distinction of the discipline whereby anthropologists are enabled to enter within the dynamics of coming to know. Being in the situation of a neophyte, who must learn from the position of no knowledge or a dynamic of 'unknowing' (see Mimica 2010), is the vital feature of anthropological work. (Kapferer 2018: 28)

Here Kapferer bases his normative assessment of the contribution of anthropology as a discipline on the importance of 'becoming external' to one's own mode of reasoning in order to challenge accepted knowledge. However, we might challenge Kapferer's ideas about what constitutes the 'external' for anthropology today. Perhaps anthropologists need not travel very far to find their most radical 'other'? We would argue that 'becoming external' is perhaps even more likely when we subject ourselves to the risk of studying precisely the kinds of people we would normally prey upon as the target of our external critique. Studying them in a way that fully retains their ability to contest and compete with our analysis rather than reducing them to 'dead empirical meat' for our own mode of thinking could paradoxically be seen as today's way of becoming external. Perhaps the kinds of people who wear suits and shiny shoes for work, dabble in excel sheets and make big decisions based on thin descriptions are by now so external to academic anthropology that they can pose the necessary challenge to accepted forms of anthropological knowledge. People who are not intimidated by our academic authority, and who have no need for us to represent them as they fully embody their own academic voices, could pose a real challenge to us as academic anthropologists and have the potential to invite us into a new and slightly more risky dynamic of 'unknowing'. Perhaps, back 'home' could be a good site for conversing with the kinds of interlocutors who are strong enough, and insistent enough, to challenge us to rethink the moral distinctions that we had naturalized in our habitual notions of good versus bad anthropology. The alternative seems to be a futile attempt to make them our prey which, as we have seen, keeps us bound within competitive loops reiterating our respective positions and preventing us from any further analytical progression. According to the normative philosophy of Stengers, the predator/prey loop would be 'bad science' (in other words, bad anthropology) in that it takes no real risk and invites no new learning about the other since it excludes what is most interesting about them: their ability to compete with us. Good anthropology, then, could be understood, in Stengers' terms, as characterized by restraint: to refrain from debunking, to resist the temptation to write behind the backs of the people we study no matter how powerful and privileged they seem to us, to engage with them – head on – as thinkers in their own right, no matter how much we disagree with what they think. Good anthropology, then, could be the nurturing of relationships where we can disagree 'in the presence' of the other, consider both sides part of the same ecology of practice and learn to live together in a relationship of divergence and danger.

Of course, any anthropologist can testify to being corrected by the people they study; this is intrinsic to learning about them. But when we find ourselves enmeshed in a field with no outside, where the counter ethnographic competition continues well into the writing process and blurs distinctions between 'our' and 'their' analysis, the temptation to retreat, make the cut and become the predator of ethnographic 'dead meat' is much greater. Our fieldwork is not just a para site in the sense that 'they do what we do'; it is disturbingly counter-ethnographical in the sense that 'they do it better' or at least they have the skills, the means and the network to persuade others to agree with them. This, we speculate, may be the most valuable challenge of the para site, one that we might as well get familiar with as the future of fieldwork in 'our own societies' is likely to require us to, increasingly, navigate more of these kinds of relationships.

Having an ecological relationship with our interlocutors would mean refraining from making that final cut predatory. It would mean accepting that neither of us can be fully defined by our respective functions (thinker versus practitioner), and that we will never really win forever. Rather than retreating to a defensive competition for the ultimate predator position, we suggest that a good anthropology of the para site would need us to think of the researcher/interlocutor relationship as a process of what Stengers calls 'reciprocal capture': 'We can speak of reciprocal capture when a dual process of identity construction is produced; regardless of the manner, and usually in ways that are completely different, identities that coinvent each other each integrate a reference to the other for their own benefit' (Stengers 2010: 36).

By seeing our researcher position as defined in such a process of reciprocal capture, we see how each party in the researcher/interlocutor relationship integrates a reference to the other, in that they take the other's presence, behaviour and habits into account. As different subspecies we each exist with our own autonomous goals and agendas but, at the same time, we depend on each other's presence in the ecosystem. Reciprocal capture, like a symbiotic relationship, is not dependent on common ground, mutual interest or agreement between the two species. Rather, it is contingent on each part integrating a reference to the other in the same way so that the prey become sensitive to the particular movement of its most threatening predators and the predator evolves to adapt to the precise anatomy and behaviours of their prey.

Contrary to the notion of collaboration that we now see promoted as a moral concept for thinking about 'good anthropology' and 'good' researcher/interlocutor relationships (Matsutake Worlds Research Group 2009; Marcus 2013), 'reciprocal capture' requires no common goal, no mutual interest and no agreement between the two parties. Their 'metastable' roles in a broader ecology take the other into account and afford a common habitat in which both species can evolve and co-exist even if they are not working towards a common goal.

An apt empirical example of this approach to 'reciprocal capture' can be found in David Mosse's call for an 'ethnography of objections' (Mosse 2006). Mosse argues that in our unwillingness to expose ourselves to interlocutors' objections, anthropology can become 'anti-social'. Writing breaks relations and establishes new kinds of boundaries. This, Mosse argues, is not only an ethical issue for the anthropologist, but also an epistemological one (ibid.: 937). Representing others in a text by connecting and disconnecting relationships is what anthropologists do (cf. Strathern 2004). However, Mosse suggests, objections to our ethnographic representations should be welcomed rather than feared or glossed over. In this sense, the objections, competitiveness and corrections that we both experienced with our interlocutors arise from their unravelling of our ethnographic representations and unpacking of our anthropological styles of evidence 'back into the relationships with them' (ibid.: 951). Objections from informants are indeed important mirror images of our own disciplinary assumptions, conventions and representational forms.

Now, is this not just the classic problem of representation, albeit here in an intensely accelerated version? It is. But our suggestion is that we tackle objections and competition as part of a scientific ecology of practices that requires us to think in the presence of those we study by becoming part of their habitat – not just while we do fieldwork but also as we publish our accounts, as Mosse suggests; not just when 'they' live in different ecologies but also when they hunt the same territories that we do and are bigger predators than we are. We would have to generate concepts that are part of – and therefore restrained by – the intimate interconnectedness of our informants' ecology (Despret 2005; Pedersen 2018). Stengers points out that an ecology of practice demands a mode of analysis where the object of study is rendered active. This sounds like classic anthropology, we know. What Stengers' normativity is asking of us now is to extend this process to every stage of the research process and to treat all interlocutors symmetrically, even if the moral economy of anthropology would consider them the 'radical other' of good anthropology (see Chapter 2). Given the impending risk of the 'death of the public university' (Wright and Shore 2017), we may need to keep our enemies closer than our friends, to integrate a reference to them under our own skin, to enter into a metastable and mutual identity construction with them in order to survive as academic researchers but also to produce a responsible and analytically productive anthropology of the para site.

Inspired by the notion of ecology and reciprocal capture, we would like to suggest that it is precisely 'the counter' of counter ethnography that makes these sites so fertile for our thinking. Collaboration based on common ground and mutual interest is nice if you want to work towards a solution to a problem that is already known and defined identically by both terms in the relationship, but common ground and agreement are perhaps not so fertile when it comes to setting a new problem. Like any good medicine, the para site can be simultaneously good and bad, productive or destructive.[4] If the future of anthropological fieldwork involves this kind of ambiguity, we might as well practise our navigation skills for this type of territory.

Whereas epistemic partnerships seem to assume that we and our interlocutors need to find common ground and shared agendas before we can enter into a process of collaboration and co-creation, we would propose that the creative evolution of our respective writings arises from the divergences, the pushbacks, the situations in which we are forced to integrate a reference to each other. Our epistemic partners taught us precisely this by affording us no outsider position we could retreat into. We found it helpful in our analysis to nurture these zones of 'the counter', to expose ourselves more to the restraints and pushbacks. In this sense, our so-called collaboration with our interlocutors depended on a certain measure of divergence in order for us to challenge each other into thinking differently from how we would have seen things had we made the cut and written our own stories about the working lives of our anthropologist-interlocutors without post-fieldwork interaction. Thinking together, then, is not necessarily thinking in unison. Rather, contestation of and constraints on our thinking are the form that productive collaboration takes.

Conclusion

In this chapter we set out to think about our relationships to interlocutors in a field where there was no going home and hence no outside academic normativity to refer to. What kind of moral position do we take in this kind of field? Stengers, like Mosse, suggests that it would be wrong of us to drag off our material and prey upon our informants behind their backs while they lay dead on our desk with no possibility to contest our analysis, resist our reframing and compete for analytical privileges. It would also be wrong of us to efface our own objections in order to simply hold the microphone for other anthropologists, be they interlocutors or colleagues. We would argue that neither option makes for a good analysis, as it would leave our thinking unrestrained by the relationships we build in the field and which we continuously have to go back to nurture. Instead, we suggest that we get as committed as we can to being entangled and engaged in reciprocal capture, that we make it as difficult as possible for ourselves before we temporarily make that cut and publish our analysis. In our case, this would mean staying with the awkward relationships we develop with our informants, doing the hard work of listening carefully to those we study while at the same time resisting their analysis full force, so that perhaps we can produce something neither of us had thought of before.

Our argument is that we need to nurture 'the counter' of the para and lateral ethnographic sites, not only to squeeze out the most creative acumen of those relations in order to produce ever more experimental ethnographic accounts that connect parallel modes of reasoning in new ways, as lateral approaches to ethnography has already effectively demonstrated, but as a way of navigating these relations in an ethically responsible manner. When considering field sites not only as sites that we travel out to, but as ecologies that we are already part of, the riskiness for us and for our interlocuters increases. There is no exit, because there was never really an entrance. Studying anthropologists at work might well be the last frontier of the genre of para ethnography: can we possibly get any closer to 'home'? But while it may be an exaggerated and somewhat myopic exercise of anthropologists gone wild in navel-gazing, it may at the same time tell us something on a more general scale about doing fieldwork in the midst of our own societies. As an analytical-cum-ethical attitude or compass, we suggest that more powerful and competitive informants' resistance and objections to our endeavours be welcomed: before, during and after fieldwork. Collaboration is not necessarily dependent on establishing common ground. The analytical spark can be lit by the friction we find in mutual competitiveness and unstable power dynamics, and we suggest that contestation is the very form that collaboration takes in this type of environment. Therefore, we welcome their unpacking of our thoughts and ideas back into relations with us and we call for integrating objections as 'capture' in our ongoing thinking about those who do like we do.

Birgitte Gorm Hansen is an independent consultant and researcher. She is trained as a psychologist from the University of Copenhagen and received her PhD in science studies and management from Copenhagen Business School in 2011. Her postdoctoral research on anthropologists working in leadership positions formed one of the four sub-studies conducted in the Department of Anthropology at the University of Copenhagen.

Lise Røjskjær Pedersen is Assistant Professor at the IT University of Copenhagen. Her PhD in anthropology focused on the instrumentalization and aestheticization of ethnographic and anthropological knowledge in a strategy and innovation consultancy. Her most recent work centres on the production and performance of data and digitalization in the public sector.

NOTES

We wish to thank all our interlocutors for their contributions to this chapter, for engaging rigorously with our thinking and writing through the years. We would also like to thank our colleagues from the Technologies in Practice Research Group at the IT University in Copenhagen as well as from the Department of Anthropology, Copenhagen University for commenting on earlier drafts of this chapter and allowing us to incorporate some of these comments as part of the presented material.

1. L.R. Pedersen conducted eight months of fieldwork for her PhD in the consultancy ReD Associates in 2013. The focus of the study was the company's different methods, work processes and practices of 'applied business anthropology', a sub-discipline that the consultants saw themselves as the founders of. The PhD dissertation is a historical as well as ethnographic description of the way in which the consultants produce ethnography-based innovation strategies for clients by systematically applying a series of aesthetic forms (see L.R. Pedersen 2018). The fieldwork was primarily conducted at the company's office in Copenhagen but included trips to New York (the company's other main office), Miami and London, where the company also operates. Prior to the fieldwork L.R. Pedersen worked in the consultancy for a period of almost two years. See Chapter 3 for more information about Gorm Hansen's fieldwork.

2. We encountered the expression 'non-anthropologist' frequently while working with academic anthropologists. It featured mostly as a label by which to identify academics from 'other' disciplines than that of anthropology. We found it in seminars, in conferences, in social gatherings where bigger groups of anthropologists meet and talk about their work and even in the curriculum given to students of anthropology. The use of the expression seems to revolve around a continuous effort to flesh out the boundaries of the discipline by contrasting it with a generalized 'other' and was by no means used with the conscious intent to render all other academic disciplines insignificant or irrelevant. It is worth noting that the anthropologists who used this expression the least were those with whom we did our fieldwork. We suspect this was due to the fact that our interlocutors, unlike our colleagues, were often the only or one of very few trained anthropologists in their workplace and hence had more experience with disciplinary diversity in their work.

3. Two of the founding partners published a book in 2014, *The Moment of Clarity*, in which they explain their approach to solving business problems. The first part of the book, entitled 'Getting people wrong', criticizes conventional consultancy and design approaches to business strategy whereas the second part, 'Getting people right', describes their own method based in the humanities,

an approach that gets people right because it starts with understanding people, the book claims.

4. In this sense, our use of counter ethnography is inspired by Stengers' work with the concept of the *pharmakon*: 'a drug whose effect can mutate into its opposite dependent on the dose, circumstance and context' (Stengers 2010: 29).

REFERENCES

Despret, V. 2005. 'Sheep Do Have Opinions', in B. Latour and P. Weibel (eds), *Making Things Public: Atmospheres of Democracy*. Cambridge, MA: MIT Press; Karlsruhe: ZKM, Center for Art and Media, pp. 360–68.

Gad, Christopher and Casper Bruun Jensen. 2016. 'Lateral Concepts', *Engaging Science, Technology, and Society* 2: 3–12.

Gad, Christopher and Brit Ross Winthereik. 2016. 'Infrakritik og Proximering: Om at finde den rette afstand', *Kultur og Klasse* 44(122): 341–56.

Gorm Hansen, B. 2011: 'Adapting in the Knowledge Economy: Lateral Strategies for Scientists and Those Who Study Them', PhD Thesis. Samfundslitteratur, Copenhagen.

———. 2017. 'Science/Industry Collaboration: Bugs, Project Barons and Managing Symbiosis', in S. Wright and C. Shore (eds), *Death of the Public University? Uncertain Futures For Higher Education in the Knowledge Economy*. Oxford and New York: Berghahn Books, pp. 117–37.

Holbraad, Martin. 2012. *Truth in Motion: The Recursive Anthropology of Cuban Divination*. Chicago and London: University of Chicago Press.

Holbraad, Martin and Morten Axel Pedersen. 2017. *The Ontological Turn: An Anthropological Exposition*. Cambridge: Cambridge University Press.

Holmes, Douglas and George Marcus. 2008. 'Collaboration Today and the Re-Imagination of the Classic Scene of Fieldwork Encounter', *Collaborative Anthropologies* 1: 81–101.

Horst, M. 2003. 'Controversy and Collectivity: Articulations of Social and Natural Order in Mass Mediated Representations of Biotechnology'. Doctoral School of Knowledge and Management, Copenhagen Business School. PhD Series 28/2003.

Irwin, A. and B. Wynne. 1996. *Misunderstanding Science? The Public Reconstruction of Science and Technology*. Cambridge: Cambridge University Press.

Kapferer, B. 2018. 'From the Outside in – Anthropology as a Dialectic of Unsettlement', *Social Analysis* 62(1): 27–30.

Madsbjerg, Christian and Mikkel B. Rasmussen. 2014. *The Moment of Clarity: Using the Human Sciences to Solve Your Toughest Business Problems*. Boston: Harvard Business Review Press.

Marcus, George. 2013. 'Experimental Forms for the Expression of Norms in the Ethnography of the Contemporary', *HAU: Journal of Ethnographic Theory* 3(2): 197–217.

Matsutake Worlds Research Group. 2009. 'A New Form of Collaboration in Cultural Anthropology: Matsutake Worlds', *American Ethnologist* 36(2): 380–403.

Maurer, Bill. 2005. *Mutual Life, Limited: Islamic Banking, Alternative Currencies, Lateral Reason*. Princeton: Princeton University Press.

Miyazaki, Hirokazu. 2013. *Arbitraging Japan: Dreams of Capitalism at the End of Finance*. Berkeley and Los Angeles: University of California Press.

Mosse, David. 2006. 'Anti-Social Anthropology? Objectivity, Objection and the Ethnography of Public Policy and Professional Communities', *Journal of the Royal Anthropological Institute* 12: 935–56.

Pedersen, Lise R. 2018. 'Fact Finders: Knowledge Aesthetics and the Business of Human Science in a Danish Consultancy', PhD thesis. Copenhagen: University of Copenhagen.

Riles, Annelise. 1998. 'Infinity within the Brackets', *American Ethnologist* 25(3): 378–98.

———. 2000. *The Network Inside Out*. Ann Arbor: University of Michigan Press.

Sismondo, S. 2011. 'Corporate Disguises in Medical Science: Dodging the Interest Repertoire', *Bulletin of Science and Technology Studies* 31(6): 482–92.

Stengers, I. 2005. 'Introductory Notes on an Ecology of Practices', *Cultural Studies Review* 11(1): 183–95.

———. 2010. *Cosmopolitics1 – Book I: The Science Wars*. Minneapolis: University of Minnesota Press.

———. 2011. 'Comparison as a Matter of Concern', *Common Knowledge* 17(1): 48–64.

Strathern, Marilyn. 2004 [1991]. *Partial Connections*. Walnut Creek, CA: Rowman Altamira Press.

Verran, Helen. 2014. 'Working with Those Who Think Otherwise', *Common Knowledge* 20(3): 527–39.

Viveiros de Castro, Eduardo. 2004. 'Perspectival Anthropology and the Method of Controlled Equivocation', *Tipiti Journal of the Society for the Anthropology of Lowland South America* 2(1): 3–22.

Wright, S. and C. Shore. 2017. *Death of the Public University? Uncertain Futures for Higher Education in the Knowledge Economy*. Oxford and New York: Berghahn Books.

CHAPTER 6

Leaving the Church of Anthropology

From Discipline to Profession in Anthropological Praxis

Steffen Jöhncke

At the core of this chapter is the concern that the representation of anthropology within academia has not kept pace with the rapid evolution and expansion of anthropological practice beyond universities in recent years. A particularly strong contrast may be drawn between, on the one hand, a particular manner of self-presentation within academic anthropology that I – with obvious polemical intent – call 'the Church of Anthropology' and, on the other hand, the long existing and still growing professional development of practical anthropology beyond academia. The Church of Anthropology preaches the moral superiority of the discipline, and as I will argue in this chapter – which is based on a study of anthropology graduates who establish professional careers outside academia – the Church does a disservice to its students and graduates as it provides them with a distorted image of the role and relevance of the discipline in the world. Graduates must leave the Church in order to come to terms with the practical value of their anthropological training.

The Church of Anthropology

How does one identify and recognize the Church of Anthropology? I would say that once one has noticed it, the Church seems to appear everywhere in anthropological texts as a form of common disciplinary doxa. Here a few selected and clear examples must suffice. In October 2015, the Executive Committee of the European Association of Social Anthropologists (EASA) published a short text titled 'Why Anthropology Matters'. This text is available on the Association's website, where it is presented on the front page as an official statement.[1] The background for the text was a meeting of the Association which, as the text says, 'brought together more than 50 anthropologists from 17 different countries, focused on discussing the ways in which the discipline of cultural and social anthropology can make a difference in Europe today'. It is further mentioned that this meeting 'took place in the shadow of the ongoing refugee crisis in Europe', referring to unfolding events that year when more than 1.3 million people sought refuge in the European Union, more than 350,000 of whom were fleeing the war in Syria. The EASA text expresses concern about this and other humanitarian crises and social problems in the world and argues that anthropology can contribute to solving these problems by offering better insights into the human (social and cultural) condition. Anthropology highlights the need for intercultural understanding across all differences and for the cosmopolitan perspective that humanity is basically one. 'Why Anthropology Matters' goes through what the authors regard as the main qualities of the discipline, the most important skills in the 'toolbox' that 'the craft of social and cultural anthropology consist in', namely, 'cultural relativism, ethnography, comparison and context', all of which enable knowledge of a unique kind. The 'need for anthropology' has never been greater, it is asserted, as cross-global interaction is only on the increase through travel, migration, technology development and the global economy, just as issues such as cultural change and cultural identity formation have never been more pertinent. Without explaining or justifying it further, the text ends with the assertion that anthropology is 'the most useful of the basic sciences'. In the text as a whole, anthropology is presented as quintessentially an activity that produces academic knowledge of a special quality and character to which the world ought to open its ears. Despite the alleged background – the refugee crisis in Europe – the authors do not identify or even consider anthropologists who may already be fully engaged in the policy and practice of refugee reception. Instead, they take the opportunity to present very broad and general claims about the potential usefulness of anthropological knowledge, particularly as it pertains to academic research.

My critical discussion here of 'Why Anthropology Matters' is not intended to challenge the deep concerns and the social indignation that may have motivated the text, nor to question the importance of arguing the social relevance of anthropology. These issues reflect interests of my own but, as I will discuss in this chapter, I suggest that we need to approach these issues from a different angle. In brief, we could begin to take all anthropologists' experiences equally into consideration, and not privilege the dwindling (but dominant) minority who are university academics such as the EASA text does. 'Why Anthropology Matters' is a short text, and my analysis of it here may seem to overburden its significance. Nevertheless, it is presented as an authoritative statement of the executive committee of the professional organization of European anthropologists, and I take it to be a very important example, as an epitome of a particular, dominant manner of thinking about the discipline itself within anthropology.

What I am concerned with here is both the explicit and implicit impressions that the text conveys of anthropology's – and, by implication, anthropologists' – role in the world. My first objection is that academic anthropology is taken to represent the discipline as a whole; my second is that anthropology is described as a voice that possesses a particular moral value as an ingrained trait of its form of knowledge; that is, anthropology is an understanding of the world imbued with a moral message about itself. At the core of this morality is the claim that anthropology comes closer to human reality than any other form of knowledge, as its ethical grounding and methodological tools unite to enable anthropologists 'to provide more detailed and nuanced descriptions of . . . [social] phenomena than other researchers'. The authors also claim that 'anthropology is uniquely a knowledge for the 21st century, crucial in our attempts to come to terms with a globalized world, essential for building understanding and respect across real and imagined cultural divides'. It should be noted that this is not a call for anthropologists to take a moral or political stance in their work according to their own views; it is, rather, a claim that anthropology itself is a source of virtue, doing and intending what is right. In this manner, anthropology becomes a self-referencing moral community – like a church.

In their discussion about the social relevance and role of anthropology, Ahmed and Shore (1995) also consider the discipline's 'moral significance': 'To put it simply, it is a discipline that is capable of doing some good – although this term may evoke church, clergy and religious preaching and antagonize academics trained in a secular tradition of scientific detachment. But without that moral dimension it is reduced to being neither a science nor part of the humanities' (ibid.: 32–33). As I see it, notions such as 'moral significance' and 'moral dimension' do evoke religious imagery, if they are taken to be characteristic of anthropology as a whole, rather than a question of anthropologists' sense of moral commitment in their particular lines of work. My concern is not rooted in a contrary belief in the merits of 'scientific detachment', as if the moral implications of anthropological work are irrelevant. The point is that it is one thing to say that anthropology can be put to effective use – that is, use that is good, bad or indifferent, depending on the intention, capability and values of its practitioners – and that we do indeed need to be concerned about this question as a scientific community. It is quite another thing to say that anthropology itself is the source of moral value. In the latter case, anthropology does become 'a quasi-religious movement' (Benthall 1995: 3).

In my interpretation, 'Why Anthropology Matters' is an example of a confessional text within what I have metaphorically termed the 'Church of Anthropology' (Jöhncke 2018). The term refers to a particular self-congratulatory way of understanding and cherishing the discipline, organized around the dogma that anthropology has intrinsic moral value, and that it has, or rather, is a superior moral message – not to say a gospel – that its disciples should bring to the world. The key point here is that texts such as 'Why Anthropology Matters' do not purport to demonstrate how anthropology has in fact produced better solutions to social problems; they merely assert that anthropological knowledge is superior, particularly by way of claiming that it is closer to human reality – to human life as it unfolds in the social world – than alternative teachings (sociology, economy, and so on). This alleged superiority has both methodological and theoretical roots: 'The ethnographic method enables anthropologists to discover aspects of local worlds that are inaccessible to researchers that use other methods', hence anthropologists' 'more detailed and nuanced descriptions', as mentioned above. The sense of superiority is rooted in anthropologists' resistance to 'simplistic accounts of human nature', common in today's world, which are presumably offered by other disciplines. The authors of the text do not seem to be concerned about the circular argument that they present: that more detailed, nuanced and complex descriptions are expressions of anthropological values of good ethnographic writing, not objective or commonly accepted standards to assess all forms of social science. One could make the contrary argument that certain and relevant forms of reductions of complexity are what all sciences must employ – anthropology merely has its own conventions of how to proceed from the complexity of ethnographic data to a select argument, usually in the form of a linear text. That scientists from other disciplines may have different accounts of their own forms of complex knowledge vanishes from view. The authors admit that even though 'ethnographic data are of a very high quality . . . they often need to be supplemented by other kinds of data', as anthropologists can study only a limited number of people in the field. Nevertheless, the text as a whole is clearly arguing that anthropological knowledge is not just different from other forms, it is inherently better – 'the most useful of the basic sciences'. The argument becomes a self-referencing, moral one: it begins and ends with the axiom that anthropology is good.

In this line of argument, if anthropology is inherently good, then real virtue and righteousness do not lie in the outward deeds of practising anthropologists, but in the inner quality of the discipline. The actual achievements of practising anthropologists become less important, because the social value and usefulness of anthropological knowledge become questions of the right conviction and faith in anthropology as an idealized endeavour. Anthropology is intrinsically good – not because it can be demonstrated to have good effects (that is, utilitarian value), nor because it is has as much scientific value as any other academic discipline. Anthropology is good in a virtuous sense; anthropology itself is the source of moral virtue. On the one hand, 'Why Anthropology Matters' claims that cultural relativism, ethnography, comparison and contextualization are methods, not ideologies; yet on the other hand, clearly they are methods for a higher cause, as the knowledge they enable is superior, not just supplementary to other forms of knowledge. In the text, Eric Wolf is quoted twice for his characterization of anthropology as 'the most humanistic of the sciences and the most scientific of the humanities'– which is, of course, to say that it is the best. My claim is that this idea is not exclusive to 'Why Anthropology Matters', it is an understanding that can be commonly found in academic anthropological writing, and it is an integral part of the teaching of the discipline.

Preaching to the Choir

It is not entirely clear to whom a text such as 'Why Anthropology Matters' is addressed. It could be read as an open message to the world – a statement about the importance of anthropology, addressed not least to policy makers and grant-awarding authorities who may well be ignorant of the value of the discipline. However, presumably, the predominant readership of EASA's website will be anthropologists and anthropology students. One may wonder then why they would need a text like this, particularly as its message is one that most of them would be quite familiar with from their academic training. Again, the metaphor of the Church of Anthropology may be useful: the faithful do not go to church to hear a new gospel, they go in order to have the gospel reiterated lest the tribulations of the mundane world have caused them to doubt. Similarly, 'Why Anthropology Matters' may be read as a piece of internal moral rearmament. It is a reminder to the already converted congregation that anthropology is important for the world: here they have it, easy to hand from eminent representatives of the discipline.

I also read the volume *Exotic No More* (MacClancy 2002) in this way – as a boost to the morale of the flock and as another example of a strong confessional text in anthropology. It was published in the wake of the controversy caused by *Darkness in Eldorado* (Tierney 2000), a book that argued how some anthropologists had been involved in less than ethical personal and research practices while conducting studies among the Yanomamo people of Amazonia.[2] Reactions to Tierney's book have varied from an initial general acceptance of its criticisms to an increasingly critical questioning of its claims. What concerns me here, though, is the response to the book from within anthropology, of which *Exotic No More* is one expression. As its editor says:

> what needs to be avoided right now is that the sensational treatment of a seemingly miscreant anthropologist be allowed to besmirch the whole profession. That many anthropologists are dedicated to research which has socially beneficial ends is evidenced on page after page of this book . . . The aim of the book is to reverse this trend in sensationalism and reemphasize the public value of the discipline. (MacClancy 2002: 2)

Quite explicitly, *Exotic No More* is an attempt to reinstate anthropology morally. The book shows that anthropologists do not behave irresponsibly and do not just study exotic rituals among small groups of people far away, as popular imagery would have it (hence the title of the book). In order to demonstrate this, the book brings together twenty-three excellent chapters by renowned anthropologists, of whom at least twenty are university-based academics and only two work in NGOs, all presenting the important research that they do, dealing with all the pressing social issues of our time, from war, epidemics and hunger, to media, migration and human rights. Many of them make strong claims for the political implications of their work and the need for advocacy and engagement. However, the point of the book is clearly not to demonstrate how practising anthropologists have helped improve conditions in the areas covered; the point is to show that academic anthropologists are responsible and study really important issues, some of which are essential for the well-being of humankind. The implicit message seems to be that what is important is not whether anthropologists are actually taking part in practical or political solutions and improvements; the objective is to show that anthropologists are 'on the front lines' of socially relevant research.[3]

As I see it, the choice to let academic anthropologists, a minority in the profession, represent anthropology as a whole is no coincidence. Indeed, it is the norm in the discipline to let the word 'anthropologist' refer to academic anthropologists, without the qualification that there may be others. There is a special kind of morality involved here – in both 'Why Anthropology Matters' and *Exotic No More* – of letting serious social and political concerns provide the background for claiming academic anthropology's value while the work of practising anthropologists is passed over in silence or acknowledged only symbolically. The effect is that the moral integrity of academic anthropology – as a certain kind of critical commentary – remains intact, while the professional dilemmas and challenges of practical work can be ignored.

This representation of the discipline is linked to another important characteristic of the teachings of the Church of Anthropology, namely the doctrine of perpetual promise and postponed potential: the real face of anthropology is now hidden (in academia), but it has the capacity to make a huge impact in the world that one day may well be realized. In the words of *Exotic No More*:

> if there is a single point that all the contributors wish to put across, it is that anthropology remains a discipline with the greatest of promise, whose distinctive approach continues to yield a diversity of significant insights into matters of contemporary import, and whose potential value for our understanding of the social world has still not yet been fully tapped. (Mac-Clancy 2002: 14)

It is a clear message of both 'Why Anthropology Matters' and *Exotic No More* that the knowledge and teachings of anthropology have the potential to help transform the world for the better. The key word here is 'potential': it is something that could happen in the future, if only the evil world would listen more. The doctrine that anthropology has potential, and as such holds a yet unfulfilled promise, is also evident from the way in which 'Why Anthropology Matters' is introduced on the EASA website:

> Anthropology provides knowledge and skills which *can be* essential for understanding and dealing with the human condition in the early 21st century. *Why anthropology matters* is a statement from the EASA Executive

Committee, which explains in simple, engaging language what is unique about anthropological knowledge, and why anthropologists *can be* key players in handling the global crises humanity is confronting, from the refugee situation to climate change and growing inequalities. (my italics)

The positive, social impact of anthropology is something that potentially 'can be', apparently not something that already demonstrably 'is'. It seems that for anthropology to make a real breakthrough in practice, more research must be done and, evidently, more preaching about the usefulness of anthropology to those – policy makers, the public, the press – who have not yet got the message. The claim of anthropology's useful potential is as old as the discipline (Malinowski 1929); over the years, the promise itself has become integral to its self-understanding and self-presentation, rather than it being seen as the basis for self-reflection, self-critique and evaluation. We could ask: has the promise been redeemed? If so, where and how? – and if not, why not? Instead, it seems that the time of redemption is never quite here yet. Anthropology's hour has not yet come, but soon, in the fullness of time, all will be revealed.

Disciples and Professionals

One of the effects of the doctrine of perpetual promise and postponed potential is that academic anthropology remains at the centre of attention in the discipline. If the work of applied and practising anthropologists were considered on an equal footing, talk would not be of potential but of actually making a difference – with all the challenges and trials that this involves. It is in the context of academic anthropology that the idea of promise makes sense, and it helps to uphold a safe distance from the world of policy and practice. It must be upon this world that anthropology wants to make an impact one day but, clearly, the world is not ready yet for our teachings. This imagery also apportions blame on an inattentive and misguided world rather than pointing to any problems with how anthropologists themselves act – including how they imagine themselves and how they relate to other disciplines.

The Church of Anthropology maintains a paradoxical disregard for the work that anthropologists outside of academia are doing here and now, and have done for decades, all over the world. For non-academic anthropologists, anthropology is not a gospel with a promise to be realized once the time is ripe. Rather, it is a professional practice and a perspective that informs their work and earns them a living.[4] It is also, for many of them, a practice that enables them to make useful contributions to social change on various scales and to improvements in other people's lives. In this, anthropologists are very rarely alone in producing actionable knowledge and perspectives, as members of other disciplines and their forms of logic and practice must be negotiated and combined with the anthropologists' own. To be quite fair, 'Why Anthropology Matters' does occasionally mention non-academic anthropologists. The authors point out that 'most anthropologists in Europe work in a multitude of professions in the public and private sectors, where they implement that [sic] specific skills and knowledges that anthropology has taught them', and they mention a few of these sectors and a few of these skills. Still, the text also claims that '[by] raising fundamental questions in a neutral, detached way, basic research can sometimes prove to be more useful in tackling the problems that the world faces than applied research'. The suggested limitations of applied research are not explicated; instead, the authors give examples of how basic research – about internet use, religion and peasants' economic rationality – may provide new and surprising insights with potential policy relevance. Yet, again, there is no indication of whether this impact on policy has been realized. It is only a potential, for others to pick up.

An implication of the perspective of texts such as 'Why Anthropology Matters' and *Exotic No More* is that, first of all, 'anthropology' is synonymous with academic research, and 'anthropologists' with academics. Other kinds of anthropological practice are relegated to a secondary and derivative position, if acknowledged at all. What the anthropologists of these texts do is to study[5] – they research, collect data, inquire and analyse. 'Anthropologists typically spend a year or more in the field', we read in 'Why Anthropology Matters', as proper ethnographic research is very time consuming. 'Typically', really? Academic anthropologists may well wonder if this description even applies to their work lives, as a whole year off other duties in order to do fieldwork seems like a rare luxury; certainly, it does not apply to any other anthropologists. The effect of such a description is to project one particular position (even if increasingly rare and unusual) as quintessential, emblematic of the anthropologist proper: the university-based researcher to whom time and money are not limitations. It also helps to maintain what I would call an academicentric world order in the discipline, in which imaginary academic work sets the standard for all forms of anthropological practice. In this manner, academic anthropologists are cast as the clergy of the Church of Anthropology, the keepers of true teachings and of model conduct.

Admittedly, historically anthropology was invented in academia, and only later became a professional practice in a broad range of occupations and organizations. In the words of 'Why Anthropology Matters': 'Unlike training in engineering and psychology, an education in anthropology is not vocational. There are few readymade niches for anthropologists in the labour market'. It may be questioned whether a degree in psychology is a particularly good example of 'vocational' training for the labour market, but it is a valid point that graduates of different disciplines face different conditions in terms of employment. One perspective is that some subjects were practices even before they became sciences in a modern sense – medicine and chemistry, for instance – while others, such as biology, psychology and anthropology have moved in the other direction, starting from academia and gradually exploring and expanding modes of professional practice other than scientific research and teaching the subject to the next generation. However, this history is in itself not a good reason to uphold the idea that (imaginary notions of) academic anthropology should remain the ideal, the standard of practice for the discipline as a whole.

The Church of Anthropology may seem to construct the discipline as a kind of calling, somewhat similar to other occupations that traditionally have been associated with the presence of conviction and a strong inner impulse, such as towards becoming a priest or a nurse. However, whereas such callings seem to be driving forces for action – i.e. towards actually doing something in the world – the call to anthropology seems to stop at the conviction: at being an anthropologist rather than advising or even imagining a course of practical action.

In order to work out an alternative, one place to start could be to discuss if 'discipline' is still a wholly adequate designation for anthropology today. In a discussion about contemporary anthropological practice, Nolan (2017: 27) makes the distinction that disciplines generate knowledge, whereas professions apply it – and anthropology covers both. I think the difference between disciplines and professions goes deeper, as an issue relating to the institutional arrangements under which various forms of knowledge and practice unfold. Fifty years ago, Foster (1969: 156) also discussed the difference between disciplines and professions, as he considered the challenges of applied anthropologists in their collaboration with 'personnel in fields such as health, medicine, administration, agriculture, and community development'. Anthropologists, he asserted, 'belong to an academic and scientific discipline, characterized by the assumption that the search for new knowledge represents the highest value'. This expresses the value system of the enlightenment that the institution of academia must uphold: scientific knowledge is valuable as an end in itself. However, as I have argued above, in anthropology this is given a moral cast concerning the discipline's special role (or dare we say, mission) in the world. Foster discusses how anthropologists in practical work confront a different set of expectations about role and performance, as the aims of the work are defined by the organization in which one is employed as a professional, rather than by the discipline:

> In contrast [to academic disciplines], planners and administrators belong to professions normally characterized by the assumption that the achievement of organizational goals represent the highest value. In doing good professional work, these specialists draw upon the scientific knowledge of a number of disciplines, as well as that of the professions, collating this knowledge to produce plans which, when enacted, will result in the solution of the problems with which their organizations are charged. Conceptions of proper professional roles, and of means, ends, and ethics, are also inculcated in planners and administrators during their professional training and ingrained in them through practice. Professional practice reflects rather more explicit value judgments than does the work of research scientists: health is better than illness; more agricultural production is preferable to less; dependent peoples must be governed. (Foster 1969: 156–57)

That Foster was writing fifty years ago is revealed by the value judgments he quotes; today we would hope to find more talk of sustainable agricultural production, and about dependent peoples becoming self-governed, but the general point still holds. The aims of professional work in policy and practice are defined by organizations – whether private or public or NGO – and it is exactly towards these aims that anthropologists working in practice are compelled to contribute, once they have accepted the task. This also means that they have to leave the Church of Anthropology and its narcissistic belief in the intrinsic goodness of anthropology, as they need to consider if they can identify with (or just live with) the aims and ethics of the organization they are working for, whether as employee or consultant, or in any other capacity (Nolan 2003: 160–66). In this line of work, anthropology is nearly always only one perspective out of several and here the valuable contribution of anthropology must be demonstrated, not merely claimed and promised. Yet, as I shall discuss below, leaving the Church of Anthropology is no simple matter for practising anthropologists who have been brought up to integrate its teachings and doctrines into their identity and capability. The morality of the Church becomes an obstacle as much as a lodestar. Non-academic anthropologists need to learn and activate many additional professional skills, and they need to challenge, adapt and expand their understanding of anthropology in order to practise it better outside of academia. At the same time, as I will discuss below, and as this book as a whole testifies to, it seems that more and more of them claim anthropology as a crucial part of their evolving professionalism. As they are moving from a disciplinary to a professional understanding of themselves, they need to reassess what exactly they can draw of practical use from their anthropology training, and what to do with the moral self-image of the discipline that has accompanied this training. Disciplines have disciples; professions have. . . professionals.

Realized Anthropology

In the Church of Anthropology, anthropology's usefulness is a question of persuasion; for practising anthropologists, on the contrary, the use of anthropology is an empirical issue, something that can be studied and assessed. If the usefulness of anthropology is not something that can merely be claimed or assumed, then it is important to identify where and how practitioners are using their anthropology. One obvious place to look is whether and how people with degrees in anthropology put their training to use in jobs outside of academia. In 2012, the employers' panel[6] of the Department of Anthropology at the University of Copenhagen asked my research unit, AnthroAnalysis, to do a study of the labour market experiences of MA graduates[7] from the department. AnthroAnalysis was set up to promote collaborative research projects and the practical use of anthropology, so the panel rightly considered that we would be interested in this issue. The purpose of the study was to gain knowledge about where and how the graduates work, and what their experiences, challenges and achievements in the labour market may tell us about their training – if and how they use it – and about the development of anthropology as a professional practice in Denmark. The report of the study (Hansen and Jöhncke 2013) was given the title 'Omsat antropologi', where *omsat* may be translated into English in various ways that all provide partly relevant connotations: realized, negotiated, renewed, converted, transformed, transposed and transplanted. The idea was to focus attention on how anthropology is recast when used under conditions and in relationships which are different from the ones in academia. The term 'applied' (Danish: *'anvendt'*) anthropology was not adopted, mainly because 'application' may seem to suggest that knowledge from anthropology can be taken as it is out of academia and applied onto some problem or situation. This is far from an appropriate account of the process of adapting and using anthropology skills professionally, according to the anthropologists of this study.

Our first task in the study was to get an overview of where the graduates were currently working, and – if possible – some indication of different career trajectories. It proved no easy matter even to identify 'the anthropological population' originating from the department, as no official records on this were kept. Training in anthropology began in the University of Copenhagen in 1963, and in the first years, the number of students and graduates was low. From 1975 to 1995, less than twenty per year left the department with the *'magisterkonferens'* degree for which seven years of studies were prescribed.[8] Since 2000, the student intake has risen to over a hundred per year, and since 2002 between forty and eighty-five have obtained the MA yearly. From 1975 till the time of our study in 2012–2013, a total of 949 *'magisterkonferens'* or MA graduates had been trained in the department. Through internet searches and snowballing techniques it was possible to reach 618 of them by email, of whom 319 replied with information about their current jobs and often volunteered a range of comments about their training in and use of anthropology. In addition, we conducted interviews and workplace visits with thirteen MA graduates of different ages who were employed in various fields. We also did eleven interviews with employers of anthropologists (not of the MA graduates interviewed). The results presented in the report were based on analyses of the whole of this material.

One may well ask if such a thing as 'the anthropological labour market' exists, or if it is the invention of a particular, disciplinary myopia. Indeed, this point came up in the course of the study, as some MA graduates questioned the extent to which their anthropology degree had been decisive at all for their careers – and hence they questioned the relevance of our study. Other experiences and competences had probably been more important, they felt, and many workplaces have no particular interest in staff members' university backgrounds – what counts are their CVs, skills and personality. Other MA graduates, however, had been employed explicitly with reference to the expectation that their anthropology background would be useful; while yet others thought they often used anthropological perspectives in their approach to tasks in their jobs, whether or not this was important or even clear to their employers. Certainly, in doing a study of this nature, there is a risk of exaggerating the role of the anthropology degree when looking at MA graduates' careers, because it is already a part of the focus to begin with. Nevertheless, the anthropology degree is the single element that the university may influence, and if the expectation of the university is that training in anthropology makes a difference – and you would sincerely hope that the university does have this expectation – then it is relevant to become wiser about what that difference may be. Obviously, for recent MA graduates, the degree had a relatively greater weight than for those with many years of work experience in their CVs. It should also be mentioned that in the first decades of this century, a degree in anthropology began to appear explicitly in job advertisements in Denmark as a possible qualification for a particular job (although rarely as the only one). It is likely that this development may continue as both the number of anthropologists and employers' familiarity with them grows.

Of the 319 MA graduates who provided information, just under 29 per cent worked in the university sector, almost all of them in academic positions. This includes doctoral students, as they are employees in Denmark. Our sample probably overestimated the proportion of MA graduates in the university sector, as it was easier for us to identify all those in university positions than those working elsewhere. We must also expect this proportion to decrease in the future, as the number of university positions does not keep up at all with the rising number of MA-graduates. This finding confirmed our expectation – and the assertion that I have made in this chapter – that academic anthropologists form a minority in the profession, at least if we take the numbers from this large university department as an indicator.

Just over a third of the MA graduates had jobs in the public sector – in local, regional or national government, in international organizations or in various institutions. Local government in Denmark has employed many university graduates in the last decades, and anthropologists have clearly been part of this current. Just over 20 per cent worked in private organizations and businesses, about half of them in consultancy companies and a quarter of them as self-employed. General expectations are that employment in the private sector will rise among anthropologists (just as among all social science graduates) in Denmark, as growth in public sector jobs is slowing down. Less than 10 per cent of the MA graduates worked for NGOs, which was a surprise, given that the NGO sector was frequently mentioned among students and university staff as a potentially attractive job field for anthropologists. Just under 8 per cent were not or no longer employed.

We decided to try to identify thematic job fields for the 294 employed MA graduates who responded in the study; this was not exactly a rigorous exercise, as possible interpretations and categorizations are plentiful, but it gave us the opportunity to obtain a general impression of main areas of practice among the anthropologists in the study. Just under 29 per cent worked with academic research (in anthropology or other disciplines), corresponding to the proportion in academic jobs mentioned above. Four fields each employed 7-10 per cent of the MA graduates: health, development or emergency aid, organizational work (including human resources and management) and design research (including product development and studies of users). A vast number of other themes were mentioned – including youth and children, the elderly, education, urban development, communication and marketing, welfare and employment, social integration, tourism, trading, art, technology, climate change and volunteers. Obviously, had we created a very broad category of 'social work', this might have incorporated several of these minor themes. The main insight here is that the MA graduates had managed to find employment in a very wide range of fields and types of work.

Given that there is no single and obvious job market for anthropology MA graduates, it is remarkable that they have managed to be employed to such a large degree. Few organizations employed more than one or two anthropologists in each location, but several MA graduates mentioned how the first anthropologist in a field often managed to open doors for others, and inspire other employers in that field about the usefulness of anthropology MA graduates. The general impression is that the anthropological labour market is created 'one job at a time', as there is little general demand for anthropologists as such. Still, MA graduates may succeed in persuading prospective employers that they have use for an anthropologist, even if they did not know this before. Very few jobs seem to require anthropological training specifically, as many are general, professional jobs suitable for graduates from diverse backgrounds, each of whom would bring a particular (disciplinary) perspective to bear on the job. A common logic therefore seems to be that one or a few anthropologists on the team would contribute to a good multidisciplinary mix. This leads to the point that interdisciplinary and collaborative working skills are essential for the anthropologist working outside of academia – which further leads to the point that the sort of disciplinary superiority complex outlined above (as an element in the teachings of the Church of Anthropology) is less than helpful in practice.

Surviving the Church

In our material from this study, there is a very large variation in terms of the character of jobs, and in terms of how and how much the MA graduates perceived themselves as using skills originating in their anthropology training in these jobs. They associated a range of professional competences with their anthropological education, but they also saw their training as the root of several problems or challenges in becoming professionals. In broad terms, it was possible to identify three different types of stance towards anthropology among the participants in our study – they do not represent three separate groups of people as much as clusters of perspectives, and certainly it is seemed possible to combine and to move between these stances during a professional career.

One approach was to downplay or relativize the significance of anthropology in one's professional life. Some of the anthropologists in the study had adopted a professional identity related to the particular trade or sector where they worked and had gradually become experts. Consequently, they saw themselves first as professionals in development, human resources, innovation, public administration, or whatever their field was, and only secondly – if at all – as anthropologists. Studying anthropology may have provided them with some of the skills that they used, but these were mainly of a generalist kind that many different choices of university education could have given them. They may seem to belong to the 'no longer anthropologist' category identified by Wright as those whom disciplinary boundary makers 'deemed to be too much involved in policy or administration' (1995: 67) to keep their designation as anthropologists. Processes of marginalization from the discipline may well be in action here, but at least for some, distancing themselves from anthropology was also a way to gain a broader professional identity. As hinted at earlier in this chapter, this stance seemed to be particularly relevant for those with long CVs and many professional experiences, but some younger MA graduates had also moved quickly to regarding anthropology as an activity of their student days rather than the core of their professional identity.

A second stance towards anthropology among the MA graduates was one of trying to reconcile the disciplinary (and moral) teachings of anthropology with the requirements and possibilities of a professional job. Some found this to be an ongoing challenge.[9] At the core of this lie the difficulties of coming from an academic discipline and transforming oneself and one's skills to the requirements of an organization with professionally defined aims. It is not a unique condition for anthropologists to feel split between disciplinary and professional approaches as they move from university to non-academic jobs; it is part of much academic training to become part of a disciplinary worldview. But I would argue that the kind of moral upbringing in the teachings of the Church of Anthropology outlined above equips anthropologists with particularly skewed expectations of what kind of professional role they might attain as they bring the anthropological gospel out into the world. They very soon realize, of course, that the professional world is less susceptible to conversion by anthropological blessings than might have been expected (see, for example, Chapter 2, this book). Instead, they are met with the expectation of needing to present how exactly anthropology may contribute to the overall aim. In this study, some graduates reacted with self-doubt about whether their work could be defended as anthropological. Others directed their criticism towards the department; we met many accounts of frustrations among the anthropologists with the framing of their university training, and doubts about whether they had learned anything of use. They had been brought up to believe that anthropology was really unique and important, and yet now they realized that anthropological skills and insights had no value in themselves, until they could relate them to other purposes and disciplines. During the study, my colleague Anne-Louise Hansen came up with the phrase 'the anthropological personality disorder' to describe this predicament, particularly of young anthropologists. On the one hand, they were still convinced of the superiority of anthropology, not least in terms of its ability to reduce anything – including other disciplines – to interesting cultural phenomena (see also Chapter 5, this book). On the other hand, all of a sudden they felt that anthropology was useless in practice and that they knew nothing about what employers were asking them for. Some reacted to this condition of self-effacing megalomania that had been inflicted upon them by distancing themselves from anthropology altogether. Others found that their way out was to reassess anthropology as a set of practical skills rather than a moral calling.

This – the focus on practical skills and on how anthropology may be a professional asset in the context of interdisciplinary collaboration – characterizes the third stance. Several of the MA graduates who took part in the study considered their background training in anthropology to be an important part of the skills they used in their work. They frequently described also how they had only realized their own anthropological 'mind-set' in relation to colleagues and work partners from other disciplines, and how interdisciplinary work had made them more aware of both the limitations and the assets of the anthropological contribution. Moreover, they had come to this stance only through overcoming a range of professional challenges and weaknesses that they would relate to their anthropology education. In the next section, I will go into some of these challenges in more detail and point out how the overcoming of challenges may also lead to an awareness of competences that derive from anthropology. Still further, I would argue that such a meta-anthropological perspective – that is, the anthropological study of anthropological practice – may help us realize that the actual character of the anthropological contribution is epistemological rather than moral.

In order to become professional anthropologists outside of academia, the MA graduates must find ways to disentangle themselves from the Church of Anthropology's moral teachings about the discipline. The conventions of promise and self-praise of the Church may appear at first as a valuable source of disciplinary self-esteem, but soon after graduation, if not before, it turns out to have the opposite effect when the harsh realities of professional life are confronted. Some experience a sense of being lacking in both professional competence and the ability to live up to their internalized disciplinary expectations. However, many succeed in overcoming this and use anthropology productively as they realize their anthropology skills in practice, though in ways divergent from those of the Church.

Professional Challenges and Competences

One aspect that was frequently mentioned as particularly hard for anthropologists at first may be summed up as 'the difficult step from description to intervention'. In a sense, this is again at the core of the move from discipline to profession. The purpose of academic anthropology is to construct as good and convincing descriptions as possible. Academic writing may well contain strong appeals to be concerned for people in need or may protest against some of the many injustices of the world – as 'Why Anthropology Matters' and *Exotic No More* illustrate. Even though their main audience, realistically, is the anthropological community itself, the appeals and protests are mainly directed to abstract others, sometimes in a very general manner – maybe to a general public or to policy makers and other responsible and practical people of the world. Academic anthropology rarely suggests a particular intervention. Yet the ability to make recommendations and suggest interventions is exactly what anthropologists in professional non-academic practice are expected to demonstrate – just like any other professional group. Anthropologists in practice can rarely limit themselves to 'study'. As a manager of a design company who employs anthropologists said in one of our interviews: 'The client does not come to us for a purely anthropological study, or a study of users – usually not, that is rare. What they come for is to get a full product', which includes suggestions for new products, design, concepts or whatever it may be. In other organizations, of course, 'the full product' may include a policy recommendation or a plan of action.

The MA graduates in the study mentioned that one of the challenges with learning to develop recommendations and interventions was that this task seemed at odds with the basic anthropological perspective of relativism – that is, the ability to see things from several angles simultaneously and not judge who and what is 'right'. Cultural relativism is crucial for anthropology as a form of knowledge, and yet, in practical terms, it can be entirely paralysing, as it gives no answers. In practice, relativism must be overcome with considerations of possible lines of action and their consequences. This means that relativism is, rather, the impetus to consider, for instance, as some of the anthropologists mention, how a product or a service may look from the point of view of different groups of users, and what the implications and opportunities of this are. This is an example of how the anthropologists reframe their approach and rediscover their skills. It also helps them realize how and where they may make a difference. Some of the anthropologists in the study mentioned how their hesitancy about an intervention may also be a professional contribution, as sometimes more research or consideration was needed before conclusions or recommendations could be clearly defined. One of them, an anthropologist in a public policy unit, even mentioned how it had become part of her job 'to take the civil servants into the field' in order to challenge their perspectives by meeting citizens and businesses directly themselves. Here the anthropologist did not provide knowledge as much as she facilitated how others may gain their own insights and, maybe, useful questioning of their own previous convictions. This was not a method that she had learned at university, but it was still an expression of an anthropological understanding that knowledge and cause for reflection may be gained from direct social interaction.

Unlike what many of the MA graduates in our study had been told at university, expert training in the use of qualitative research methods was not a particularly decisive asset for them in the job market. Today, professionals from many different backgrounds have training in qualitative methods, and even though anthropologists may deplore the conceptual deflation that they feel has hit such terms as 'ethnography', there is no way of luring the genie back into the 'anthrobottle' again. Several of the anthropologists in this study had realized, however, that what they could offer was not so much technical competence in research methods as such; rather, it was ideas about how to use them. It seemed that a certain 'explorative mind-set' of the anthropologists – the interest and ability to explore social phenomena empirically – was what some of the employers in the study particularly valued from them. This, rather than qualitative methods as such, was what the employers mentioned as an important anthropological contribution. Often the anthropologists would bring in a broader perspective; as one said: '[Another] staff person in the organization may resort to two or three tools to solve a problem, but an anthropologist may say, "maybe we haven't understood the problem correctly"'. Another employer seconded this view, that anthropologists' outlook was often broader. Referring to anthropologists involved in the study of consumer preferences, he said,

> this may sound negative, but the output that we get [from anthropologists] is not so much 'on-target', on the other hand it is much more valuable. Because it makes us understand, 'OK, . . . if *that's* what gives value to the consumers, if *that's* how they live or think about these things', then it gives us a wholly different perspective to the answers that they [the anthropologists] are bringing.

A third employer, this time of a public policy unit, even thought that this broader and more explorative approach from the anthropologists had influenced his organization as a whole: 'It is important to be curious about things we don't know about beforehand. It is important not to bring prejudices, hypotheses and narrow reply options [into a study]. We do not come [to do interviews] without some form of an interview guide, but we try to keep it as open as possible'. This is an illustration of how the anthropological contribution may fuse with the interdisciplinary activity of organizational life.

What these employers had found was that anthropologists provided a particular understanding of how to use qualitative research methods. From an anthropological perspective, we would say that this understanding is informed by anthropological epistemology: it draws on theoretical understandings of society and culture, and hence on theoretically informed notions of how these issues may be relevant as well as how they may be explored, not least by questioning limitations in existing views, including one's own. This is not the outcome of any one anthropological theory in particular; it is rather the summary effect of theoretical learning in anthropology. In our report of the study, we used the phrase 'implicit, subtheoretical assumptions' as a description of what the anthropologists in our study base their practice on. They rarely make explicit reference to any particular anthropological theory in their work, yet there is a degree of common understanding of the questions that are usually worth asking about the social world – covering issues such as the meaning of social relations, categories, power, values, organizing, negotiations, conflict, exchange, and so on, in any given field. In that sense, anthropology is a set of particular kinds of empirical interest – in combination with a knowledge of how this interest may be pursued methodologically, if the opportunity for study is there. In professional terms, practising non-academic anthropologists further need to be able to scale and direct this interest to the requirements of the organization they are working for; they need to draw conclusions to be more specific in terms of recommendations and interventions; and they need to be able to disseminate their knowledge in multiple manners and genres to diverse audiences.

I would suggest that the anthropological epistemology very briefly outlined here is what anthropologists in different lines of professional work – inside and outside of academia – share, even when research is not part of their job. What anthropological training has provided them with is a particular kind of curiosity about the social and cultural world around them, or what I earlier called 'the questions that are usually worth asking'. This applies to anthropologists in all types of organizational roles, not just those doing research. I would say that it is an approach to anthropological praxis in the terms suggested by John Comaroff: 'the discipline ought to be understood as a praxis: a mode of producing knowledge based on a few interrelated epistemic operations that lay the foundation for its diverse forms of theory work, mandate its research techniques, and chart its empirical coordinates' (2010: 530). Certainly, this praxis has a wide variety of expressions in various lines of anthropological work,[10] and there is good reason to explore further how different circumstances and purposes of this work – we may call it different relations of production in the anthropology industry, inside and outside of academia – provide different conditions and opportunities for its practitioners. Fortunately, there is a growing literature about the non-academic practice of anthropology that we may draw on in this pursuit of a broader basis for defining the profession – such journals as *Annals of Anthropological Practice* (formerly *NAPA Bulletin*) in the US, for instance, as well as accounts of practitioners' work in Pink (2006), Cefkin (2009) and MacClancy (2017), to mention but a few.

The examples that I have drawn on in this chapter indicate how practising, non-academic anthropology professionals realize anthropology in continuously new ways that are creative and competent responses to professional challenges. Crucial in this context is the character of non-academic anthropological practices as unfolding almost invariably in interdisciplinary settings, in professional organizations where the ability to learn and communicate responsibly across disciplinary lines and backgrounds is essential. Many of the anthropologists in the study discussed here said that they have learned this 'the hard way' – that is, with little preparation from the university. Now, they are expanding the remits of the profession into practices that are way beyond what they have learnt at university, and they are raising professional questions to which academic anthropology does not have the answers. For instance, whereas academic anthropology may seek to define the discipline from the perspective of notions of cultural relativism and complexity, professional anthropologists in practice may point out that these are valuable ideas that sometimes also have adverse practical consequences. The main point is, I think, that we must acknowledge that academia alone can no longer define what anthropology is and becomes.

Conclusion: Expelling the Spectre of Compromise

During the study discussed here, anthropologists (and indeed, employers) regularly regretted that what they were doing was probably *ikke rigtig antropologi*, which may be translated as 'not real' or 'not the right' anthropology. This reaction may well reflect the fact that the study was carried out by researchers based in an anthropology department, who, presumably – given the prevailing distribution of rights to definition in the discipline – were representatives of 'real anthropology', and who may be the judge of whether others lived up to their standards. We did what we could to put this suspicion to rest, and I think we succeeded in convincing participants that we only wanted to learn from them. Nevertheless, the high frequency of excuses about deviations from the (perceived) norms of academic anthropology made it clear that this was an important concern for many MA graduates in the study, particularly the younger ones. Some even talked about practical work as involving many 'compromises' in terms of standards of methodology, such as time in the field, or not having the freedom to pursue any line of interest in their work, but having to work within the remits of the organization of their employment. Of course, one may experience a personal sense of compromise, if individual circumstances force acceptance of an unsatisfactory job. The point is that 'the spectre of compromise', as I call it, also appeared among anthropologists and employers who were visibly very successful and justifiably happy with their work.

The spectre of compromise is an expression of how criteria deriving from one line of work (academia) are used to make value judgments in other lines (professional work in practice). The point is, of course, that imaginary working conditions in academia are even more irrelevant as standards for non-academic work. It is a sad effect of academicentrism in anthropology to hear how anthropologists who are competent at expanding and adapting their professional skills to new tasks and conditions feel compelled to apologize for their imagined inadequacy. Fortunately, it is likely that they too will realize eventually that the ability to make responsible compromises is itself a professional competence. In the meantime, the findings and observations discussed here have implications for anthropology training at universities. We need to do away with the misconceived notion that anthropology makes a constructive difference in the world through acting like a church, a self-referencing community preaching about its own moral superiority. It is doubtful whether there is much external audience for that line of missionary work anyway. Even worse, however, it has adverse effects on practitioners of anthropology, as discussed in this chapter, as well as on students of anthropology who are given a false image of the role and significance of their profession in the world. In order to improve that, we need to think about how we present and teach anthropology, how we may broaden our perspectives of professional work to be included in teaching, and which professional experiences we require of those who teach.

Steffen Jöhncke is senior lecturer in social anthropology at the School of Global Studies at the University of Gothenburg, Sweden. He practised for ten years in social policy and social work before returning to academia to pursue doctoral studies. In 2008–2018 he was head of AnthroAnalysis at the University of Copenhagen, Denmark.

NOTES

I want to thank my former colleague in AnthroAnalysis, Anne-Louise Lysholm Hansen, for her excellent work in the study of MA graduates discussed here. Anne-Louise was a driving force in every step in the study, from its design to the final revisions of the report. Any elaborations of our analyses discussed here, however, are my responsibility. I also want to thank Professor Susan Wright at the Danish School of Education, University of Aarhus. I have had the immense privilege to discuss issues relating to the theme of this chapter with Sue regularly since 1989, including her extremely useful comments on this text. Finally, I want to thank the editors of this volume, Hanne O. Mogensen and Birgitte Gorm Hansen, for the opportunity to contribute to this book and for their valuable editorial feedback and suggestions.

1. https://easaonline.org/, retrieved 15 August 2019.
2. Interestingly, Tierney's book (2000) is not referenced formally in the Introduction to the volume by its editor Jeremy MacClancy, maybe because he does not want to add to its notoriety. But the reference is clear enough in his mentioning of how 'the more eye-catching studies' in anthropology tend to gain more public attention than serious scholarship does: 'A particularly ugly example of this bias occurred in 2000 when an expert on Amazonia published a book accusing a senior anthropologist of grossly exploiting his position among the Indians he has lived with for the sake of his own selfish ends' (MacClancy 2002: 1–2).
3. In a later book, MacClancy (2017: 38) mentions how *Exotic No More* was criticized by reviewers for being 'Thatcherite' and 'too pragmatically framed'. My critique here is rather that it was not pragmatic enough. Yet, in his introduction to the 2017 volume MacClancy presents a range of useful observations and comments about the practical relevance of anthropology.
4. It is not just practising anthropologists who make a living from anthropology, of course. The moral teachings of the Church of Anthropology both cloaks and legitimates the fact that anthropology is a way to earn a living for university academics too.
5. The American Anthropological Association also defines anthropology as a 'study': 'Anthropology is the study of humans, past and present' (retrieved 15 August 2019, https://www.americananthro.org/). So does the Royal Anthropological Institute in the UK: 'anthropology (the study of humankind)' (retrieved 15 August 2019, https://therai.org.uk/about-the-rai). Even Strang's (2009) otherwise useful book on anthropological practice focuses on anthropologists in academic research roles.
6. The employers' panel is a body that each university department in Denmark is required by law to set up for advice about conditions and demands in the labour market, which may be useful for the development of curricula and the employment of MA graduates.
7. 'MA graduate' is my translation of the Danish '*kandidat*' degree, usually awarded after five years of mono-disciplinary training (three years at bachelor's and two years at postgraduate level). Very few students leave university with a BA degree only, making the '*kandidat*' degree both the norm and the expectation.
8. This degree was gradually supplanted by the MA degree in the 1990s, and finally made defunct in 2007.
9. It is my impression that many of the anthropologists in the studies presented in the other chapters of this book take this stance, often expressed as an ongoing concern with whether their work is anthropological (enough) or not.
10. See also Baba (2000).

REFERENCES

Ahmed, Akbar S. and Cris N. Shore. 1995. 'Introduction: Is Anthropology Relevant to the Contemporary World?', in Akbar S. Ahmed and Cris N. Shore (eds), *The Future of Anthropology: Its Relevance to the Contemporary World*. London: Athlone, pp. 12–45.

Baba, Marietta L. 2000. 'Theories of Practice in Anthropology: A Critical Appraisal', *NAPA Bulletin* 18(1): 17–44.

Benthall, Jonathan. 1995. 'Foreword: From Self-Applause through Self-Criticism to Self-Confidence', in Akbar S. Ahmed and Cris N. Shore (eds), *The Future of Anthropology: Its Relevance to the Contemporary World*. London: Athlone, pp. 1–11.

Cefkin, Melissa (ed.). 2009. *Ethnography and the Corporate Encounter: Reflections of Research in and of Corporations*. New York: Berghahn Books.

Comaroff, John. 2010. 'The End of Anthropology, Again: On the Future of an In/Discipline', *American Anthropologist*, New Series, 112(4): 524–38.

Foster, George M. 1969. *Applied Anthropology*. Boston: Little, Brown and Company.

Hansen, Anne-Louise L. and Steffen Jöhncke. 2013. *Omsat antropologi: En undersøgelse af det antropologiske arbejdsmarked i Danmark* [Realized Anthropology: A Study of the Anthropological Labour Market in Denmark]. Copenhagen: AnthroAnalysis, Dept. of Anthropology, University of Copenhagen.

Jöhncke, Steffen. 2018. 'Antropologikirken' [The Church of Anthropology], *Tidsskriftet Antropologi* 77: 143–46.

MacClancy, Jeremy. (ed.). 2002. *Exotic No More: Anthropology on the Front Lines*. Chicago: University of Chicago Press.

_____ (ed.). 2017. *Anthropology and Public Service: The UK Experience*. New York: Berghahn Books.

Malinowski, Bronislaw. 1929. 'Practical Anthropology', *Africa: Journal of the International African Institute* 2(1): 22–38.

Nolan, Riall W. 2003. *Anthropology in Practice: Building a Career Outside the Academy*. Boulder: Lynne Rienner Publishers.

_____. 2017. *Using Anthropology in the World: A Guide to Becoming an Anthropologist Practitioner*. New York: Routledge.

Pink, Sarah (ed.). 2006. *Applications of Anthropology: Professional Practice in the Twenty-first Century*. New York: Berghahn Books.

Strang, Veronica. 2009. *What Anthropologists Do*. Oxford: Berg.

Tierney, Patrick. 2000. *Darkness in El Dorado: How Scientists and Journalists Devastated the Amazon*. New York: Norton.

Wright, Susan. 1995. 'Anthropology: Still the Uncomfortable Discipline?', in Akbar S. Ahmed and Cris N. Shore (eds), *The Future of Anthropology: Its Relevance to the Contemporary World*. London: Athlone, pp. 65–93.

Conclusion

Hanne Overgaard Mogensen and Birgitte Gorm Hansen

In the Introduction we presented some of the political and societal factors that have shaped the development of anthropology as a university discipline in Denmark since the 1980s, and its headway into the labour market outside of academia. We showed that the development of anthropology as a discipline is closely related to political reforms during this period, some of which were also seen outside of Denmark. In concluding this book, we want to ask whether the shape of the moral project of Danish anthropology also relates to some of the same societal factors.

We started out by referring to the opening ceremony of the 116th Annual Meeting of the American Anthropological Association (AAA) in 2017 where a call was made for anthropologists to work for what is right and just and use their critical skills to empower subaltern voices and practices. We ended the book with a chapter by Jöhncke on 'the church of anthropology' (Chapter 6) referring to a text from 2015 by the Executive Committee of the European Association of Social Anthropologists (EASA) titled 'Why Anthropology Matters', where anthropology is described as a voice that possesses a particular moral value. Both of these instances seem to refer to a moral project akin to the one described in the chapters in this book. But we cannot, based on the studies we have carried out, comment on how widespread or pervasive this moral project is among the many anthropologists and many kinds of anthropology that are carried out around the world. What we do suggest though, is that a certain kind of moral project has had favourable conditions, particularly in Denmark where anthropology is taught in state universities that are being asked to contribute to society, to train people to implement and administrate the welfare state, to document the societal impact of their teaching and research; and where most of the public funding of research is devoted to topics defined as strategically important to society. In addition, the employability of university graduates is a concern of all university departments in Denmark, since the financing of individual departments can be influenced by unemployment rates. As shown in Chapters 1–6, many anthropologists already do work outside of academia and perceive of themselves as working for a better society. And what is distinct about Denmark is the way in which anthropology has indeed been positioned as both a societal resource and an economic asset at a particular moment in time. Is anthropology's moral project – as we see it in Denmark – related then to anthropology's ongoing attempt to justify itself, its importance and relevance in society and its place on the labour market?

Or could we at least say that a moral project – which can also be identified in anthropology more generally speaking – has been given particularly favourable conditions in Denmark? Before attempting a preliminary answer to this question, we will return to the analytical framework presented in the Introduction and compare the different kinds of moral work that have been identified in the chapters.

The Moral Work of Anthropologists

In the chapters we have shown that anthropologists put a considerable amount of effort into generating and re-enacting a division of the world into spheres and assess the moral value of their work according to these. The world is divided into two spheres: 'things as they are' in concrete everyday human practice and 'things as they seem' in abstract or numerical representation or calculative logic. We have also suggested that a distinction is made between anthropology as an identity and anthropology as a set of tools. We visualized these two divisions as two axes of a coordinate system which we presented in the Introduction (see Figure 0.1).

What we have shown in the chapters is not where in our coordinate system particular anthropologists are positioned. Rather, we have shown the ongoing re-enactment of these distinctions. Our interlocutors' moral work consists of an endeavour to position themselves as spokespersons for what takes place in concrete everyday human practice rather than as instruments for what takes place in abstract or numerical representation or calculative logic. This continuous effort of interlocutors to position themselves in relation to a less morally defensible 'other' is what we call 'the moral work' of anthropology.

Let us review how this positioning – or moral work – is related to two themes: that of anthropological identity and that of the varying intensity of the moral work that our interlocutors do across different types of organizations and job functions.

Anthropological Identity

The moral work of anthropology was not on the agenda when we initially set out to study anthropologists at work. Questions of morality emerged as a theme that clearly ran across the different materials collected for this project. As pointed out in Chapter 3, there is a possibility that morality became a predominant theme due to the fact that our research set-up made our interlocutors acutely aware that they were being studied 'through the eyes of their own discipline' and this may explain our material's gravitation towards interlocutors' self-representations. The chapters of the book have analysed these self-representations and the ways in which anthropologists at different points in their career and in different kinds of working conditions ask themselves moral questions.

As pointed out throughout the book, we do not claim that anthropologists are more or less moralistic than other professional groups. What does seem to characterize anthropologists and set them apart from most of their colleagues from other professional groups is, however, the conflation that often takes place between personal identity and academic discipline, especially during their education and their first years on the labour market. The moral project of anthropologists seems to be woven into their professional as well as their personal identity project. The analytic skills of anthropologists often do not feel like a professional skill you can switch on and off; rather, it seems to become part of the anthropologist's sense of self. 'As an anthropologist I must', 'as an anthropologist I feel', 'as an anthropologist I would always' are statements which show that academic and personal identity tend to merge. Many interlocuters talk of doing continuous or permanent fieldwork, or of their training having endowed them with an ability to 'read' patterns in human groups that has become second nature and cannot be switched off. We have argued, based on the ethnography presented in the chapters, that this conflation of discipline and identity embodies a moral world of anthropological practice where the anthropologists tend to position themselves as marginal or even exotic to the organization in which they work, a critical position from which they offer an alternative view that questions the dominant order.

Even though this ability to stand 'outside' the workplace and reflect on what is happening within it seems to give the anthropologist a unique profile and a valuable ability to provide original insights to the organization, it also has a downside. Our interlocutors may, more than other professionals, get themselves into situations where they feel torn or pressured to compromise on what they see as 'good' or 'right' and therefore show more hesitation in their decisions than their colleagues would do. They are especially hesitant to 'go fully native' in their respective work practices as this seems to pose a threat to the anthropological identification with the role of an observant, critical and somewhat exotic outsider. Hence the need to invest energy in generating a distinction between themselves and what is seen as the 'non-anthropological' or 'evil other'.

Our interlocutors seem to consolidate their sense of an anthropological identity by way of this dissociation. This accounts for the repeated tendency to compare themselves with perceived 'others': They are decidedly not 'djøfer' (Chapter 1); they are not profit maximizing consultants (Chapter 2); they are not any kind of mainstream corporate managers (Chapter 3); they are not data scientists (Chapter 4); and they are absolutely not 'data' (Chapter 5).

We did also find anthropologists who identify less with their discipline and are less troubled by the thought of becoming part of a system, and for most of them the tendency to dissociate from the practices they are part of diminishes with time. In other words, our fieldworks among anthropologists at work have also shown that over time many of them increasingly come to identify with the organization they work for. But still, this act of dissociation helps our interlocutors to define more clearly what anthropology as a profession can look like in comparison with other more well-defined professions in their workplace (see Chapter 6) and therefore also what their own particular contributions at the workplace consist of. In addition, there seems to be something more going on. More specifically, this act of dissociation seems to do important 'moral work' for our interlocutors.

Moral Workload of Varying Intensity

All of our interlocutors without exception place immense moral value on the ability to accurately represent the concrete human everyday practices they engage with in their daily work. This morally valued position of being a faithful spokesperson seems to be part of the reason that anthropologists are wary of fully merging with the professional identities offered to them as medical professionals, consultants, corporate managers or interdisciplinary researchers. Becoming identified with the practices and organizational goals of their workplaces threatens not just our interlocutors' identification with being anthropologists, but also the moral value of the work they do as spokespersons for that which is concrete, lived, real and in need of proper representation.

This also explains why the consultant, the manager and the academic anthropologists we meet in Chapter 2, 3 and 4 have a more intensive 'moral workload' than the anthropologists-cum-medical-professionals we meet in Chapter 1. The latter seem to be protected from the threat of 'moral injury' by lines of transversality that connect the organizational goal of the health care sector with the moral imperatives of a caring medical anthropologist. Hence, the 'evil others' of Chapter 1 seems to be abstractly presented by the remote 'djøfer' residing much higher up in the organizational hierarchy. The anthropologists working as consultants, interdisciplinary researchers or top managers, however, are under gradually increasing pressure to maintain their separate identity. The closer our interlocutors get to the top of an organizational pyramid or formal hierarchy, the more they might be expected to identify with the goals of their organization, and the more moral work they will have to do in order to maintain the role of spokesperson for the people on the ground. More effort needs to go into maintaining the distinction between their own anthropological identity and the organizational identity offered to them in their everyday engagement with excel sheets, budget lines, profit maximization, calculative logic and 'nonanthropologist' colleagues, employees, collaborators or managers.

The chapters of this book thus show the kind of moral work that interlocutors charge themselves with across all four fields, but also the differences in its urgency and intensity.

The Moral Economy of Anthropology in Denmark – and Beyond

Anthropology in Denmark is a relatively large discipline in a small country. In the Introduction we showed that the welfare state and its neoliberal reforms provide an important context for the development of anthropology as a discipline in Denmark, in particular the rise of medical anthropology, design anthropology and business anthropology, and the increased focus upon interdisciplinary research in Danish universities, since the 1990s. They also explain the move of anthropology from academia to the labour market outside of academia in the course of the 1980s and 1990s.

We suggest that this is an important part of the background, not just for the growth of the discipline, but also for the particular shape of the 'moral work' we have identified among anthropologists in Denmark. The separation into the two spheres that we have referred to as 'anthropology as a tool' and 'anthropology as an identity' is closely related to these developments, and the horizontal axis in our coordinate system (Figure 0.1) may be more prevalent in Denmark than in other countries. A demand for anthropology and its 'tools', such as qualitative methods, participant observation and other means of mapping human behaviour, increased in the 1990s and the university departments responded to this by becoming protective of the discipline and arguing for the need to recognize it as a profession and not just a set of tools that other professions can easily adopt. Thus, the strengthening of anthropological identity took place alongside the discipline's move into a broad range of collaborations inside and outside of academia.

Another contextual factor that may have contributed to the shaping of the moral project, or more precisely the vertical axis (Figure 0.1), is the ease with which anthropologists in Denmark (as well as other academics) have accepted that the university as an institution, and thus also anthropology as a discipline, are justified through their contribution to society. It would be interesting to further investigate the connection between the high level of trust in the (welfare) state in Denmark, and Danish anthropologists' self-perceived role of being a critical voice whose ultimate purpose is to contribute to the ongoing work towards a better and more just society.

We have discussed the difference it makes in the working lives of our interlocutors whether they approach anthropology as an identity project or as a profession. The ones who approach anthropology as something they are, rather than as something they do, feel required to put a considerable amount of effort into critically reflecting on their own practice to ensure that they stay on the right side of perceived moral distinctions. Feeling morally marginal or identifying as an outsider who feels marginal but morally superior is not likely to be the best positions for anthropologists who want to create change in the world. But as we suggested in the Introduction, the strong identity among anthropologists may also have helped them to move into the labour market and make a brand for themselves. And as mentioned above, for many anthropologists at work, the importance of anthropology as an identity project decreases over time and they start to perceive of anthropology as something they do. And maybe anthropologists' desire to work towards what they perceive as good, just and right is more likely to come to fruition if they become aware of their own moral economy and are clearer on when to do anthropology and when to be an anthropologist. We hope that this book will help to create such awareness and encourage a debate about these issues.

We have taken our starting point in Danish anthropology as it is practised at this point in history, an anthropology which is grounded in an international, primarily anglophone, northern European anthropology, but which also has its own particular shape. Still we hope that this attempt to direct the torchlight at the discipline will encourage others to ask similar questions about the way in which anthropology is practised in other parts of the world and the direction in which anthropology is heading in a changing world.

Hanne Overgaard Mogensen is associate professor at the Department of Anthropology, University of Copenhagen. Her main topic of research is medical anthropology and international health, primarily in Africa. She has also published literary anthropology based on her research. She teaches medical anthropology at the University of Copenhagen.

Birgitte Gorm Hansen is an independent consultant and researcher. She is trained as a psychologist from the University of Copenhagen and received her PhD in science studies and management from Copenhagen Business School in 2011. Her postdoctoral research on anthropologists working in leadership positions formed one of the four sub-studies conducted in the Department of Anthropology at the University of Copenhagen.

Index

Lightning Source UK Ltd.
Milton Keynes UK
UKHW022235130522
402993UK00003B/204